Llewellyn's
2003
Magical Almanac

Featuring

Karri Ann Allrich, Barbara Ardinger, Elizabeth Barrette, Chandra Moira Beal, Stephanie Rose Bird, Mavesper Ceridwen, Nuala Drago, Denise Dumars, Ellen Dugan, Marguerite Elsbeth, Ember, Ed Fitch, Emely Flak, Karen Follett, Therese Francis, Anna Franklin, Lily Gardner, Magenta Griffith, Natalie Harter, Elizabeth Hazel, Eileen Holland, Jonathan Keyes, Kristin Madden, Mary Magpie, Edain McCoy, Ann Moura, Dr. Jonn Mumford, Jenna Parsons, Robert M. Place, Diana Rajchel, deTraci Regula, Roslyn Reid, Laurel Nightspring Reufner, Sheri Richerson, Sedwin, ShadowCat, Cerridwen Iris Shea, Susan Sheppard, Lynne Sturtevant, Carly Wall, Jim Weaver, Abby Willowroot, and S Y Zenith

Llewellyn's 2003 Magical Almanac

ISBN 0-7387-0072-X. Copyright © 2002 by Llewellyn Worldwide. All rights reserved. Printed in the United States.

Editor/Designer: Michael Fallon

Black & White Cover Illustration: © Merle S. Insinga

Color Application to Cover Artwork: Lynne Menturweck

Calendar Pages Design: Andrea Neff and Michael Fallon

Calendar Pages Illustrations: © Kerigwen

Interior Illustrations © Helen Michaels, pages: 17, 22, 26, 35, 37, 41, 49, 51, 61, 69, 72, 75, 80, 86, 98, 105, 111, 113, 120, 123, 135, 139, 158–9, 163, 166, 237, 242, 247, 251, 255, 262, 267, 276, 281–2, 286, 296, 303, 305, 307, 331, 345, 351, 355, 368

Clip Art Illustrations: Dover Publications

Special thanks to Amber Wolfe for the use of daily color and incense correspondences. For more detailed information, please see *Personal Alchemy* by Amber Wolfe.

You can order Llewellyn annuals and books from *New Worlds,* Llewellyn's magazine catalog, or online at www.llewellyn.com. To request a free copy of the catalog, call toll-free: 1-877-NEWWRLD, or click on "Catalog Request" under the Online Bookstore heading on our website.

Moon sign and phase data computed by Astro Communications Services (ACS).

Llewellyn Worldwide
Dept. 0-7387-0072-X
P.O. Box 64383
St. Paul, MN 55164-0838

About the Authors

KARRI ANN ALLRICH is an author, artist, and eclectic cook who weaves her Goddess path through all aspects of her life. She shares her Massachusetts home and studio with her husband and their two sons. Her published books include: *Recipes From a Vegetarian Goddess, A Witch's Book of Dreams,* and *Cooking by Moonlight.* Ms. Allrich has also written articles for numerous publications.

BARBARA ARDINGER, PH.D., is the author of the book *Goddess Meditations* (Llewellyn, 1998), and *Practicing the Presence of the Goddess* (New World Library, 2000). An initiated Dianic Witch and member of the Covenant of the Goddess, Barbara currently lives in southern California.

ELIZABETH BARRETTE is managing editor of *PanGaia* and assistant editor of *SageWoman.* She has been involved in the Pagan community for over twelve years, and lives in central Illinois. Her other writing fields include speculative fiction and gender studies. Visit her website at: http://www.worthlink.net/~ysabet/index.html.

CHANDRA MOIRA BEAL is a freelance writer in Austin, Texas. She lives with a magical house rabbit named Maia and has authored hundreds of articles on topics ranging from mermaids to law. Chandra also self-published *Splash Across Texas,* a guide to aquatic recreation in her home state. *Chandra* is Sanskrit for "moon."

STEPHANIE ROSE BIRD, a.k.a. Mojo Rose, is an artist, writer, conjurer, root doctor, and educator. She has been on faculty at the School of the Art Institute of Chicago since 1986. She is also the founder of her own herbal haircare line designed for black women, and she has written for such publications as *Herbal Companion Magazine.* Stephanie is a mother of four and an avid prairie wildflower gardener who shares her home with butterflies, wild birds, a cockatiel, and a black cat.

MAVESPER CERIDWEN, a.k.a. Marcia Bianchi, is a Brazilian Wiccan of the Dianic Tradition. She is also a lawyer, teacher, and mother who dedicates her life to helping beginners learn the Goddess Path. Visit her websites at: www.templodadeusa.com.br and www.abrawicca.org.

NUALA DRAGO is an author, musician, folklorist, and self-initiate who has practiced her own form of Witta for more than thirty years. She has been a life-long student of ancient cultures and languages and speaks Irish Gaelic. She and her husband live in the country with their German Shepherd, three cats, and an agouti Holland Lop.

DENISE DUMARS is a member of the Fellowship of Isis who practices with several Isian groups in the Southern California area. She teaches college English and has written much about modern myth and magic in such publications as *SageWoman, Fate, The Isis Papers,* and various editions of Llewellyn's annuals.

ELLEN DUGAN, also known as the "Garden Witch," is a psychic-clairvoyant and practicing Witch of more than fifteen years. She and her husband raise three magical teenagers and tend to their gardens in Missouri. Ellen received master gardener status in the spring of 2000. She is will be publishing a "Garden Witchery" book with Llewellyn in 2003.

MARGUERITE ELSBETH, also known as Senihele and Sparrowhawk, is a hereditary Sicilian Strega and Lenni Lenape (Delaware Indian). She is a professional astrologer, tarot reader, and spiritual healer specializing in crisis counseling, spiritual troubleshooting, and difficult relationship issues. She has written numerous articles for Llewellyn's annuals, is the author of *Crystal Medicine,* and coauthor of *The Grail Castle: Male Myths and Mysteries in the Celtic Tradition.* She currently lives in the Southwest desert.

EMBER is is a solitary Witch, writer, and poet. Her interests include gardening, reading, music, crystals, and creating handmade soap and candles. An advocate for the environment, Ember enjoys spending time in nature and working to preserve precious natu-

ral resources. She lives in the Midwest with her husband and two feline companions.

ED FITCH is a scholar of modern Paganism. Initiated into the Gardnerian Wiccan tradition in the mid-1960s, he has written much about the background lore of Wicca and Paganism.

EMELY FLAK is a writer on Pagan, magical, and folkloric topics who lives in Brighton, Australia, in the province of Victoria. By day, though, she works as a flight attendant safety trainer. This is her first time contributing to Llewellyn's annuals.

KAREN FOLLETT has been a practicing Witch for thirty years, and was first taught by her great grandmother, a healer and midwife. Currently a member of the local coven of the Georgian tradition, she works as a nurse specializing in maternal and child health. In addition, Karen is an empath, medical intuitive, and reiki practitioner. She has been married for twenty years and has two sons.

THERESE FRANCIS, PH.D., is an author, astrologer, folklorist, herbalist, and public speaker. Her two most recent books are *The Mercury Retrograde Book, 20 Herbs to Take on a Business Trip,* and *20 Herbs to Take Outdoors* (One Spirit). She is author of numerous articles on herbs, astrology, and New Age topics, and has written for Llewellyn for several years. An active member of the Sante Fe Astrology Forum, she teaches astrology, psychic and intuitive development, self-defense, and the integration of body, mind, heart, and spirit. She currently resides in Sante Fe, New Mexico.

ANNA FRANKLIN is a third-degree Witch who has been a practicing Pagan for more than twenty five years. She is the author of six books, and coauthor of four more. She was cocreator of the popular *Sacred Circle Tarot,* and wrote the forthcoming book *The Fairy Ring,* Anna has contributed articles to Pagan magazines; she lives and works in an English Midlands village where she grows her own herbs and food.

LILY GARDNER is is a lifelong student of folklore and mythology. She is a priestess in the Daughters of Gaia coven and a member of the

Fat Thursday Writers. Lily lives with her husband, two corgis, and an ancient cat in Portland, Oregon. She is currently working on a novel.

MAGENTA GRIFFITH has has been a Witch for over twenty-five years, an ordained priestess for thirteen years, and is founding member of the coven Prodea. She leads rituals and workshops in the Midwest, and is librarian for the New Alexandria Library, a Pagan and magical resource center (http://www.magusbooks.com/newalexandria/).

NATALIE HARTER has degrees in anthropology and women's studies, and has been fascinated by female figures in religion and mythology for as long as she can remember.

ELIZABETH HAZEL is an astrologer, tarotist, and rune reader. When she is not writing and making art, Liz enjoys music and gardening.

EILEEN HOLLAND is a Wiccan priestess who lives in New York. She is the author of *The Wicca Handbook* (Weiser, 2000). Her website at www.open-sesame.com has had over 3 million visitors.

JONATHAN KEYES is a health astrologer who works with herbs, diet, stones, and animal totems to help harmonize planetary influences for health and well-being. He writes a regular "lunar health" column for Stariq.com and has written for *Mountain Astrologer*. He also writes a bimonthly health horoscope that can be found at: www.astrologicalhealth.com.

KRISTIN MADDEN is a homeschooling mom and wildlife rehabilitator. She is the author of *Shamanic Guide to Death and Dying, Pagan Parenting,* and the forthcoming *Shamanic Guide to Health and Healing*. She was raised in a shamanic home and has explored Eastern and Western mystic paths since 1972. She sits on the governing board of The Ardantane Project, a Wiccan/Pagan seminary, and is a Druid and tutor in the Order of Bards, Ovates, and Druids.

MARY MAGPIE is a self-initiated Witch with a great interest in the Norse Heathen traditions. She is a member of a coven in the English Midlands and has written articles for various Pagan magazines, including *Silver Wheel* and *Quest*.

EDAIN MCCOY has practiced Witchcraft for more than twenty years, during which time she has studied many magical traditions including Wiccan, Judaic, Celtic, Appalachian, and Curanderismo. By day, she works as a stockbroker, and by night she writes (when she's not ballroom dancing). She is the author of sixteen books, including: *A Witch's Guide to Faery Folk, Celtic Myth and Magick, Celtic Women's Spirituality, Astral Projection For Beginners,* and *SpellCraft For Covens.*

ANN MOURA has practiced as a Solitary Witch for nearly forty years, and now focuses on the green level of Witchcraft working with the elementals and the divine in nature. She enjoys writing poetry, drawing, painting, and gardening. Her published works include: *Green Witchcraft: Folk Magic, Fairy Lore, & Herb Craft; Green Witchcraft II: Balancing Light & Shadow;* and *Green Witchcraft III: The Manual.*

DR. JONN MUMFORD (Swami Anandakapila Saraswati) is an international lecturer and author of many books for Llewellyn, including *Ecstasy through Tantra* and *The Chakra & Kundalini Workbook.* For more information about Dr. Mumford, visit his website at: http://www.jonnmumfordconsult.com.

ROBERT M. PLACE is a visionary artist, and the designer, illustrator, and author of several tarot decks for Llewellyn. He is an expert on Western mysticism and the history of the tarot, and he has taught divination at the New York Open Center, Omega Institute, New York Tarot School, and the World Tarot Congress. He has appeared on the Discovery Channel and the Learning Channel. Visit his website at: www.crosswinds.net~alchemicalegg.

DIANA RAJCHEL is a third-degree priestess who studies with Ocean-Wind coven. Along with her interests in Paganism, she studies creative writing at Minnesota State University in Mankato and is president of a Pagan group at the school. She also runs a website located at www.medeaschariot.com in partnership with her husband.

DETRACI REGULA is the author of *The Mysteries of Isis* (Llewellyn, 1996), and has written numerous articles and books for Llewellyn

through the years. When not writing and lecturing, she enjoys traveling to sacred sites. Her Mysteries of Isis website is located at: www.geocities.com/detraciregula.

ROSLYN REID is a Discordant Druid and a member of the Richard P. Feynman Memorial Cabal in Princeton, New Jersey. She lives on a former farm, where she grows a variety of fruit, raises Great Pyrenees dogs, and teaches yoga and tarot. She is a long-time contributor of art and articles to Llewellyn, as well as to publications such as *Sage-Woman* and *Dalriada*. Her work has also appeared in consumer magazines such as *Tightwad Living* and *Thrifty Times*.

LAUREL NIGHTSPRING REUFNER has been a solitary Pagan more than a decade. Currently, she writes articles for various publications, along with whatever else seems too interesting to resist, from her home in southeastern Ohio. Her website can be found at: www.spirit-realm.com/Melinda/paganism/html.

SHERI RICHERSON has more than twenty years experience in newspaper and magazine writing for numerous publications and websites. Her range of writing expertise has included astrology, herbs, aromatheraphy, and tropical and exotic plants. She is also a lifetime member of the International Thespian Society. Her favorite pastimes are riding her motorcycle and her horse, and gardening.

SEDWIN is a writer and explorer of ancient Goddess spirituality. She teaches a workshop called "Understanding the Language of the Goddess," based on the work of Marija Gimbutas, and she lives near New York City where she enjoys drumming circles with friends.

SHADOWCAT is a priestess and Witch in the American Celtic Tradition of Lady Sheba, but she prefers solitary work. A self-taught, self-proclaimed gourmet cook, ShadowCat spends her days acquiring new manuscripts for Llewellyn Publications.

CERRIDWEN IRIS SHEA is a tarot-reading, horse-playing, dragon-loving urban writer Witch who lives in Manhattan and works on

Broadway. Her plays have been produced in various locations throughout the world, and her writing has been published under various names in various genres. She is currently owned by four cats.

SUSAN SHEPPARD is the author of three books, and is also WTAP-TV's "Daybreak Astrologer." She appears on live television on the first Friday of each month to give astrological readings to anyone who calls in. She is the creator and owner of the Haunted Parkersburg Ghost Tours in her hometown of Parkersburg, West Virginia. You can view her website at: http://magick.wirefire.com.

LYNNE STURTEVANT is a freelance writer specializing in folklore, mythology, fairy tales, and the paranormal. She has been a solitary practitioner following an Eclectic path since 1970 and holds a bachelor's degree in philosophy. She is a regular contributor to Llewellyn's annuals and to *Fate* magazine.

JENNA TIGERHEART is a member of the Covenant of Unitarian Universalist Pagans and the Unitarian Universalist Association. She has practiced Witchcraft and appreciation for our Mother the Earth for many years. She is also a Pagan songwriter and a member of the women's chorale group "Chantress."

CARLY WALL is author of the soon-to-be released *Psychic Scents: Edgar Cayce's Approach to Using Scent in Psychic Development* (A.R.E. Press), and has written numerous books on aromatherapy and herbs. A regular article contributor to Llewellyn's annuals for the last eight years, she holds a certificate in aromatherapy and is member of the National Association for Holistic Aromatherapy (NAHA). She lives with her husband and cat on a farm in Ohio.

JIM WEAVER writes and paints at his home in the beautiful hill country of southern Ohio. He has a degree in history, and has authored numerous articles on the folkloric traditions of Greece, the Near East, and the Appalachian mountain region of the United States.

ABBY WILLOWROOT is an archetypist, artist, priestess, and mother whose life for the past thirty years has been dedicated to bringing Goddess imagery and consciousness back into contemporary culture. She is the founder and director of the Goddess 2000 Project and the Spiral Goddess Grove. Abby's art and articles have appeared in *WomanSpirt*, *SageWoman,* and *GreenEgg* magazines. Nine pieces of Ms. Willowroot's jewelry are in the permanent collections of the Smithsonian Institution in Washington, DC.

S Y ZENITH is three-quarters Chinese with a dash of Irish in her ancestry. She is a solitary Pagan who has lived and travelled extensively throughout Asia. For the last seventeen years, S Y has been based in Australia. Her fascination with folk traditions both Eastern and Western has resulted in numerous articles in different genres under several names. Her work has been published both in Australia and the United States. She is currently working on a book titled *Malay Folk Magic.*

Table of Contents

Introduction to Llewellyn's Magical Almanac

Number 13 usually brings to mind sinister things—bad luck, and black cats, and broken mirrors, and terrors in the night. Of course, the notion is entirely random, right? Or as Emely Flak writes in her article on "Number 13 Lore" (page 362 in this edition): "Superstition about this number persists in Western society, despite the fact that there is no logic for fear of any particular number. Fear of this number has even earned its own name—triskaidekaphobia."

In honor of this fact, we've unofficially taken to calling this extravaganza edition of Llewellyn's *Magical Almanac* the triskaidekaphobic edition. In this, the thirteenth edition of a now-old book, we are taking some new looks at magic in everyday life, and tapping into some of the world's most ancient knowledge—the magic and healing power of crystals, for instance, as well as the lore regarding tattoos, dandelions, even the color green. And we bring to these pages some of the most innovative and original thinkers and writers on these subjects.

This focus on the old ways—on the lore of men and women around the world knew and understood the power of their ancestors—are important today, as it seems the balance of the world has been thrown offkilter; sort of like having a thirteenth guest at the table. Terrorists, water shortages, hatred, internecine battles, and militant religious fervor all seem to be holding sway over us. While we don't want to assign blame or cast any other aspersions, this state of affairs perhaps is not surprising considering so many of us—each one of us—is out of touch with the old ways. Many of us spend too much of our lives rushing about in a technological bubble—striving to make money, being everywhere but here, living life in fastforward. We forget, at times, that all of this has happened before, and it will happen again.

Still, the news is not all bad. People are still fighting to make us all more aware of the magical, beautiful things in the world. Pagan and Wiccan communities, for instance, are thriving across the country and throughout the world. In this edition of the

Magical Almanac, writers from far away as Australia, Brazil, and England contribute to an expanding volume of knowledge, lore, and magical ritual.

In the 2003 edition of the *Magical Almanac,* we pay tribute to and homage to the ideals of magic and beauty and balance of our ancestors. This may sound a bit corny for some, perhaps a bit too idealistic, too, but those who say so likely have never put what has been written in this almanac over the past thirteen years to good use.

Magic is an ancient tool whose time has come back around to help us restore balance in our lives. More and more people are using magic, celebrating the elements, praying to the Goddess and the various incarnations of the divine, and studying the myths and legends, lore and tales of the past. In the end, one person at a time, using ancient wisdom, we can make a new world.

Articles for Winter

The Magic of Urban Legends

by Shari Ann Richerson

Urban legends seem to be just about everywhere these days, spurred by the explosive communicative speed of e-mails and websites. Some of the legends are pretty gruesome; others are very interesting. What is the impulse that makes these legends seem so magical to some people?

In general, a legend is a story told over and over. Sometimes these stories are verifiable through newspaper clippings or other similar sources, sometimes not. Naturally some legends are more intriguing than others. But the biggest factor that determines whether or not an urban legend stays around has to be its believability.

According to Blake Cahoon, publisher of the "Beyond Infinity" online magazine (at www.amthyst moon.com), one of the most famous urban legends is the story of the hitchhiking ghost. This legend is found all over the country, but essentially it is the same story everywhere. In the tale, a young girl is picked up as a hitchhiker by a naïve young man, who drops her off somewhere and then finds out that the girl died long before. In Chicago, the girl even has a name: Resurrection Mary. She was killed long ago coming home from a ball.

Another interesting urban legend is a story of flesh-eating bananas, which goes like this. An e-mail states that flesh-eating bacteria has been found on a recent shipment of bananas. Since we all know bananas come from a foreign country, this gives the story a kind of xenophobic shock value. As with many other such e-mail warnings, this tale begins: "This is not a joke—please read and pass it on! Please forward to everyone you love!" The story continues with a warning—that shipments of bananas from Costa Rica have been infected with "necrotizing fasciitis, otherwise known as flesh-eating bacteria." Readers are advised not to purchase bananas for the next three weeks, or, if they have, watch for a sudden onset of fever followed by a skin infection. The story continues with great verve: "The skin infection from necrotizing fasciitis is very painful and eats two to three centimeters of flesh per hour. Amuputation is likely, death is possible." And readers are advised to burn off flesh in advance of the infection in order to stop its spread.

The e-mail warns that up to 15,000 Americans could be affected by this deadly epidemic. Of course, the reason that such a thing has not yet been announced through regular news channels is due to the government's fear of a nationwide panic. The e-mail concludes, as such e-mails often do, with an appeal to readers to "please forward this to as many people as you care about."

A characteristic of urban legends spread by e-mail is that they are very difficult to verify. Most often, there are reasons given why such information is not already widely know. Furthermore, the source of the information is usually very distant—a foreign country, or a friend of a friend. Almost always, there is an appeal made to the reader not to discount the information.

Another urban legend that I found fascinating had to do with the film version of the *Wizard of Oz*. I had never heard of this before, so maybe you haven't either, but according to lore there is an actual suicide filmed in the movie. The event in question is said to occur just after Dorothy meets the Tin Man and before the group meets the Cowardly Lion. Just as the three characters (Dorothy, the Tin Man, and the Scarecrow) say, "To Oz," and then begin to dance, there is movement over Dorothy's left shoulder. Some say this is a man hanging himself, others say it's a bird. I'll let you decide for yourself.

While we're on the subject of movies and legends, I should mention *The Blair Witch Project*, which was based on just such lore. The movie covers the legend of Elly Kedward, who in February of 1785 was accused of drawing blood from several children she lured into her home. Found guilty of witchcraft, she was banished from the village. After an extremely harsh winter, she was presumed dead. But then, by November 1786, the children who accused her, along with half of the town's children, vanished. The Blair townspeople fled out of fear.

In November 1809, the *Blair Witch Cult* was said to be published, recounting this legend. However, no known book by this title exists. By 1824, Burkittsville was founded where Blair used to be. Through the years, there were a number of reported sightings of a woman, or parts of a woman's hand, and accounts of missing children in the area. Then, of course, there are the disappearances of the three documentary filmmakers of the *The Blair Witch Project*. Did they really disappear, or was the movie simply the creation of yet another urban legend?

Blake Cahoon sums it up very well: "Urban legends are all over the country and take on various shapes and sizes from monsters to the serial killers lurking and scratching on a car hood. They serve to stimulate the imagination and to frighten us on those cold winter nights as we huddle around the fireplace, or on a cool summer night huddled around a campfire."

Urban legends definitely come in all sizes and shapes. Some legends can scar you for life, while others will have you laughing. They definitely make for interesting conversation and if you dare, interesting research. Many urban legends seem to focus on nature or people, sometimes a combination of both. When I inquired as to why this was, Ram Varma, a meditation teacher, author, and seminar leader, responded: "Everyone has some unique talents. One who truly knows one's uniqueness, shares it with the rest of the world preferably in an unselfish way for the benefit of the community, will effortlessly become a legend in (due) course of time. That appears to be the law of nature."

Whether urban legends are a law of nature or a manifestation of mankind can only be determined by you and your beliefs. Regardless, they still make great fireside stories.

Lilith Rituals for Modern Pagans

by Ellen Dugan

Lovely are the curves of the white owl sweeping
Wavy in the dusk lit by one large star.
Lone on the fir-branch his rattle-note unvaried,
Brooding o'er the gloom, spins the brown eve-jar.
——George Meridith

Lilith is the Divine Lady Owl and the original bad-ass chick, the archetypal seductress and the personification of the dangerous feminine glamour of the Moon. Lilith is the wanton winged goddess of erotic dreams. She is a symbol of forbidden pleasures and beguiling sorcery. Is it any wonder she is so popular nowadays?

Our most familiar image of Lilith comes from a terra-cotta relief from Sumer, dated to around 2000 B.C. Here, she is depicted as an attractive, winged woman with clawed feet, sur-

rounded by owls and standing on two lions that face in opposite directions.

Generally speaking, Lilith has ties to the mythologies of the Sumerians, Babylonians, and Hebrew cultures. To the Babylonians she was known as *Lilitu;* to the Sumerians, *Belit-illi* or *Belili.* A Sumerian fragment recorded her name and described Lilith as a maiden, "the hand of Innana." She was sent by Innana to bring men into the temple. In Hebrew mythology, she was known as a screech owl or night hag.

Lilith was the first wife of Adam, and she demanded equality in all things. When she refused to lie submissive beneath him, Adam complained to his creator about Lilith's "shrewish" behavior. Having had enough, Lilith spoke the hidden name of God and flew away to her home in the Red Sea. The more docile Eve was created to take her place.

Lilith was also associated with the Queen of Sheba, and in medieval France she was known as *La Reine Pedauque,* which translates, "the queen with the bird's foot." Lilith was thought to fly at night along with her twelve daughters, the Lilim. Together, they enticed young men who slept.

To modern Witches and Pagans, Lilith is a patroness of Witches and the goddess of the waning Moon. Lilith was described by the author Doreen Valiente in her book *ABC of Witchcraft,* as an enticing sorceress, a beautiful vampire, and the ultimate femme fatale. Lilith stands for desire, pleasure, and sexual love—not for the purpose of procreation but simply for enjoyment. Besides her obvious associations with sexuality, Lilith represents wisdom, renewal, equality, feminine power, and independence. Lilith encourages us to live on our own terms. She is a powerful role model for women, and as long as we remember that sex, like magic, should never be used to coerce, harm, or control another person in any way, we can use Lilith energy to improve our lives and relationships.

Lilith's sacred animals are the owl and the lion. Owl magic or medicine has an interesting connection to Lilith. Because it has a noiseless flight, the owl traditionally symbolizes secrets, wisdom, and silence. The owl swoops silently down on prey, just as Lilith was believed to, and so people who carry the owl as a totem animal often are a little spookier than average. Their natural clairvoyance leads them to perceive and detect what other folks want to keep hidden.

Lilith Clairvoyance

People who are close to Lilith therefore often experience an owl-like insight, seeing pictures or receiving images of people and places. Learning to control this "talent," for those of us who have always had it, takes effort and discipline. Being a clairvoyant, though it can be useful, is not always a barrel of laughs—many images can be overwhelming and or disturbing. When I was younger I couldn't even shake a person's hand without receiving a fast shuffle of images and feelings. I had no type of shield or buffer to mitigate the swirl of emotions. When I began to avoid touching anybody, people misinterpreted that as being rude or snobbish. I wasn't until I grew older that I learned a few shielding techniques to protect myself.

For instance, learning to work with owl medicine was a great help to me. The owl is all-seeing, certainly, but she is also wise enough to be still, and to watch and wait. Furthermore, working with dark goddess energy taught me the value of acceptance. If you need help learning to deal with yourself just as you are, then Lilith can be a powerful ally.

If you care to try magic with Lilith, her magical correspondences are:

Planetary association: Saturn

Moon Phase: Waning Moon

Oil: Patchouli (also a sexual stimulant for men)

Plants: Lily, willow tree, and red roses

Animals: Owls and lions

Crystals: Carnelian for desire, and ruby for power

Colors: Red and black (use in candles and perhaps in lingerie)

A Psychic Lilith Ritual

Light both a black candle and a white candle for balance. Set out your tarot cards or other divinatory tool between the candles as you ask for Lilith's blessings on your psychic work. Say:

Lilith, wise woman ahead of your time,
Help me now to interpret symbol and sign.
I call on the owl for knowledge of outcome,
May I be blessed with truth and inner vision.
With wisdom, my lady, help me to see the unknown,
In strength, Lilith, help me to accept what I am shown.

Meditate for a few moments and then perform your divination. Remember to thank Lilith for her assistance when you are finished.

On the other hand, if you simply want to spice things up with your partner in the bedroom, Lilith's your best bet! But be careful, she has a wicked sense of humor. Calling on Lilith for some extra spark or desire works very well, but you may feel a magic hangover in the morning. A small price to pay perhaps, just don't say that I didn't warn you.

Speak this invocation:

Lilith, goddess of the night, teach me to love and to be wise,
Aid me under the dark Moon and sail through the skies.
Give me gifts of love and seduction, passion and desire,
As I will this, so shall it harm none. By the powers of air, water,
earth and fire.

Call on Lilith some enchanted evening, to make you feel more sexual and attractive. (Between the job, the kids, and housework, a woman's got to have a few tricks up her Witch's sleeve.) Light the candles. Start some patchouli incense burning. If you want to go all out, open a bottle of wine and sprinkle the sheets with some crimson rose petals. Ask for Lilith's blessing and then race each other down the hall to the bedroom. Have yourselves a Lilith moment.

Channeled Writing

by Karen Follett

Remember Friday night sleepovers? Remember the frivolous candlelight séances? And girls giggling around the Ouija board? For many of us, these adolescent games were actually our first attempts at channeled writing.

Channeling is the ability to reach across our normal plane of physical existence to the planes of the otherworldly entities that surround us. Channeled writing, then, is the conscious or subconscious transcription of messages channeled from the other side.

The Real Process of Channeling

The late night Ouija-board sessions are a simplification of the process of channeling, an activity which primarily involves the abstract right brain reaching out into unknown spheres of existence. As writing involves the analytical left brain, by the time these messages appear on paper, it is very easy to rationalize and analyze them beyond all comprehension.

The fact is, entities of the other realms don't necessarily communicate in words, sentences, or even phrases. If you are channeling correctly, sometimes you will perceive symbols or what appears to be nonsensical gibberish. In general, channeling should be undertaken in such a way that you just let the images and perceptions enter your consciousness. It is important that you maintain your focus and your breathing, and transcribe what is entering your perception, whatever it is. I can't stress enough that you not let your left brain take over. Remember always, you are acting as a pathway, or channel, for information.

Most of us passively channel in "hunches" and intuition, but most of these messages end up in the inner consciousness (what most people refer to as the subconsciousness) and never have the opportunity to surface to the conscious mind. Active channeling requires a quiet, listening mind that is in an open and receptive alpha state such as you try to foster while meditating.

As with channeling, meditation is the act of listening to the universe. The imagery that I find most useful in channeling involves opening the chakras (particularly the crown), and clearing the pathway between the subconscious and conscious minds. When you open the crown chakra, imagine golden rays emanating from your crown. Focus on these rays reaching into the other realms. Focus to a two-way flow between the rays extending from your crown to the other realm and back to your crown. As you feel the rays intensify, take a deep breath and relax. Some people have no physical sensations when contact is made. Others, myself included, feel a tingle from the crown to the neck. Now just let your mind relax. Let the rays and images flow. Visualize the flow entering your crown and radiating from your pencil as you begin to write.

Here are some more tips for you to keep your channeling efforts on target:

> Keeping a channeling journal is extremely helpful in learning how to interpret messages from beyond. And not only can you review the messages, you will be able to see an evolution of your communication skills between you and the entities of the otherworld. As with any skill, when you increase your expertise you will notice an increase in the strength of connection. Ultimately, you will be able to request specifics from the entities. You will be able clear the channeling pathway and quiet the mind almost any time or anywhere. Your communication with your "spirit" will gain clarity, and you will gain the wonderful knowledge that you have earned the gift of wisdom that transcends all boundaries of life and time.

If you find aromas helpful to inducing meditation, use them. Some good choices are mugwort, lavender, and valerian. Candles can provide a good focal point. Make sure that you stay alert enough that you do not leave the candles unattended. Good color choices include white, blue, or purple. Any object that you use for scrying (crystals, bowls, candle flame) will also provide a good focal point. However, if you find the inclusion of any of these objects intrusive, don't use them. The ability to channel is within you. With the exception of pencil and paper, you don't need any external "props" to connect with the otherworld.

Happy Channeling

The most famous channeled writing events ever are perhaps the channeled messages of Patience Worth, received and written by Phyllis Curran. This event occurred during the turn of the last century in St. Louis, Missouri. Patience Worth introduced herself to Phyllis Curran during a Ouija board session. Initially the Ouija board was used to transcribe Ms. Worth's messages. However, as the strength of their contact grew, Ms. Curran could perceive and transcribe messages without the use of any "props," trance states, or environmental conditioning. Over the years of their relationship, approximately four million words (including poetry, plays, and novels) were transcribed and published.

You may be wondering who you will be encountering on this plane of existence. A lot of self-help books enthrall the reader with stories of the "fluffy bunny" spirit guide that is just waiting for you to contact them. While that wonderful being is there and is waiting, you will probably encounter several lesser evolved beings on your travels.

In fact, there are countless entities in the other planes. Some are task-oriented and may only be able to mirror the images that you project. Other are entities are still growing to wisdom. And others still have never touched our earthly plane.

You will find entities in your travels that will feel emotionally close to you (perhaps relatives who have crossed over), and you will discover entities who are of the "light"—highly evolved and happy to guide you down the path to personal success and enlightenment.

On our earthly plane, like attracts like. Vibratory auras reach toward auras that compliment them. This attraction also occurs on the spiritual plane. As you spiritually grow, you will notice that you may still run into lesser evolved beings, but you will have a greater ease in reaching the more highly evolved guides.

In any event, all information you discover in your travels is potentially useful. Knowledge is a good thing.

Sure, some information may indicate that you need to look inward for growth. Other information may be based on your wants, not necessarily on what is good for your growth. Always take care: If something you channel seems too good to be true, chances are you won't want to bet the mortgage on this information. There is an old Persian proverb that is useful when trying to discern the evolutionary wisdom in messages channeled from beyond. Loosely translated, this proverb states, "Trust in the gods, but tie your camel tight."

In other words: Open up to the information, but use your head. If it don't feel right, chances are it ain't right. In these cases, you might be well served to acknowledge the information, dismiss the entity, and move on, seeking and asking only for wisdom.

Unearthing the Great Goddess

by Abby Willowroot

The many images and icons of the Great Goddess that come to us from our ancient past give us glimpses into another world—a world where the mothers and elder women were held in great respect; a world that worshipped the Great Goddess in all her fullness and abundance.

Many so-called experts have discounted these goddess figures as "fertility figures," but there is evidence that refutes this assessment. With their pendulous breasts, full bellies, and buttocks, these goddess figures suggest women of some age and wisdom (not fertility). The features of these goddesses also display age and gravity, suggesting these were figures of veneration that celebrated the Mother and Crone stages of life, rather than the Maiden or young woman.

The World of the Great Goddess

The mysteries of our human and planetary past are currently being unraveled. As such, we are discovering more about the Great Goddess and her world. Archaeologists around the world are making new discoveries and looking at old finds with a fresh eye. Many statues of the Goddess once relegated to museum basements are being dusted off and put on display for all to see. The word "goddess" is slowly replacing the words "fertility figure" in exhibits, books, and magazines.

What is emerging from the distant past in all parts of the world is evidence of the presence of goddess-centered religious traditions. For instance, the recently discovered Cussac Cave in France has revealed a great number of female figures, along with animals, that tell us more about the ancient world, the Great Goddess, and her people. It will be many years before we are able to see all the images that have been found at Cussac Cave, but the ones shown so far have great subtlety and sophistication.

France has more large caves than any other country on earth. To date, 144 caves have been discovered in France. Many of the caves are decorated with ancient cave paintings and carvings, and most contain goddess images. The Goddess has also been found in caves in Africa in beautifully stylized engravings, although these seldom get the attention that the French images do. In fact, Africa has a very rich heritage of sophisticated ancient cave art. In Australia, too, many caves have been found with female images shown as figures of reverence and respect. In fact, all over the world there are a great number of images of sacred female forms.

The similarities in the look and feel of goddess images found in all parts of the world are quite remarkable. Goddesses from the Baltic are similar to goddesses found in Central America. Many African, Scandinavian, and Australian goddess images share striking similarities. The more we learn, the more we see that humans share a common vision of what is sacred, what is important, and essential to survival.

The work of Marija Gimbutas has made many of these amazing goddess images accessible to us. Her research into the ancient worlds of the Goddess have brought us all nearer to understanding why the Goddess is important today. As she once wrote:

> Through an understanding of what the Goddess was, we can better understand nature and we can build our ideologies so it will be easier for us to live.

If you want to see ancient goddess figures first-hand, most museums have at least two or three in their collections. You will probably be amazed at the unheralded beauty of these figures. In fact, many goddess treasures still go unnoticed. At Mound City in Ohio, I discovered a beautiful copper goddess figure in their museum. It has not appeared in books, but it is clearly a goddess discovered here in America. If you are lucky enough to live in Ohio, Florida, or anywhere along the Mississippi, know that many goddesses have been found in your area. If you live in New Hampshire, Massachusetts, Maine, or Vermont, visit Mystery Hill in Salem, New Hampshire, and experience an ancient American sacred site replete with goddess energy. If you live in the Southwest there are many petroglyph carvings and sites that contain goddess or female images. In the plains states, there are ancient mounds and stone circles.

Modern Goddess Finds

Many years ago my husband visited the Lascaux Cave in France, when it was still open to the public.

What struck him most profoundly was the sense of safety and security he felt. The cave, he said, was nestled deep in the body of the Earth, and he felt a mysterious and overwhelming sense of sacredness and peace surrounding him.

In recent years, many new goddesses have been found. Here are just a few of the recent monumental discoveries:

1994–Ardeche Gorge Cave complex found

1996–New caves and cave art found in Italy and Spain

1999–Ancient tools found in Edmonton, Alberta, Canada

2000–Giant Crystal Cave found in Spain with large crystal geode

Cussac cave with hundreds of images

Ancient pre-Mayan Temple found in the rain forests of Guatemala

An amazing 5,000-year-old Sumerian burial site found in Iraq.

2001–Pre-Incan Moche tombs discovered in Peru

In Egypt a 3,000-year-old tomb discovered

Archeologists discover what they think is Genghis Khan's tomb

The sunken city of Ro Heneth (a.k.a. Heraclion) discovered in Greece

All of these recent discoveries will yield an amazing amount of new information about the distant past. Statues and artifacts of the Goddess will be found at many of them. The visions and wisdom we have gained from the already-found artifacts teach us that our ancestors were far more like us than we ever could have imagined. Each new discovery gives us a fuller understanding of those who came before us. As we grow in this understanding, the culture and wisdom of the Goddess is returning to our own time and informs our own twenty-first century values.

Even now, contemporary artists are creating new art based on the ancient symbol language of the Great Goddess. Groups like the Goddess 2000 Project are actively promoting the creation of new sacred goddess art. People everywhere who honor the Goddess are celebrating her presence in a thousand ways. This is a time of great discovery and great change. May we have the wisdom to learn to value what is truly important as we continue to discover new art and images from the past in caves and tombs.

There is still much to discover from the past as we move forward into the future. The ancient goddesses deep in the earth are waiting to share their mysterious secrets with us.

La Llorona, Legend of the Weeping Woman

by Edain McCoy

A few years ago, on a clear and moonless night littered with stars, I was driving with my friend Maria through rural south Texas, heading home to the city of San Antonio from the remote village where we had just taken a class on herbal lore. The warm autumn air was dry and still, and we had the windows open as we made our way down a one-lane caliche road that, in flood-prone south Texas, often crisscrossed low-water crossings over small creeks and arroyos.

I slowed the car as we came to yet another deep dip in the road that went over a creek. I could hear the burble of the water as it passed through the channels cut beneath the road.

Suddenly, without warning, a wisp of white flew across our path. I slammed down the brake pedal with the Pavlovian instinct of a south Texan who lived where deer and cars collide on an hourly basis. Before my mind could register that deer don't leap across bridges and that what passed before us was not any kind of animal, the silence of the night was rent by a faint wail as the fog-like mass faded as it moved downstream.

Maria grabbed my arm with a grip like a vise-clamp.

"Vaya, vaya!" she urged. *Go, go.*

I drove on, knowing that Maria was not easily frightened, and that, when she was, there was usually a very good reason. As I drove on, she was quiet, and when I glanced at her I noted that she hugged her bare arms as if cold.

Later, after we pulled onto Interstate Highway 10, and the peril had faded into the night, I pressed Maria for answers.

"Haven't you ever heard of La Llorona?" she said after some time, an incredulous look on her face.

I thought I was familiar with most of the major Mexican and Southwestern folk legends, but this one was new to me.

"Llorona?" I asked.

"The Weeping Woman."

"Weeping. That makes sense." The name Llorona [lah-yah-RO-nah] was taken from the Spanish verb *llorar,* meaning "to cry." Still, this tidbit of etymology did not explain why this La Llorona was wandering above a meandering creek late at night. Maria sighed and patiently explained the story to me.

The Story of Beautiful La Llorona

"A long time ago there was a young woman," Maria began her story, "She was very beautiful, but she was jealous of her children. Her husband adored them, and she felt she was second in his affections.

"After he died, she fell in love with another man who wanted her, but not her children. Her children, she decided, would never cost her the love of another man, and so she took them down to the creek and drowned them. When she told her lover what she'd done, he was horrified, and told the leaders of the town. They drowned her in the same creek in which she killed her children, and now she's doomed to wander the rivers of Mexico and Texas for eternity seeking her dead children."

A shiver passed through me as Maria finished her story. Sure, it was a typically titillating ghost story, but as with most folk legends, I sensed there was something more profound at its root. I determined to uncover the roots of La Llorona.

To my delight La Llorona's legends were well documented in a variety of versions. Maria's was one of the most recent accounts, but most depicted the young woman as a killer, someone who couldn't be trusted because she was envious of the attention paid to her offspring. She was the epitome of the devourer goddess who typically eats her young. In fact, I knew then I was on the right path to unveiling the true La Llorona as I began to suspect that this was a perversion of a much older myth, like the ancient Celtic banshee, or the Washer at the Ford, a fallen goddess who wails and cries when a member of the family she is protecting is about to die.

La Llorona's Ancient Roots

The next-most recent tales of La Llorona told of her drowning herself when she discovered she was pregnant with the child of a married man with whom she'd been having an affair. Older versions, meanwhile, told of her being drowned by her father when he discovered his daughter's pregnancy. Another told of La Llorona's husband drowning the children himself because of his own jealousy, and then blaming the deaths on his wife. This again was a theme of many familiar myths, particularly that of Rhiannon in the Welsh tradition.

As the pages of Meso-American history turned back, La Llorona emerged more as a victim than a criminal, and I began to feel an empathy with her. Yet I was sure I was not at the root of the legend yet.

I began talking to everyone I met about La Llorona and found many, like myself, who believed in her existence. They had heard her, they said. They had seen her. They knew when she was near because they felt her cold, desolate presence. Thus, they avoided creeks, arroyos, and low-water crossings after dark.

All of them feared her.

But she only sought her children, I told them. I wondered why they were so afraid? What archetypical message was she sending that made people fear her rather than weep in sympathy with her over her plight?

The answer was to be found in the pre-Columbian world of old Mexico, in the great civilization of the Aztec people.

In the great Aztec city of Tenochtitlan, the leaders of the Aztec people thrived. Their gods and goddesses provided all that was needed, and they were worshipped and honored with a violent passion.

At the dawn of the sixteenth century, the prophets began telling legends of metal-clad men with long beards, riding fast on four-legged beasts across the sea. With them would come death and the downfall of their civilization.

According to the stories, the wails of the goddess Chuacoatl were often heard at this time, and the prophets and priests channeled her words to the people:

My children. My beloved children.
I cannot hide them.
Where can my children go?

The warning was the wail of a living mother, a goddess who foretold the coming of the Spanish Conquistadors who eventually destroyed the Aztec way of life with their European weapons, diseases, and religion.

Is Chuacoatl, I wondered, the same woman as La Llorona—still searching in vain for the civilization who loved her and whom she once protected. Or, if she is merely the ghost of a jealous young woman who drowned her own children out of jealousy, why then do people still fear her so?

Even today, I still sometimes hear her cry in the night. It is a mother's lament, and maybe. . . maybe, she is—like the Celtic banshee goddess—a little bit more than a mother.

For Further Study

The most absorbing tales of La Llorona are found in children's books. The Internet also has some interesting sites dedicated to her origins. Search for a site called "The Spirit of La Llorona" (www.lallorona.com), in which her tale is called a Mexican "Blair Witch Controversy," for the most complete look at her stories. You can also find more information about her in the following books:

Carrasco, David L. *Quetzalcoatl and Irony of Empire: Myths and Prophecies in the Aztec Tradition.* University Press of Colorado, 2001.

Hayes, Joe. *La Llorona: The Weeping Woman* (for young children). Trails West Publishing, 1987.

Villanueva, Alma Luz. *Weeping Woman: La Llorona and Other Stories* (for older children and adults). Bilingual Press, 1994.

Ghost Powder Spell

by Eileen Holland

This simple powder will divert unwelcome ghosts and spirits when placed in their path. It is best made while the Moon is waning.

> 1 part   dried rosemary leaves, ground
> 1 part   sea salt
> 1 part   garlic powder
> Dried black beans

Blend the first three ingredients and seal the powder in a glass container. Store the beans in a separate container. Beans are an ancient charm against ghosts, and black is the best color for banishing. Keep the beans handy for emergencies. Throw or spit beans at a ghost to drive it away.

If there is a ghost or spirit in your home, try to observe its behavior. Note in which room it is most often seen, felt, or heard, and pay special attention to its comings and goings. Sprinkle the Ghost Powder so as to make a barrier across the places where it enters your space. Also sprinkle the powder where it exits, but be sure to do this when it is not present, so that you will not trap it in your home.

Spirits are easy to call but can be hard to get rid of, so Ouija boards and séances are dangerous. If you insist on calling spirits despite this warning, be sure to cast a circle first, to protect yourself. Ghost Powder could be sprinkled to mark the circle on the floor. If the Ghost Powder cannot banish the ghost or spirit at your house, you are dealing with something very strong and need professional help. Look for a Witch, psychic, or other practitioner who has experience and expertise in banishing ghosts, or helping spirits to move on into the light.

The Mysterious Black Dutch

by Susan Sheppard

Nearly one thousand years ago, a mysterious group of small, fairy-boned people arrived in eastern Europe, bringing with them various mystical arts, a colorful style of dress, and expert skills in magic and fortunetelling.

The native Europeans did not know where the strangers came from, but because of their dark skin and black hair the Europeans speculated their origins were in Egypt or Turkey—and the group's new name, Gypsies, comes from this misunderstanding of their origin. (Their own name for themselves is "Rom," or "Roma" in the plural.) When these traveling bands came upon an area called Wallachia (in present-day Romania), they settled for a time and their numbers began to grow. For a few hundred years the Wallachians and the Gypsies lived together in relative peace until an evil prince assumed his throne and began a reign of murder that set the two groups against one another.

The Travelers and the Impaler

The traveling Gypsies brought with them a tradition of magical arts, spellwork, and enchantments and divinations. There is also evidence that they believed in vampires (from India legend) and shapeshifters such as werewolves. This is ironic, given that one of the first tormenters of these

people was Vlad Tepes, prince of Wallachia, otherwise known as Dracula.

Vlad Tepes was not a vampire but a mere mortal with a twisted mind and soul. The kind of evil Vlad bestowed upon his own people was more gruesome than any vampire's. During his reign Vlad murdered or impaled at least a half a million people (mostly for the pleasure of watching them die slowly). At the time, Vlad Tepes made war on surrounding lands, in an effort to wipe out infidels. Vlad especially hated the Turks who had earlier imprisoned him.

The Turks, meanwhile, fought him so valiantly that Vlad, enraged, slaughtered thousands of captured Turks. Because Vlad thought the small, isolated traveling bands of Gypsies were related to the Turks, or Egyptians or other infidels, he enjoyed killing them. In fact, he gave orders to his soldiers to, "Go out and kill all of those little dark people who look like Egyptians, and do it well." In time, hundreds of Wallachian Gypsies, or Roma, were rounded up. Three Roma men were butchered, and their parts cooked into soup. The remaining Roma were forced to eat the men.

The Roma in Europe

Despite their trials, the Roma remained a resilient group, and they escaped into the Black Forest region of Germany to recover their losses. To the Germans, the Wallachian Gypsies became the Zigeuner. Depending upon your source, *zigeuner* meant "Egyptian," or "Go away thief!" The Zigeuner traveled over Germany in painted wagons and practiced their usual crafts—soothsaying, silver and copper-smithing, horsetrading, stargazing, strumming, dancing, and basketmaking. Many Zigeuner Gypsies became famous horse-trainers, acrobats, and musicians in German circuses.

The Zigeuner were renowned in Germany, but were they popular there? Not hardly. The German genocide of the Zigeuner Gypsies ended up being far worse than Dracula's had been earlier. In the 1700s, weekend Gypsy hunts were held in the German countryside. A bounty was placed on each Gypsy's head. The more Gypsies you killed, the more money you earned. Typically, Zigeuner men were drawn and quartered. Women and children were decapitated. Their heads were then mounted and displayed in German drawing rooms.

By the mid to late 1700s, many Zigeuner Gypsies fled Germany. They were led by dreams of another land, one where they could live freely, practice their mystical arts in peace, and find some measure of acceptance (knowing full well there would never be complete acceptance.) This took the Zigeuner to Rotterdam in the Netherlands—a city undergoing a mass immigration of other German peoples who had suffered persecution in their native land.

The Roma in a New World

In the late 1700s, the Zigeuner headed for a port in Philadelphia. The Roma had heard streets in America were paved with silver and gold, and perhaps even copper to hammer into jewelry and cooking pots. On the ship over, the Roma sang, danced, and made their plans. Unfortunately, their reputation as Gypsies preceded them to the New World.

A ways from shore, the Roma were forced off the ship and made to swim to land where a crowd awaited to beat them with clubs and boat hooks. However, the Roma outsmarted the whites, some heading to isolated parts of New Jersey to later join the Rominichels, or English Gypsies. Others headed for the blue, floating Alleghenies of south-central Pennsylvania. What more beautiful place for a Gypsy to hide than under that region's airy slopes and pure starlight?

And then the Roma hit upon their first stroke of good luck. In Pennsylvania, the Roma found a people who had many of the same cultural traits as they. The Pennsylvania Dutch were a people with traditions of hexing and spell-casting, of speaking to ghosts and spirits and reading signs, and of training and trading horses just like the Gypsies.

So around 1800 was a time for the Roma to changes names and wardrobes again. The Zigeuner Gypsies became Chikkeners (in the Pennsylvania Dutch language). But this time there was a trade-off, something the Zigeuner-Chikkeners would have to give up forever—their identity as Gypsies. In the past, the Roma had maintained their identity mostly by keeping a prohibition against marrying or having families with non-Gypsies. In fact, such a thing was considered quite taboo. But in America, a natural cultural mixing pot unlike much of Europe, Roma numbers quickly fragmented, and the Chikkeners couldn't keep the Gypsy lifestyle up. The Pennsylvania Dutch were good to them, providing them a haven unlike any time in their history. The Pennsylvania Dutch admired Rom skills in metal and glass crafts, horse-raising, and magical arts. So it was a natural step for the the Chikkeners to "marry in" with the them.

As a result, this small group of Roma-Gypsies, who had survived just about every atrocity offered up in Europe (even Dracula!) came to be known in America, especially in the mid-Atlantic region, as the "Black Dutch," and sometimes "Dirty Dutch" (in parts of West Virginia and Pennsylvania).

This is where our tale takes another turn and deepens even more. Like the Melungeons of Tennessee and Virginia, the term "Black Dutch" began to be used as a cover term. The Chikkeners had been so successful in covering up their true identities as Gypsies, that other groups began to claim they were also Black Dutch. These imposters included tri-racial groups of white, Indian, and black blood.

Why? In thirty-six states it was a felony to marry a person of another race. And as the Black Dutch were considered European by this time, in many cases a prosecution of a dark-skinned person was avoided by claiming to be Black Dutch. This was a convenient way for families with black or Indian blood member to stay together. Census takers questioning racially ambiguous families were known to say: "Black Dutch? Ah, I see. Swarthy Germans."

Later some Black Dutch married African-Americans and mixed bloods. Although the Chikkeners were not friendly with Indian tribes when they first came over (locals kept mixing them up with natives because of their dark skin and habit of wearing feathers in their hair) many Black Dutch today have strong lines of Native American Indian blood. Such a mixing of cultures could only take place in a country as diverse as America. After all, the Gypsies never found real acceptance in Europe, and had hardly ever lived with whites before. However, in America the Black Dutch Gypsies would thrive and mix in as they never had before.

Black Dutch Magic

The Black Dutch Gypsies took on the dress and customs of the Pennsylvania Dutch, but their culture did not disappear. In fact, the Black Dutch never gave up their native interest in the occult and the mystical. The spirit world was in their blood and there was no getting it out of them. In the end, the Pennsylvania Dutch incorporated many Gypsy customs and beliefs in their own culture, thus enriching it immensely.

In 1819, a compelling book of folklore was published which covered the spells, hexes, folk remedies, powwow medicines, and enchantments of the Pennsylvania Dutch. Called *The Long Lost Friend,* its author was John George Hohman, a German Catholic. What is interesting is that Hohman claimed he had gathered much of the folk and occult lore in the book from a "European Gypsy." Remarkably, this book gained much popularity in the south when a Jewish salesman bought copies of it and sold them to freed blacks in New Orleans. Magic in *The Long Lost Friend* involves using parts of black roosters and chickens and bat's hearts in spells—items that are normally associated with Hoodoo in the South.

Evidence is mounting of just how much the Chikkener, or Black Dutch Gypsies, influenced the practice of magic in the eastern United States. In the powwow magic of the Pennsylvania Dutch in the north and the later in Hoodoo practices in the south, the rich and varied magical practices of the Roma are clearly evident.

One of the more interesting facts that surround Black Dutch or Chikkener magical beliefs is the way unrelated cultural traditions are blended. That is, Black Dutch magic combine African/Hoodoo practices in the American South, Asian Indian or Hindi root practicies, a dash of the Native American magic and remedies, and European charms, witchcraft, and occult lore.

I never understood how this could be true until I embarked on a curvy path of unraveling my own Black Dutch heritage. Here are just a few connections I found.

In recent years there has been a resurgence of a wedding custom called "Jumping the Broom," where the bride and groom jump over a broom after reciting the wedding vows. "Jumping the Broom" has been a part African-American weddings for hundreds of years (perhaps longer) dating back to the slave days. It is popular today in Pagan and Wiccan handfastings.

Remarkably, the first documented reports of the "Jumping the Broom" ceremony was among Romanian Gypsies in the 1400s. Even today in the hills and mountains Appalachia, where the Black Dutch had a strong influence, there remains a "Jumping the Broom" wedding custom that survives.

Here's another connection. A belief in the crossroads as a place of spiritual danger, where devils and ghosts lurk, is common among European Gypsies and African Americans in the South. How this idea turned up in the American South and eventually found its way to the Mississippi Delta as a part of Hoodoo practices and beliefs (as in the famous tale of blues guitarist Robert Johnson) begs more research. Other world cultures believe in the dark powers of the crossroads as well, and likely it is the Roma people who spread this idea in their travels across Europe, the Middle East, and parts of Africa. It appears too that the Roma brought the idea of vampires and other shape-shifters to Europe from India, where such ideas originated. The Pennsylvania Dutch have long been known to hex, cast spells, and practice a type of sorcery that has to do with summoning ghosts, ancestors, and spirits of the dead. Such practices are strongly prohibited in Jewish and Christian law, and it's pretty hard to get around this fact. Delving into the world of ghosts, little gods, and ancestors would not be a sin to the Black Dutch since such practices are based on an old tradition of using spirits to cast spells. That is, sorcery involving summoning spirits, spells, and hexes are not at all prohibited in the Roma culture.

So it makes sense that the influence of the Roma is what caused the Pennsylvania Dutch to break the most fundamental laws of their sacred book, the Bible, in summoning spirits. In Christian religions, there are strong warnings that forbid such sorcery, yet the Pennsylvania Dutch referred to their bibles as "conjure books," and used them to invoke magic and unleash spirits. This only makes sense when consideringing the Pennsylvania Dutch's deep connection to and involvement with Gypsies.

Black Dutch Heritage

As one-eighth Black Dutch, for most of my life I did not know what the term meant. I couldn't imagine and was only frustrated when I tried to find out. Part of my family had dark and exotic features but thought this was because there was a Native American blood in the family tree (which there is). I can remember my Black Dutch grandmother calling a deck of playing cards "the devil's book" and worrying when I taught myself to read fortunes with cards the Gypsy way. She never told me not to learn such a thing, though.

When I inquired of my grandmother what Black Dutch meant, she, herself, did not know. Grandma's mother died when she was small, but she remembered her as dark-skinned, with snappy dark eyes and a heavy German accent. Grandma also recalled her aunt coming to visit one time wearing an unusual, colorful blouse. This was all Grandma knew of her mother's Black Dutch family.

About twenty years ago, I dreamed I was visiting a historical town, perhaps Philadelphia, and in my dream I was browsing in an antique shop. I wandered across an old oil painting of a brown-skinned woman wearing a red turban. She had delicate, dark hands and tapering fingers that looked as though they had been carved from wood. She was a handsome woman but not pretty. I could not decide whether the subject of the portrait was a Gypsy or an American Indian. She could have been either. I wanted the painting, but couldn't afford it. Yet I knew the woman in the portrait belonged to me just as I belonged to her.

Years later, when I was doing family research I received an e-mail from my father's cousin. He said he believed he had located a picture of my great-grandparents. He mentioned the photograph was quite worn, as if someone had lovingly carried it in a wallet for nearly a lifetime, but he would be happy to scan the photo and e-mail it to me.

When the hundred-year-old photograph popped up on the computer screen I burst into tears. There was my dark angel—the one that had watched over me in my dreams. At well under five feet in height, she was just an elf, but her face, so like my fathers', was as dark as a chestnut. She was the mysterious one who spelled out my name over the Moon, one who gazed down at me from silver spangled stars, whose cries I had long heard carried on the wind.

And she had always lived in me, had informed my behavior as I danced with my Gypsy tambourine as a four-year-old, read fortunes with plain old playing cards at the fall carnival each year, interpreted the signs and studied the stars, held séances, belly-danced, and started my ghost walking tour company.

Through the picture I had come to realize the Black Dutch were in my blood, and would always be. My wise body and heart knew this long before my mind ever did.

Now, on this long journey of my life, I know I am at a cross-roads where any answers I find are only slivers of the mysteries suggested by the ancestors. But I know I will keep looking to the ancient ones who offer us their guidance and love, and always I will seek the voice of the little dark one who whispered to me—"all roads lead to you."

For Further Study

Griggs, Linda. *Wayfaring Stranger: The Black Dutch, German Gypsies, or Chicanere, and their relation to the Melungeon.* The Patrin Web Journal (http://www.geocities.com/Paris/5121/melungeon.htm).

Tattoo Consecration Spell

by Ed Fitch

Although this ritual is intended primarily for the very common Celtic or Teutonic interlace tattoo that people have put about theirs upper arms, it can be applied too to most tattoos on the arm that are intended as protective talismans.

At the dark of the Moon, go to a place of solitude. Take with you an image of your patron diety (with a female aspect that appeals to you), a candle, an iron knife (or athame), and a small bottle of rum or similar god-power elixir. Dress as befits a warrior.

Set the images of your male and female patrons in a place of honor, and set the rum and the knife before them. Sit before the images, gaze on them, light the candle, and meditate for thirty-nine heartbeats upon your connection to your protective patrons.

Then open the bottle of rum and liberally wet your finger with it. On your tattoo draw the "Tyr" rune (with arrow pointing upward), then on the opposite side of the tattoo draw a sun-wheel (a circle with an X drawn in it). Say:

O High Ones, hear my call!
Grant that this sacred and powerful
Marking upon and within my body
Be consecrated in your honor,
To be a shield, an armour,
And a protection

Against all harm
To the mind and to the body.
May the High Ones grant me
The endurance that I may need
To be victorious
In any time of peril.
In the names of the Great Ones, so be it!

Pick up your blade and lay it across your tattoo in three places, saying in these or similar words:

May the armor of protection
Ever be stored
Strong and vital
Within this ancient
And sacred symbol. So be it!

If you have a tattoo on the other arm, repeat this spell on that side also. Then hold the bottle of rum up before the image of your patron, saying in these or similar words:

My friend and lady, my guardian,
My good and strong companion,
I drink this in your honor,
For strength, for courage,
And for the most powerful
Of protection. So be it!

Pour a little of the rum before the image of your patrons, drink some yourself, and relax for a while. You may wish to talk with your patrons about your life and about the protection that you desire. When you feel that the time is proper, put out the candle, and depart.

It is well to repeat this spell whenever you feel the need of it, and in times of stress or danger. Also, at the dark of the Moon each month it is a good idea to "feed" your tattoo by anointing it with rum.

Whirling Dervish Meditation Ritual

by Jim Weaver

Our whirling endures.

—Mevlana Celaleddin Rumi

Dance is one of the oldest forms of human expression. The people of primitive civilizations danced for many reasons—to celebrate a successful harvest or hunt, to keep away evil spirits, to remember ancestors, or bring life-giving rain. Whatever the reason for the dance, there is no question that many early dances were inspired by magical and religious beliefs. Dance was viewed as a way people could temporarily relieve themselves of earthly ties, and for a while, rise to the realm of spirit.

Although dance has been used since ancient times to express religious and spiritual feelings, it was the great poet and mystic, Mevlana Celaleddin (or Jalaluíddin) Rumi, who raised dance to a sacred religious rite.

The Whirling Dervishes

Over 700 years ago, Rumi founded the great Moslem religious order known in the Western world as the "whirling dervishes." *Dervish* is a Persian word, which means "doorway." This order, which was based in the cultural center of Konya, Turkey during the 1200s, became famous for its *sema*, a twirling trance-like dance noted for its exquisite turning, or whirling, movements.

Unlike other religious systems that occasionally use dance as part of their ceremonies, the whirling dervishes look upon dance as the core of their mystical and religious experience. In fact, the dervishes themselves do not think of their whirling ceremony as a dance at all; instead, they believe the dance-like movements to be part of their spiritual and religious observance.

The dance is a form of celebration. As the dervishes turn, they cast off all earthly passions—they "sacrifice them"—so they can connect with the divine. As they whirl to the music of the *ney*, or reed flute, and *kudum*, or small double drum, they align themselves with the cosmic order. They also show their faith in the circle of birth, life, death, and rebirth. Above all, their ceremony is an expression of harmony and universal love, and a time to connect with the spirit of Mevlana (Master) Rumi, who created the whirling dervish ceremony.

A Dervish Meditation

The meditation that follows is not part of the cycle of religious ceremony performed by the whirling dervishes. Instead, it draws upon the rich mystical symbolism found in the sema dance. When the dervishes perform the sema the number whirlers may vary widely, from as few as three to as many as thirty. Your meditation may be performed alone or with a group.

For the meditation to be more enriching, you should understand the deep mystical significance of the basic movements involved in the turning. Before the actual ceremony, the dervishes walk in a circle past the musicians and the spiritual leader known as a sheikh three times. This walk honors Rumi's son, Sultan Veled, and recognizes our place in the eternal circle of life and resurrection. A prayer to Rumi and a chapter from the Koran are then chanted.

Understanding the Movements

Before the turning begins, the dervishes remove their black robes and let them fall to the floor. This action symbolizes the release of earthly cares and passions. Their arms are crossed over their chests, each hand placed on the opposite shoulder. Then the music begins, and as each dervish begins to turn, they raise their arms. The right palm must face up; the left palm down. It is believed that the divine power enters the right palm and is directed through the body into the earth from the down-facing left palm. In Western magical traditions, positive energy is typically raised by turning deosil, or clockwise; however, the dervishes turn counterclockwise. They believe that by turning in this manner, each dervish is turning towards their own heart. Each turn is done on the left foot.

A complete ceremony consists of four *selams,* or sections. During the final selam, the sheikh joins the turning by moving to the center of the floor in a very beautiful moment. In this formation, the sheikh represents the Sun, and the dervishes turning about him represent the planets of our solar system.

Dervish Ceremonial Clothing

You don't need to obtain special clothing to perform the meditation. In fact, during the early to mid-twentieth century, when the whirling dervish order was banned from publicly performing in Turkey, dervishes frequently practiced in private in their street clothes. If you do have a simple white robe and you're comfortable in it, use it. Traditionally, the flowing white dervish skirt symbolizes the future, which is veiled in mystery. The wool-felt cylindrical hats represent tombstones, not in the physical sense, but in that each dervish has put to rest their worldly cares and egos and be open to receiving the divine power.

Dervish Music

The music of the whirling dervishes is rooted in Turkish classical music of the Ottoman period. It is hypnotic and rhythmic, and instruments include the ney, Oriental violin, kudum, and, perhaps most important, the human voice. Even though you may not understand the language, the chants are thrilling to hear.

Since music is at the center of the dervish ceremony, you should obtain a CD or cassette of dervish music for your ritual. In music stores they may be found under Turkish, Middle Eastern, or New Age sections. I've also ordered dervish music from local music stores.

The Meditation

It takes years of training to actually become a whirling dervish. This meditation is only meant to be used for personal spiritual growth and increased awareness. Now is a good time to mention that the whirling dervish experience is not for men only. Over the centuries women have also taken part in the ceremonies and have held the position of sheikh.

To begin, cast a circle and purify it according to your beliefs. The altar should be covered with a blue cloth. On the left, light a black candle, to absorb all negative thoughts and passion. On the right, light a white candle; this is Spirit. In the center, light an orange candle, this is the Sun. In the front center of the altar, place a small stone. This stone represents the resting place of all your cares and worries.

For the moment, you should be open only to the healing power of the Divine. Begin the music, then ground and center. Free your mind for awhile, forget the daily grind and the stress it causes. Banish negativity by walking three times counterclockwise around your circle. Stop in front of the altar. Feel the music and sway in time with it. Raise your arms—right palm up, left palm down. You are the Earth in microcosm. Slowly, and I mean slowly, begin turning counterclockwise around the circle, perhaps three times. Stop and rest, kneel or sit. If you wish, continue turning. Always turn with your left foot as your axis. You will experience some dizziness; be very careful.

After you have finished turning, sit before the altar and think of any problem or habit you wish to get rid of. Since many dervishes practiced healing magic, now would be a good time to say words of power for healing purposes.

Don't be surprised if you achieve a light trance-like state. Let yourself return to a normal frame of mind. To close the meditation, thank each candle and extinguish it. Thank the stone for accepting and absorbing your negativity. Thank each direction, including the heavens and Earth. If you wish, continue listening to the beautiful music. Release your circle. You should feel calm and balanced. Record any thoughts or impressions you felt during the meditation in a journal. Put aside the ritual candles and stone, save them for the next time.

Getting used to turning takes time. Keep your meditations short and gradually lengthen them. If you ever begin to feel tired or dizzy, stop and relax within your circle.

I hope this meditation ritual will open new doors of opportunity for your spiritual growth. Feel free to add your own ideas as you go to make it right for you.

For Further Study

Friedlander, Shems. *The Whirling Dervishes*. State Univerity of New York Press, 1992.

For an introduction to dervish music:

Returning: Music of the Whirling Dervishes. Available in compact disc and cassette tape formats. Planet Earth Music, 1994.

Saami Spirit Ally Song

by Kristin Madden

The Saami are a people who live north of the Arctic Circle in Scandinavia and the Russian Kola Peninsula. Commonly known by the derogatory terms "Lapps" or "Laplanders," the Saami are nomadic herders who follow the migratory path of reindeer through the seasons. Some Saami are more settled, relying on fishing and hunting to survive.

Magical Saami

The Saami have been recognized for their magical and shamanic culture for thousands of years. Known in the Western world for their sorcery, the Saami people were reputed to be able to stop ships under full sail, thereby keeping foreigners from their shores. Saami diviners were also able to foretell events, know what was occurring at great distances, and even bring back tangible evidence of their out-of-body journeys to far-off lands. Saami wind wizards were both feared and sought for their magical ropes. These ropes were said to hold three winds of increasing strength that might be used by sailors—though with great caution.

The Saami were first described by Tacitus in A.D. 98. He called them the *Fenni* and placed their lands north of the Germanic tribes. The Fenni had no horses or weapons, and their homes were mobile. Fenni women joined the men in hunting and held equal power in society.

Like other native peoples, the Saami hold an animistic worldview in which all things are imbued with a type of spirit or energy. The Earth itself is seen as a living, sacred being. Nature is thought of as a gift to the people. For everything that the Saami take, they must give something back. In this way, they can continue the cycle of blessings. Children grow up with an understanding that Nature will teach them if only they will listen.

To the Saami, the spirit world is *saivo*. Saivo spirits are either nature spirits taking the form of wild creatures, or little people that live under the earth, similar to the Little People described in folklore throughout the world. These beings are known to work with humans under certain conditions as guardians or guides.

Much of the anthropological literature about the Saami focuses on the saivo allies of the *noaidi*, the Saami shamans. In 1975, Louise Backman became the first outsider to describe the saivo. Although she believed that only the noaidi could have a truly interactive relationship with these beings, she described the saivo as aiding all Saami people. At that time, so much study had been done on Saami shamanism and sorcery as an exclusive element of the culture that many early scholars assumed that these helping spirits were not a part of the lives of the rest of the people.

What researchers failed to see for so long is that the spiritual life of the shamans is not separate from that of the people. Spirituality is completely integrated into Saami life, and it permeates all aspects of the culture. It is true that the noaidi, or Miracle Men as they are now often called, have been drawn to a higher level of interaction with the spirit world. However, they are not alone in their interactions with the saivo.

In fact, the Saami worldview is fairly similar to that of Native North Americans in that there are several Saami "tribes." Each tribe has its own dialect, and its own vision of the supernatural world. In some cases, a person's saivo ally is believed to be inherited. This was true with the *Skolt Saami kaddz*, which functioned much like the clan guardians of some Native North American peoples. This guardian spirit was passed on from father to son and mother to daughter for generations.

Saivo Songs of the Saami

Many Saami grew up with a deep understanding of the close relationship between songs and the saivo that aid us. The Saami understand that the saivo do not communicate as we do in this reality. Therefore, we need an uncommon method of communicating with them. These songs, which connect common folk with the saivo, are called *juoigos* or *joik*, and are best thought of as a kind of special song that wells up from the depths of one's deepest soul.

Thought to have the ability to possess one's mind and therefore deeply feared by Christian missionaries, the Saami joik was long banned by Scandinavian and Russian governments as a song of the devil. Indeed, among the Saami the joik is deeply spiritual. It as seen as circular, with no real beginning or end, and was often used to facilitate the journeys of the shaman into the otherworlds. Joiker and joik are integral parts of the whole essence of being.

To start, a Saami would choose one or more of the saivo to work with. The Saami would come to one of the sacred mountains in the region and sing the sacred song, invoking the saivo and attempting to attract its attention. This effort was always undertaken with utmost seriousness of purpose, as it was believed if the Saami joiker was not fully committed to the joik and later attempted to get out of the relationship, the saivo could severely injure the singer.

In other cases, Saami youths would be approached while out in nature by a saivo spirit. The saivo would teach this young Saami a song, and the youth would return in a day's time to the same spot to meet the saivo again. If the spirit was ready to work with this individual, it would also return and expect the Saami to share in the song once more. On the third day, the singer would again return and share in the song. From that point on, the saivo spirit could be called upon by singing the learned song. And for the remainder of the youth's life, this saivo will act both as guide and guardian.

The Saivo Ally

For the noiadi, the saivo ally, once found, may be brought into magical workings through dreaming and shamanic journeying. In fact, many of the Saami people meet their saivo during dreaming, which is understood to be the journeying of the free soul while the physical body sleeps.

When the saivo are not with their Saami, they can be found at *siedde*. Siedde are sacred places, usually stone sites. The siedde may also take the form of sacred mountains or natural stones, or they may be man-made stone altars. The Saami go to these places to make offerings to their saivo and ask for their assistance.

In general, the noiadi is protected by the saivo on journeys to the Land of the Dead. These spirit allies also teach the noiadi the shamanic arts and thereby increase the personal power of the noiadi. This power may be used later in healing or in fighting other shamans or sorcerers who threaten the people. The saivo aid the noaidi, often through the use of the drum, in making the best determinations regarding judgment or punishment of the people who commit crimes against society.

Other Saami receive luck from the saivo. The saivo teach curing, the ways of plants, food finding, and more. They guide us to people and places that are beneficial and help us avoid potentially destructive situations. As most Saami children are taught early on, nature has much to teach us if we only listen.

For Further Study

Ahlback, Tore, ed. *Saami Religion*. Donner Institute for Research in Religious and Cultural History, 1987.

Backman, Louise. *Sajva*. Stockholm Studies in Comparative Religion, 1975.

Frankincense and Myrrh

by Elizabeth Hazel

The Roman author Ovid provided a vivid story of the origin of myrrh in *The Metamorphoses,* written circa A.D. 10. Myrra was a young woman who had the great misfortune to fall in love with her father. Her nurse discovered her dark secret, and arranged for Myrra to join with her father on a dark night when her mother was worshipping at the temple of Ceres. Afterward in the light, her father was horrified to discover that his young lover was his daughter. Anguished with torment for her impiety, Myrra left home pregnant and wandered the world. When she was nearly ready to deliver her baby, Myrra begged the gods to give her some other form. Juno Lucina delivered of her a son, Adonis, who was in turn raised by Venus, and Myrra became a tree which sheds sap like tears from its wood—the resin later known to us from the nativity story, wherein it was one of the gifts of the Magi, myrrh.

Myrrh, and its Biblical and botanical counterpart frankincense, had been in use for thousands of years before the days of the Roman caesars. The *Egyptian Book of the Dead,* written 3,500 years ago, mentions a variety of uses for frankincense and myrrh as offerings, incense, anointing oils, perfume, and as an ingredient in the embalming of corpses.

Why are these substances so precious? What qualities have made them so desirable throughout history? Ovid's story suggests that the gods created myrrh as proof that the gods listen to sincere prayers. But even more important may be these resins' botanical origins, their medicinal properties, and their long use in religious ceremonies.

Magical Resins

Frankincense is derived from the plant *Boswellia carterii* or *Boswellia thurifera*. It is a shrub-like tree with fern-shaped leaves and white or pink flowers. Its ancient name was olibanum. Myrrh, meanwhile, comes from a shrub-like tree, *Commiphora myrrha*, that has broad aromatic leaves and white flowers. This tree's ancient name was karam. Both of these species belong to the *Burseaceae* family, and are native to Africa, Asia Minor (Persia), southern Asia, and China.

Technically speaking, frankincense and myrrh are gummy saps, or resins, collected from these plants that become solid as they dry, and are easily crushed and powdered. Myrrh resin is a pale, smooth ivory color; frankincense resin is a darker, rougher resin that dries into multiple shades of amber and gold. The resin can be used and processed in a number of ways.

As medicinal substances, frankincense and myrrh have internal and external uses. Myrrh is used for weak gums and teeth, and is even now added to some brands of toothpaste. It is also a disinfectant used to pack wounds, and to wash sores and hemorrhoids. It soothes coughs, colds, and sore throats, and at one time it was used to treat leprosy. Frankincense is a bit gentler on the skin, so it is used cosmetically for wrinkles and skin diseases. It was also utilized to cure respiratory and urinary infections, and as an anti-inflammatory agent for rheumatism and arthritis.

Both substances are mildly sedative and have an uplifting quality. This has led to the use of frankincense and myrrh for sacred purposes—as an incense component and as an anointing unguent. The Egyptians burned the raw resins in their elaborate funeral ceremonies to propitiate Anubis, Osiris, and Ra. Their fragrances are richly warm, sweet, thick, and cloying. They can be overpowering when burned in an enclosed space. A few pieces of resin on a charcoal brickette will burn for several minutes, cleansing and purifying the altar space and opening the mind. In fact, the Catholic Church's incense is made with frankincense and myrrh, along with a third ingredient—either sandalwood powder or copal resin.

The magical qualities attributed to frankincense and myrrh are related to their medicinal qualities: altering states of consciousness, nurturing, purifying, and communicating with gods and spirits. When burned, these resins create a sacred space for meditation and communion with higher powers. They work particularly well during invocations, carrying words or thoughts to the gods in the thick smoke.

Frankincense and myrrh can be rendered into essential oils through steam distillation. As oils, they are thick, sticky, and powerfully aromatic. For use on skin or as an anointing unguent they need to be diluted with a carrier like sweet almond or sesame oil.

The change from a solid resin to an oil puts them under the rulership of the great goddess Isis, and imbue them with different therapeutic qualities than the resins. Frankincense and myrrh oils accent the more feminine and receptive qualities in magical use, in contrast to the active and masculine properties of the solid resins. As pure essential oils, frankicense and myrrh are superb in oil diffusers, attracting the attributes of Isis—protection, security, and abundance, and as a remedy for urinary or genital ailments. Wearing an oil blend or unguent made from them stimulates the aura of animal magnetism and potency. The fragrance clings for hours, and gives a silky texture to the skin when blended with cold-pressed vegetable oils like jojoba, coconut, and sweet almond oils.

As either an oil or resin, frankincense and myrrh are appropriate for sacrifice or god-gifting. They act as an attractant in prosperity spells, as both have the virtue of great value. They increase the power of other ingredients when added to ritual incense or oil blends.

For a purification or protection incense, blend frankincense and myrrh with sage, rosemary, and thyme. As an incense for invocation, blend the two resins with sandalwood powder or copal. For wealth and prosperity spells, frankincense and myrrh can be combined with yarrow, clover, cinnamon, and cloves. For attraction, blend with lavender; with rose and peony for lasting love; with mandrake root or vetivert root for sexual magnetism.

The astrological and magical attributions for these resins are diverse. The Qabalistic attributions to the Sephiroth give myrrh to Binah (Saturn) and frankincense to Tiphareth (the Sun). Frankincense is solar; attributed to Ra and Baal, and is an ingredient for exorcism blends. Myrrh is considered feminine and lunar, sacred to Isis. It is a component of healing spells, and is used to bless amulets, talismans, and tools. Both are used in rituals to expand magical power and concentration. Agrippa designates all resins generally to the rulership of the Sun. Though Aries, a sign where the Sun exalts, rules myrrh, and Leo, as sign where the Sun rules, rules frankincense.

In general, frankincense and myrrh are very versatile, and will fit into any sort of sacred ceremony. Using them continues the timeless tradition of using these special essences to carry sincere prayers to the heavens.

For Further Study

Agrippa, Henry Cornelius. *Three Books of Occult Philosophy.* Edited and annotated by Donald Tyson. Llewellyn Publications, 1993.

Translation and introduction by E. A. Wallis Budge. *The Book of the Dead: The Hieroglyphic Transcript of the Papyrus of Ani.* Bell Publishing Company, 1960.

Cunningham, Scott. *Encyclopedia of Magical Herbs.* Llewellyn Publications, 1985.

Ovid. *The Metamorphoses.* Translated by Mary M. Innes, Penguin Books, 1965. (The story of Myrra is in Book Ten—page 233 in this edition.)

The Magical Bully
by ShadowCat

When you think back to grade school, are your clearest memories of the bullies in your class and their endless and insidious torments? This is probably true of middle school and high school as well. Some things never change, even into adulthood bullies seldom change their ways. Well, I'm here to tell you, the longer we allow the bullying to continue without confronting the behavior, the more it will always continue.

Note: For the purpose of this article, I will be using the masculine pronoun "he" in discussing the characteristics of the bully. The archetypal bully is a masculine energy, but of course bullies can be either gender, and even cross-gender.

Bullies in Magical Communities

Those of us who belong to a coven or who are active in magical communities no doubt have come in contact with what I call the magical bully. These are people who, like their forebears on the playground, endlessly brag (about all of their magical affiliations) and (as if anyone really cares) seek to "one up" anyone else who will listen to them. They will feign interest in asking you about your training and how you came to the Craft, and the moment you open youself up they will snicker. Despite the fact that you long ago left the playground behind, the magical bully almost always leaves you feeling down and out of place.

In general, the magical bully always has to be heard. He wants the first word and the last, even if he contradicts himself or is simply wrong. Whether he actually knows more than everyone else doesn't matter, because he is certain he does. Typically, a magical bully sees himself far differently than others actually see him—usually as a great benefactor rather than a manipulator. If he is reading this, he will not see that this applies to him.

The magical bully criticizes everyone and everything. His view of life is essentially negative, and eventually no one wants to be around him except those individuals who are just like him. The magical bully is an emotional batterer. You can never do anything right; he is here to correct you and make you better as a result.

Ultimately, his goal is to control those closest to him—the magical community he claims to embrace. If you disagree with him, the magical bully will fly into a tirade, perhaps even a rage, until you just shut up and he "wins."

General Bully Traits

To help you recognize a magical bully, here are some general traits he typically exhibits.

The magical bully is:

A master liar, especially when confronted. He often will blame others for any misunderstandings. The magical bully excels at deception and should never be given the benefit of the doubt.

A charmer. But this is the false charm of a "Jekyll and Hyde" quality. He does not show his vicious side publicly whenever possible, but tells his true feelings to a confidant. He employs charm to gain things he wants. It is generally excessive in nature. He is a sycophant.

Glib, verbose, and says a lot about nothing. In the end, his point is often lost in his wordiness, and you leave feeling he's stuffed your head with a lot of nothing. The bully usually only possesses superficial knowledge, and relies more on hearsay than on actual study.

Illogical and flighty, even contradictory, in his thinking, often contradicting himself. Confront him with his contradiction and watch him squirm.

Exceptionally gifted at knowing what someone wants to hear and at presenting convincing arguments.

Irresponsible and not to be relied on. The magical bully is not capable of sustaining intimacy in relationships.

Emotionally immature. He may speak like an adult, but he reacts like a five-year-old. Tantrums are not uncommon.

Deeply prejudiced, exhibiting a hatred of the opposite sex, of different religions and races. Typically, he tries to hide this from the community, though it is often very obvious to everyone.

Arrogant and opinionated, yet projects a sense of being untouchable. Rules do not apply to him, though he loves imposing rules on others.

Compulsive and a control freak. He wants to control what you say and do. If you act independently, he will attempt to restrict you and even damage your standing in the community.

Ruthless. He will do anything he can to undermine or destroy the standing of the person who sees through his bravado. He usually does this by unconsciously projecting his own character flaws on to this person.

Adept at creating conflict between individuals whom he sees as his enemies.

False in making claims about education, knowledge, expertise, and experience. He lives in a false reality and fabricates his existence to be what he really wishes it could be. The magical bully is a phony, but excels at presenting a believable self to the community. He also appears to truly believe in his fabrications.

Selfish and self-aggrandizing. The magical bully has only self-preservation in mind at all times. He is not a team player.

Callous and insensitive to the needs of others. He will gossip, backstab, and start rumors to discredit others. If confronted, he will deny he said anything.

A lousy and ungenerous giver. He will never volunteer to do anything for the sake of the community. He'll always be around to "advise," but never to do any sort of work.

Be Magical in Dealing with a Bully

Does this sound like anyone you know? Bullies cause a great deal of stress wherever they live, work, worship, and play. This stress becomes unhealthy for people who have to deal with them on a daily basis. So, the question is: How should we deal with such a person? Is there anything we can do to protect ourselves?

First and foremost, once you make a determination based on the character points above, you should not hesitate: Vote him out of your coven or community. Do yourself a favor and keep him from threatening you and your spiritual beliefs ever again. And do not let him charm his way back in to your circle or community. He is not going to change. This behavior is a pattern that no doubt goes back to his childhood.

As a special warning to coven and community leaders: The magical bully will want to be your special friend. He wants to have your authority and respect, but he doesn't want to work to get it. He will present one face to you and another to you coven members or community. The end result is that your coven members and community will resent you for not seeing through this bully. And once you lose your standing in the coven or community as a result of constantly praising, rewarding, or defending your bully while your coven and community members are being maligned by him, the magical bully will move on to another group or community and he will have nothing good to say about you.

After reading this, you may be thinking, well, this bully behavior applies to people in my workplace, in my family, and in my circle of friends who have nothing to do with the magical community. All I can say is: Bingo!

Bullies are bullies. You must recognize them where you find them and get them out your life. They are everywhere.

The European community is miles ahead of the United States in recognizing the destruction that bullies cause. They have legislation for dealing with such people in the workplace and community. I can only hope the United States will follow their example some time in the near future.

Healing Auras with Crysals

by Ann Moura

An aura is the surrounding energy field exuded by all matter. It is evident in different forms, and can be sensed intuitively and psychically, or sighted visually as a surrounding glow or haze of different colors. Learning to detect auras can be useful in certain healing circumstances where no other treatment may apply.

Learning to See Auras

The auric layer closest to the body is the generally the easiest to see, appearing as a thin outline around the object or person. Further out from this, the aura spreads into a wider band that is bordered with a diffused glow, possibly colorful, white, or dark. Whether the background is light or dark may affect your ability to see the energy fields, so try experimenting with this, using your own aura for practice by looking in a mirror. Once you are able to see your own aura, try seeing those of trees, plants, and animals.

Once you are more practiced, you can begin to use auras to determine the nature of a person's health or illness. The colors of auras are affected by the physical and psychic health of an individual. Yellow is the color of elemental air, and indicates intellect. Red is associated with elemental fire, and in an aura this could show vitality or rage. The blue of elemental water shows psychic energy, while the green of elemental earth is associated with nurturing. White is the color of spirituality.

When the green of earth is vibrating

with tiny sparkles of spiritual white in a person's aura, a pregnancy is indicated. Pink shows love and affection. Orange displays the energy from fire blended with air. Colors that are dingy show depression; while grays imply closeness to the otherworld and the ability to work magic with the energies of wind, rain, and storm. Dark spots in an aura indicate weaknesses or gaps in a person's energy field, and these are what may benefit from the healing input of crystal therapy energy.

Healing with Crystals

Quartz crystals are potent generators, transformers, and transferers of energy. They are commonly included in radios, lasers, and other technological equipment for such purposes. Their use in psychic healing traditionally concerns amplifying brain and body cell activity and cleansing auras.

For healing auras, you will need five quartz crystals in all, and these should be ones that you connect with prior to purchasing. See what crystals draw you, then address the entity within by mentally projecting your compassion and your desire to work with it. If you sense a warm glow from the crystal, then it is attracting you and wants to bond with you, but if not, leave the crystal for someone else. Once you have found your crystals, cleanse them in spring water (bottled is fine) and rock or sea salt. Lay the crystals on a bed of amethyst to dry off, then wrap in black cotton cloth or silk and let them rest.

The cleansing process is vital as it removes from the crystals the extraneous energies picked up from being mined, handled in a store, and imprinted with other people's energies. Without cleansing, you may open a channel between yourself and someone else who may interfere with the healing. Cleansing the crystals creates a balance between you and the crystal. After cleansing you do not want other people touching or handling the crystals, but if this happens (as during a healing session), the crystals can be purified quickly by immersion for half an hour in warm water mixed with sea salt and vinegar. In these cases, remove the crystal and rinse under cool running water, then dry and store as usual. Toss out the soaking water since it now contains the purged energies. You should also place your crystals under the light of the Full Moon periodically for energizing.

When healing auras, you need to have two clear crystals, two cloudy crystals, and one larger crystal to act as the healer. The clear crystals project god (or male) energy that activates energy flow, aids in clarity of thought, and is good for energizing, focusing, and stimulating alertness. The cloudy or milky crystals project goddess (or female) energy that relieves stress and tension, cleanses and restores equilibrium, aids with sleep, and hones intuitive skills. After finding and cleansing the right crystals, program each by holding them to your third eye (center of forehead just above the nose) and projecting into the crystal your desires for each of them.

The primary method of bringing an aura back into balance is to move the energy in a circular motion around the body, adding energy where needed. To start, have the person needing healing lie on his or her back. Point a cloudy quartz crystal toward the feet, and a clear quartz crystal toward the top of the head. Next, place a clear crystal in the palm of the open right hand pointing down (towards the feet), and a smaller cloudy crystal in the palm of the open left hand pointing up (towards the head). You, as the healer, now wave the healer crystal in a slow, circular motion over the body. There is no need to touch the person being healed—the energy flow occurs through the crystals.

Move the healing crystal down the right side of the body and up the left side. When the crystal feels heavy in your hand, it is indicating the need to pause over areas needing healing. The crystal will become heated, and you will feel a prickling sensation. This is your cue to project an image of light and compassion into the crystal. Radiate this image radiates through the crystal and into the person you are treating.

Once balance is restored in the affected area, the crystal will cool and lighten; move on when this occurs. When the front is completed, have the person roll over and repeat the process for the back. After this, the person may roll over once more and lie still with the crystals in place. You may want to discuss the areas over which the crystal paused to transmit healing energy, then take away all the crystals from around the person to indicate the healing is complete. Cleanse all the crystals, wrap them in their cloths, and put them away. If you have a generator crystal, one dedicated to refocusing the energies of other crystals, you should set it on each crystal for a few minutes before you put them away.

The Ladies of the Library

by deTraci Regula

Almost any modern magical practitioner lives surrounded by books. These private libraries often grow to take up every spare corner of the house. But you should know too that any collection of books may also include an invisible component as well as the visible part—that is, your own Lady of the Library. And while the goddesses of the library are many, knowing which one likely watches over your library, and invoking her aid may help keep those sacred tomes in better order.

For instance, presiding over the ancient and renowned Library of Alexandria along with her consort Serapis, Isis may be the best known of these book-loving deities. Rare among ancient goddesses, she is also associated with two books: *The Book of Breathings,* which comprise the magical words used to revive her husband Osiris, and *The Virgin of the World,* an alchemical text.

Isis was not the only Egyptian goddess associated with books and libraries. At the training colleges of the temples of Egypt, scribes were under the domain of Seshat, the sacred chronicler of the life of the pharaoh, and who inscribed his name on the leaves of the Persea tree. And Nephthys, somewhat mysteriously, also could claim the title of "Lady of Books," though her shadowy mythology is unclear as to why this is so. In China, there is a painting of the Lady of the Library who presents a book, her divine robes swirling around her in a dance of color. Her libraries smell of the rich, black Chinese inks made of soot and incense. Some volumes are scrolls wrapped around ornate dowels; other books are printed and folded accordion-like, packed in segments held together by silk bindings. There is the book she offers in her hand, and the mystery of her own divine figure; wise scholars study both.

Sometimes Miao Shan, a Chinese divinity who is seen as an emanation of the Bodhisattva Kuan Yin, the goddess of mercy, is also associated with reading. This young woman allowed herself to be mutilated to create a healing potion for her father, who had rejected her and her quest for spirituality. She joyously received, as a gift from a dragon king, the night-shining pearl, which she used as a kind of "itty-bitty book light" to illuminate sacred texts so she could read them at night.

In Greece, the Muses decided who would receive inspiration. They inspired the great authors of antiquity, including Homer, Plato, Euripedes, and many others. Images of Clio, the muse who inspired historians, still appear in libraries. She is usually shown sitting wearing flowing garments, with a book propped open on her lap.

Before the advent of writing, goddesses of inspiration were usually goddesses of memory as well. The swirling liquid in Cerridwen's cauldron of inspiration could transform the lips of a poet, forever giving words to transform, inspire, or indict society. Perhaps her successor is not at work in the library, but presiding behind the local coffee bar, doling out "inspiration" to the new age of writers who have set aside quill, pen, or pencil in favor of the laptop keyboard.

Next time you sit down to write or even just to read, say a small word of thanks and praise to your library goddess of choice.

Using a Magical Intermediary

by Robert M. Place

As long as I can remember, I have been interested in magic. For instance, I was fascinated as a boy by movies with supernatural themes.

One of the movies that most captured my youthful imagination was the 1950's version of *The Seven Voyages of Sinbad*. The original tale of Sinbad was part of *The Arabian Nights* collection of stories. Sinbad was a rich old sailor living in Baghdad, recounting the hardships of his seven fantastic voyages to show his discontented porter that wealth can only be obtained through personal enterprise and risk. In his seven voyages, Sinbad lands on an island that turns out to be a whale, is carried off by a giant bird called a roc, and has to escape from the cave of a cyclops before he is eaten. In all the adventures, he manages to escape the dangers and always reaps a reward.

In the movie version of Sinbad, the screenwriters were not concerned with the accurate portrayal of their historic model. They freely deviated from the text and even added elements from another Arabian Nights story, Aladdin. Like Aladdin, the movie Sinbad managed to win the heart of a beautiful princess and to obtain a lamp containing a wish-fulfilling genie. When Sinbad wanted to summon the genie he would rub the lamp in the customary fashion, but in this movie version, he first had to recite an invocation:

From the land beyond, beyond,
From the land past hope and fear,
I bid you genie now appear.

As we can see in the words, real magic power lies beyond our desires, hopes, and fears in an interior land. Whoever wrote the script to this Hollywood movie understood the basic paradox of magic; to obtain our desires we must go to our inner place of power, and so beyond desire.

Magical Intermediaries

We all like to think that we are in charge of our lives. However, it is not the ego that is the master of us—most of our lives are consumed by the pursuit of our desires and the flight from our fears. The real power in charge is our unconscious interior that controls these emotions.

Here, beyond hope and fear, lies our higher self. The higher self has the power to draw to us whatever we desire, but the only way to approach the higher self is to enter a deep meditative state wherein we let go of our hopes and fears. When we get to this state, we will no longer want what we wanted when we started. That is, we have let go of our desires even to make the journey. Difficult stuff, but there is a traditional way to go around these difficulties. The answer to this problem lies in an intermediary.

An intermediary is a personification of our inner power that is easy to converse with. It is a go-between between our ego and our higher self. In the Sinbad movie, the intermediary was a genie, but in different traditions it has also manifested as various gods, angels, demons, and fairy godmothers.

Introduction to Magic

By the 1960s, I was in college and in the midst of a search for some power that could grant my wishes. In those days, I would often go downtown to Greenwich Village to a small occult bookstore. It was here that I was introduced to the Western magical tradition in the books, blended incense, and jars of powered ingredients sold in the shop. In 1970 I graduated from school and moved to Passaic, New Jersey. In a small occult publishing company called Wehman Brothers in Hackensack, I found reprints and translations of old Qabalistic magical texts that contained actual antique incantations for summoning spirits, complete with recipes for perfumes and numerous magical diagrams.

I was finding my way to my genie, but many of the magical operations in the books contained distasteful details—such as pulverizing black pepper, hogsbane, mandrake, loadstone, and myrrh into a paste with the blood of a bat and the brains of a black cat. To make such an incense not only went against my vegetarian sentiments, but gathering the ingredients—especially when combined with the astrologically calculated timing—was beyond the limits of my youthful perseverance.

However, one day I came across a humble little book with a pale-green paper cover and and the title in dark blue lettering, *The Sixth and Seventh Books of Moses, or Moses' Magical Spirit-Art.* This was a work translated from a German text, which in turn stated that it was translated from ancient Hebrew and from the Cuthan-Samaritan language in the early 1700s. The book was filled with numerous magic formulas for summoning angels and planetary spirits to accomplish a magician's desires—in other words, genies. The instructions were accompanied by curious prints of magical hieroglyphs with geometric designs and inscriptions in Hebrew, Latin, and alchemical, astrological, and magical symbols that appeared to be reproductions of engraved designs from the original text. Some illustrations had symbolic characters such as the crowned serpent and the serpent on a staff. Some were circular mandala-like diagrams.

Despite my lack of knowledge of Hebrew, the instructions in this book seemed straightforward and practical to implement, especially a chapter near the back that contained a no-nonsense approach to using the psalms in the Bible as magical charms. The author listed each psalm telling what its magic virtues were, what angel ruled it, and how and when to recite it. The necessary ingredients were mostly wholesome things like olive oil, black ink, and clean sheepskin parchment. The recommended timings for the rituals were based on the cycle of the Sun—such as, before sunrise, after sunset, or after morning prayer. It was with the help of this book that I began my first magical operations and summoned angels to deliver me from my fears and so on.

At the time, I was working at my first full-time job as an investigator for the state welfare board. My supervisor had put in a bad report about my work—which I did not deserve—and I had been ordered to appear before the director the following morning. I was sure that I was going to be fired, and I wanted to do something if only to guarantee a fair hearing. That night just after sunset, with my Bible in my hand, I went into a vacant lot across the street from my apartment. Facing west, I called on the appropriate angel, read a psalm, and threw soil over my left shoulder.

The next morning in the director's office, I found that my suspicion was true. The director informed me that my employment was being terminated because of the bad report that I had received. In my defense, I said that I did not think that the report was accurate and that if he would call in my supervisor she would confirm this. In the interest of fairness, the director obliged me and called her to our meeting, and, sure enough, my supervisor said that she had changed her mind and my work was now up to par. The director reinstated me. Just like that, with the angel's help the magic had worked.

Granting Wishes

I was hooked. I began using psalms to fix up my life, and I found that as long as I followed the directions in the book and addressed the psalm to the correct angel, they always worked—though the degree of success varied. For example, when my girlfriend broke up with me, I used magic to arrange a spontaneous meeting and restore her affections for me—at that time, I was not above this kind of manipulative behavior. The accidental meeting happened the next day in the park. Her anger had subsided, but we did not get back together as I had hoped. Luckily, there were limits to what I could accomplish with magic. This woman was not meant to be with me for several reasons, including the fact that she did not want to. My genie seemed to have the good sense not to override another person's free will.

A genie is a personification of the place of unity from which all opposites, such as hope and fear, converge. This place of unity and creation is one with the intelligence of the universe. As such, it has a plan. If I ever succeeded in overriding the plan, I would only have made more of a problem than I started with. Although I did make a mess at times, the genie preferred to grant my wishes in a way that was more deeply satisfying and in keeping with the energies of the universe. As I stated at the beginning, our desires are not entirely ours; they come to us from a normally inaccessible area deep in our unconscious. Jung called it by its alchemical name, the "unus mundus," which means "the world of the one."

A skeptic may complain: since not all of my magic worked, how can I be sure that any of it worked? Maybe it was just a coincidence when it worked. In answer, I can say that the magic always made something happen, but it was not always what I expected to happen. Also, the results had that miraculous acausal quality that Jung called synchronicity. When I magically arranged to meet my ex-girlfriend, she appeared at the park at exactly the same time that I did— as if it had been planned. But we did not get back together because it would not have been right for either of us. Eventually, through magic, I drew to myself the woman who was right for me and to whom I am still married. In this way, magic had provided real long-term fulfillment.

In time, I stopped using the psalms for magic and began experimenting with other techniques. I burned candles, created words of power, and practiced psychic healing. Slowly my approach changed from one of ego-centered control to one of letting go of control and looking for direction from within. I began to think of my inner self as my higher self. With this realization the magical path became one with the path to higher consciousness.

For Further Study

Anonymous. *The Sixth and Seventh Books of Moses, or Moses' Magical Spirit-Art*. Wehman Brothers, year unknown.

Von Franz, Mary-Louise. *Number and Time*. Northwestern University Press, 1974.

———. *Psyche and Matter*. Shambala, 1992.

Dream Rituals

by Karri Ann Allrich

For some, dreams are merely fantasies, peculiar and disconnected to daily living. For many of us, however, dreams are a source of inspiration, and hold the key to self-awareness. Dreams offer us an opportunity to heal old wounds and resolve lingering conflicts.

In our conscious daily life we may too readily shelter ourselves from our deeper shadow self, ignoring our personal underlying issues. In our dreams, however, we are often forced to face our fears, confront our contradictions, and eliminate obstacles that stand in our path. Many Witches and seekers believe in the power and insight of this separate reality: the elusive realm of dreams and visions.

Working with Dreams

As a Jungian dream Witch, I wholeheartedly believe in honoring the insight and instruction of dreams. I keep a dream journal next to my bed and record my most vivid dreams and daydreams. Over the years, my dream journal has proven to be an invaluable tool for personal and creative progress. I have used my dream images in many ways: magically, creatively, and intuitively. They have inspired paintings, solved artistic dilemmas for numerous artists, and healed wounds or solved problems from the past. On more than one occasion, they've even fanned the flames of desire!

By understanding that our subconscious mind is actually our deepest intuition, we begin to fully grasp the value of working with our dreams. Dreams are the language of the soul, tapping into our primary instinct, our original self. Using the images offered up in our dreams is a magical way to help ourselves heal, expand our creativity, and embrace possibility. Using our dreams in ritual can be a very powerful and moving experience.

Enhancing Intention

Most of us are familiar with the concepts of positive thinking, visualization, and focusing our intention on our goals. Affirmative magic is empowering and energizing, and dreams can certainly be used in this manner.

For example, I once had a lovely dream about a beautiful beaming baby. He was absolutely radiant! Upon waking, my intuition informed me that he represented the birth of a new creative project. I was, at the time, beginning work on my second book for Llewellyn, and quite excited about the concept (a book on dreams!). As chance would have it, the very next day an ad insert fell out of a bill envelope. As I bent down to pick it up, I found myself gazing into the eyes of a merry little infant, very much like the wonder baby in my dream. I immediately taped the photograph above my writing computer.

This uncomplicated act was magic in its simplest form. The baby's image became the icon of positive reinforcement for my fledgling newborn project. Whenever I had a whisper of doubt, just looking at that tiny face, sparkling with pure joy, filled me with the confidence to persevere. Using the picture of the baby from my dream gave my intention more energy. If I had chosen a rune or crystal assigned to foster self-confidence and perseverance, it wouldn't have contained half the power this visual contained—a personal archetypal symbol, born from my own subconscious.

The Fine Art of Banishing

A compelling way to utilize our dreams is to create a banishing ritual using a personal dream symbol. Oftentimes our dreams will reveal old anxieties, attachments, or obstacles that we need to conquer, let go of, or banish before we can accomplish something. Working with dream images, we may craft simple yet powerful rituals to help us let go of old hurts, deadening relationships, or inhibiting fears.

Let's imagine that you have just dreamed of an old lover from the past, someone who wasn't a healthy choice for you. In the dream, you are filled with an old familiar longing and desire to reconnect, yet in pursuing it you find only frustration and apprehension. The lingering attachment to this person sustains a hold on your spirit. What can you do about it?

To start, you can plan a banishing ritual during the phase of the waning Moon, when diminishing lunar energies support the process of letting go, or removing. Begin by choosing a symbol from the dream: a gold ring, a telephone, sunglasses, anything that you intuit has meaning for your relationship and symbolizes the core problem. For example, a broken telephone might reveal a lack of real communication. A lost ring may indicate that you've neglected your sense of self and autonomy. A vampire bite or loss of blood could symbolize the frightening suspicion

that your energy is being drained by a narcissist. If you have trouble coming up with a symbol, meditate on your dream and allow your intuition to guide you in finding the right one. Once you've decided on the symbol, find an example of it. This may be an actual object or a depiction, such as an image cut from a magazine or catalog. If what you want to banish is a feeling, a psychological state or habit, write it down on a piece of paper. To enhance the power of the word, include a visual in some form: a doodle, shape, or mark of some kind that expresses the dream in a nonverbal way. Think of runes and ancient glyphs, and make up your own. This adds power to your magic.

Once you have your symbol, you have a choice: to bury or to burn. There are many valid ways to approach rituals of intention. They may be as simple as writing down the dream symbol you wish to banish and burning it, or as intricate as creating a collage of memories and inviting in friends to help you bury it with ceremony. Obviously, if you have chosen an actual object, the practical choice may be burial. I've performed quite a few burials in my day, leaving aspects of my past behind in tiny burial grounds, tucked away beneath hedges or thick patches of herbs. A number of graves even sport elfin-sized grave markers—a reminder of my intent to bury specific issues once and for all.

To do this, meditate on the object first, holding it in your hands and visualizing it's lessening power over your life. You may even bind it with ribbon in specific colors in order to strengthen your intention of limiting its influence. Black is a good basic color for banishing and protection. Purple is a good choice for spiritual issues. Red is appropriate for old hurts and anger. Yellow supports healing an old wound. Then, wrap the object at least three times around, and verbalize your binding intentions out loud. As the object is buried, I like to toss in a few coins. This reminds me of the price I've paid for my newfound wisdom, and acknowledges the cost of my past mistakes. I usually burn a sage stick afterward to cleanse away any lingering pain or negativity. I let the rising smoke carry my intention to the spirits.

If you choose to burn a dream symbol illustration, this is best done outdoors in a fireproof cauldron. That said, I do realize many dreamers live in apartment buildings with no access to a yard. If there is no balcony, you may do the ritual inside, using a fireplace, or, if you have enough space, by placing a fireproof cauldron in a well-ventilated area (away from flammable curtains and materials). A friend of mine even burns small paper banishings in her enameled bathroom sink; for this, an older cast-iron tub will also work (but not modern fiberglass tubs). Being a lover of irony, I can even see the value in utilizing a flushing toilet for this purpose. Typically, I use a large Turkish copper bowl I found once at a flea market.

For purposes of banishing, either cut a symbolic image from a magazine, draw a small picture, or even write a farewell letter of intent. Inscribe any symbols, words, or intentions on the image that express what you desire to accomplish. Fold the paper three, six, or nine times, verbalizing your goal out loud, if you wish. Place it in the fireproof cauldron and light it with a wooden match. As the paper burns, visualize your obstacle, pain, attachment, or habit going up in smoke. Follow with a sage smudge stick afterward to clear the space of any lingering energies. Put on some music and dance. Celebrate the banishing!

After the Banishing

After your banishing ceremony, water magic works wonders and is one of my personal favorite ways to turn my attention forward. Make sure your ceremony has occurred on the eve before the New Moon. Prepare a warm bath with a good handful of sea salt (for purification). Light black candles for protection, yellow for healing, and lavender for spiritual cleansing. Immerse yourself in the warmth of the bathwater and add six drops each of rosemary and lavender oil for cleansing and spiritual healing. Meditate upon your dream symbol until it is clear in your mind. When you are ready, pull the plug and envision the dream symbol leaving your body, and departing down the drain. As you rub your body briskly with a clean fresh towel, visualize yourself shedding your old skin and beginning anew.

Work with your dream symbols as simply or elaborately as you wish. Magic not only happens, it heals.

The Jersey Devil

by Denise Dumars

Monsters are sighted in many places around the globe, and the United States is no exception to this rule. One of the longest-lived American monster legends is found in what is, perhaps, an unexpected place.

Scary New Jersey

When Americans think of New Jersey, they think of large suburban centers and seaside resorts. But New Jersey also possesses an unusual geographical feature—the Pine Barrens, a wild wooded area not unlike the one depicted in the film, *The Blair Witch Project*. Located in the southern part of the state, approximately between the towns of Freehold and Millville, the Pine Barrens is home to the Jersey Devil.

The earliest tale of the Jersey Devil goes like this—In 1735, a hard-working woman named Jane Leeds, living in the marshlands of Leeds County, New Jersey, found herself pregnant with her thirteenth child. Her family was not wealthy, in fact they all worked hard just to make ends meet. Despondent at the idea of bearing yet another child, she cursed the infant by saying: "I wish this child to be born a devil!"

The legend says that Jane Leeds' thirteenth labor was a normal one, with a midwife in attendance and a healthy baby boy delivered. But almost immediately, the child's appearance began to change. He sprouted horns and a tail, his face became distorted to resemble a horse's head, and his body was elongated grotesquely. He grew wings on his back and claws on his now-deformed hands and feet. The creature slashed the midwife's throat and was never seen again, supposedly escaping into the Pine Barrens.

Many think that the Jersey Devil was really just a deformed child who was hidden from view by his parents. His legend has merely increased with the embellishment of gossipers. But others are convinced that this creature is an actual monster

There are various legends related to the origin of the Jersey Devil; the Leeds legend is the most prominent and widely accepted story, but new legends have come up over time. Supposedly, the creature was really a cryptozoological anomaly, an undiscovered species of wild creature, a survivor of the Jurassic age, or something supernatural or even extraterrestrial. Other legends throughout the nineteenth and twentieth centuries told stories similar to the Leeds' cursed child, updated to fit the times. In time, strange folklore surrounded the creature; Captain Kidd and other disreputable visitors to New Jersey were supposed to have befriended it or to have gone in league with it as if it were some agent of the "real" Devil.

The Jersey Devil Today

Whatever the Jersey Devil is, sightings of it have been reported consistently for over 250 years. The Devil has also been seen outside of New Jersey, in parts of Pennsylvania and New York. What makes this indigenous monster so unusual is its consistently bizarre description. It has a horse-like or donkey-like head, wings, thick black fur, red eyes, and sometimes a barbed or forked tail and clawed feet or cloven hooves. Its body has been described variously as that of a dog or a kangaroo. The creature has a piercing cry and hot, rank breath. It is unlike no other creature ever sighted in the United States.

Eyewitness accounts usually are written off as the hallucinations of drunken or otherwise impaired witnesses. Some people suspect that the locals keep the story alive in order to discourage real-estate developers from paving over and building subdivisions on their wild lands.

Still, not all sightings of the Devil can be linked to purposeful hoaxes or unreliable witnesses. In fact, over the years prominent businessmen, police officers, and elected officials have sighted the monster. One of the most famous people to have seen the Devil is nineteenth-century war hero Commodore Stephen Decatur. Another is Joseph Bonaparte, brother of Napoleon and a resident of Bordentown, New Jersey, from 1816 to 1839, who is said to have sighted the Devil while on a hunting trip through the woods.

The Jersey Devil is a powerful symbol for the state—so much so that New Jersey's National Hockey League team is named the Jersey Devils! One former governor of New Jersey, Walter Edge, reported that when he was a child the Jersey Devil was used like the "bogeyman" to frighten children into being good. Needless to say, many have tried to capitalize on the legends of the Devil. One sideshow promoter claimed that he had captured the Jersey Devil, but that it had escaped, and offered a reward for whoever found it and returned it. Another rented a kangaroo from a menagerie, painted green stripes on it, attached artificial wings, and tried to exhibit the creature. Unfortunately, the green paint made the kangaroo ill, and the attraction never made it off the ground.

Chilling tales about the Jersey Devil abound. Many report following odd tracks in the snow or mud, only to find them disappearing up onto rooftops or into treetops. The Devil's cry is particularly piercing, and its wings make an odd sound, which has been variously compared to the sounds of insects buzzing, a record being scratched, or wood being sawn. The Devil is often blamed for mysterious attacks on domestic animals and livestock, although wild animals of a more pedestrian variety could easily be the source of these attacks.

Every now and then, people find mysterious piles of bones and feathers; of course, these are attributed to the Devil. One Jerseyite found the remnants of wings along with bones like those in a dog's legs, and declared the Jersey Devil dead. And of course, some ever-enterprising huckster compiled a composite skeletons and exhibited it as Jersey Devil remains.

Don't bother the people of Leeds Point if you go looking for the Jersey Devil. The residents are tired of tourists who come knocking on their doors and asking about it. But if you actually see the Devil, you might want to drop into one of the local bars or restaurants and cope with the horror by ordering the powerful mixed drink named after it.

Like the fabled phoenix, the Jersey Devil—which many residents say is properly called the Leeds Devil—keeps rising from its own ashes. Like any good legend, it never really dies.

For Further Study

McCloy, James F., and Ray Miller, Jr. *The Jersey Devil.* Middle Atlantic Press, 1976.

Website: "The Jersey Devil of the Pine Barrens." http://www.strangemag.com/jerseydevil1.html. Includes an article by Anthony Perticaro.

The Tools of the Witch

by Anna Franklin

The following seven implements are crucial to the daily workings of today's Witch. Here are some suggestion about how you can make each of these tools your own with a brief magical ritual or activity.

The Athame

Witches use a black-handled knife called an athame to cast a circle, to invoke the axis mundi, and to call up the four quarters. Generally, the athame is made from iron or steel, giving this tool power over the invisible realms, and is kept blunt in keeping with its use for ceremonial purposes.

Ordinarily, you should consecrate your athame, once you choose it, at the time of your initiation. In the old days, each Witch was called upon to make his or her own knife. The forging of metal was considered a magical act, and the blacksmith was a magician who took the raw materials from the womb of Mother Earth and transformed them with air, fire, and water. Shaping metal was equated magically to shaping the flow of life; to make and use the knife was to shape destiny.

While forging a blade is not possible for most, you can carve your own handle in a magical way. To start, take a block of wood and roughly sketch on it the shape of the handle you want to carve. Remove the bulk of the unwanted wood with a saw. Fix your work in a clamp, and, taking a large gouging tool and mallet, gradually chip away small parts of the wood, working away from you, cutting with the grain. Keep working around the shape evenly, turning it until you get the desired rough shape. Then using a flat chisel begin rounding the handle. You also will need to carve a channel inside the handle to take the prong of the blade. When you have the shape, smooth it with a rasp, then rub with coarse sandpaper, finally finishing it off with fine glass paper.

The Herb Knife

Herbs are never cut with iron or steel. Druids used golden sickles, representing the power of the Sun (gold) and the Moon (crescent), to cut herbs. But not many of us could afford such an implement. Herb knives are usually made of copper or silver. If you are lucky you may be able to find an old piece of silver cutlery in an antique shop, or persuade a friendly silversmith to make you a silver or copper blade which you can fashion a handle for. Consecrate your herb knife with an incense, oil, or tisane of centaury, the patron plant of herbalists.

The Cauldron

A cauldron is essentially a vessel which transforms the raw ingredients of life, through cooking, into something new. The earliest cauldrons would have been made from clay, though later they were made from metal. Whether made of clay or metal they consist of materials from the earth, transformed by the fire of the kiln or forge. There are many cauldrons in Celtic myth, owned by various gods and goddesses. Some mysteriously produce sustenance, some transform, and some hold the fruits of the harvest. In essence, all these cauldrons represent the transformative womb of the Goddess, in which seeds germinate and growth, and return in death to grow once more.

The cauldron is a symbol of initiation, renewal, rebirth, and plenty. It may contain water, fire, incense, or flowers as the occasion demands. Fill your cauldron, once you have it, and perform a quick leaping ritual. Leaping over the cauldron, like leaping over the broomstick, is a fertility rite.

The Cup

The symbolism of the cup is many-layered. On one level, the cup is a similar tool to the cauldron, representing the nurturing and loving womb of the Goddess. The sharing of the cup during a ritual exemplifies this. When we drink we make a direct connection with Mother Nature. The cup is mythically connected to the White Goddess of the Moon, who is seen as a vessel filled with physical and emotional food for the world.

Fill your ritual cup with wine, a drink that gives inspiration, vitality, and expanded consciousness. The cup demonstrates the need to satisfy the thirst for knowledge as well as for liquid nourishment. During the time of the persecutions, no special magical equipment was marked or set aside in any way, lest a search reveal it. The cup used in a craft ceremony was simply the best cup in the house, consecrated only with a sign of the pentagram drawn upon it in charged water. Today, mark your cup, made of silver, wood, or clay, with such a pentagram. The best time to purchase your cup is at the time of initiation.

The Pentacle

A copper or clay disc marked with the sign of the pentagram is an essential element of a Witch's altar. It represents the sign of the Goddess, humankind, and the

element of earth. Earth is solid; it supports and nourishes us. In token of this, bread is placed on the disc during the ritual, and is blessed.

While it would be difficult for most people to gain access to the equipment to make a copper disc, a simple clay disc is an effective alternative. Roll out some modeling clay, cut into a nine- or twelve-inch circle and inscribe with a pentagram. This should then be fired and glazed. A variety of modeling clays can be obtained from art shops that need no firing. Alternatively, a handsome disc can be made from a sheet of slate. This does not have to be round, and can easily be incised with a sharp tool. You can also use a flat sheet of rock; just paint the symbols on it.

The Witch Necklace

The necklace represents the continuous cycle of being—life, death and rebirth. Many goddesses are depicted with strings of beads that stand for the circle of the heavens, with jewels as stars. The thread that joins the necklace is the oneness that holds the cosmos together.

Traditionally, Witches wear a necklace of amber and jet. Amber holds both a magical and electrical charge and relates to the powers of the Sun, the God, and the masculine, while jet relates to the powers of the Moon, the underworld, the Goddess, and the feminine.

Witch necklace beads may be made from many things: seeds, crystals, pressed flower petals, any appropriate gemstones, and the seeds or fruits of a tree or plant that you have built up a relationship with. To make your necklace, just take a piece of twine at least six inches longer than the necklace you intend to make. Slide the first four beads onto the twine. Thread the loose end back through the first bead and knot firmly. Repeat with the other beads, knotting each time. Thread the remaining beads onto the other end of the twine, incorporating the loose end, and loosen the other end and tie both together firmly. Take the loose end and rethread it through the last bead, knotting as at the beginning of the necklace. Do the same with the next three beads and thread the remaining twine back through the next four beads. Clip off any spare thread.

The Wand

The wand represents the fertilizing phallus, which joins opposites and creates life. On a deeper level, the wand joins the physical and the spiritual realms and transmits energy from one to the other.

The function of the wand largely depends on which wood it is made from. For example, ash connects with the sky god and invokes the axis mundi; apple, depending on when it is cut, may connect to the summer goddess and her gifts of love and fertility, or to Samhain and the underworld with its secrets of transformation. A bay wand is connected with the Sun and its power of healing, while rowan connects to the goddess Brighid and rites of divination.

Cut your own wand from living wood, keeping aware that the time of the cutting affects what the wand will be good for. If you wanted to cut an oak wand, for example, you should go out before dawn at Midsummer and seek your chosen tree as the Sun rises. The wood should be virgin, of one year's growth only, and the wand should be cut from the tree at a single stroke. It should measure from elbow to fingertip. Make a small hollow in the end that you will hold in your hand and insert of piece of cotton thread with a drop of your own blood into it before sealing it with wax.

Found Goddesses, An Introduction

by Barbara Ardinger

In 1988, Morgan Grey and Julia Penelope wrote that the "underlying principles of language and magic are transformational." Faced with the new realities of our modern world, they invented new goddesses to deal with it. In the introduction to their book, *Found Goddesses*, they describe how they started playing with the idea of creating their own goddesses who not only respond to the specific needs of the twentieth century, but whose very naming calls into being the power of our will and envisioning. After all, who else do we invoke for modern dilemmas such as keeping safe in traffic, dealing with modern teens, and coping with computer crashes? The goddesses we need for modern issues and challenges are the Found Goddesses.

Like Gray and Penelope, I have come to recognize the fact that we can change our realities with the words we use. That is, we create new worlds and realities by spinning our webs of words. Here are a few guidelines for finding goddesses yourself. First, these goddesses are generally situational. They appear for specific purposes—traffic, computer woes, and so on. Second, their names are usually based on puns, as this brings them more readily to mind when you need them. And finally, Found Goddesses are fearless; they are everything you need them to be whenever you need them—so go ahead and evoke them, and do not fear or worry. You have the power of magic at hand.

Jollity, Goddess of Holidays

by Barbara Ardinger

There's a old joke about Unitarians that I think applies equally to neo-Pagans. It goes like this: Unitarians are so fond of having any cause for celebration, they celebrate everyone's holidays. Thus we are blessed to know Jollity, Goddess of Every Possible Holiday.

It's that time of year, after all. Can't you just feel the excitement in the air, the quiver of anticipation? Down on Main Street, everyone in town has gathered, singing in front of shops on which lights flash and twinkle.

And here comes Jollity, perched on top of her rolling pink throne, bubbles blowing behind her. Dressed in cloth of gold and pink, with elbow-length satin gloves and a feather boa, Jollity waves her starry wand at one and all. The crown upon her head is tall and sparkly, and a banner across her bosom proclaims, in scarlet letters, she is Miss Congeniality.

Arrayed round her rolling throne are a holiday tree bedecked with twinkling lights, tinsel, multicolored ribbons, a piñata in the shape of a frog, dozens of painted eggs, and bushels of glittery glass balls. Wire garlands in a rainbow of colors whip and wave in the breeze, and Jollity flings nosegays and bridal posies in every direction.

Behind the rolling throne marches the New Year dragon, carrying dreidels and gelt, candles and pots of shamrocks, flowers and a basket of first fruits, and beautifully wrapped gifts for all. The gifts are tossed in heaping handfuls and armfuls to spectators by Jollity's helpers, the elves and the grandmothers and the inventors. Some spectators jump in front of other spectators to catch the gifts. Others, more polite, hand them off to those standing behind them.

Behind the dragon marches the brass band and the proud civic spirits, holding their banners and tasseled hats. They try to shake hands with every spectator and kiss every babe.

In good order follows Jollity's little red wagon, heaped with the holiday food—cakes and ice cream, golden roast turkey, succulent ham, roast beef with Yorkshire pudding, apple and peach cobbler, pumpkin and mince pies, lamb and flat bread, hummus and tabouli, stuffed grape leaves, chicken soup with matzah balls and potato latkes, tamales and turkey mole, and exquisite noodles and sauces and spices from every land. Grandfather hurls the edible gifts of Jollity into the crowd. Some of the people catch these gifts. Some of the people throw them at other people. Some people fling them back. You have to be very good at ducking.

Near the end of the parade comes another marching band with about seventy trombones, and at last we can see the flowery last floats of princesses and princes, wizards and prophets, winning sports teams, and the civic officials. Some of these people, having no food to throw, toss articles of clothing into the rows of spectators.

Jollity's parade has given us an entire day of celebration. Night has fallen and flashy sparkles fill the skies above us and rise into the sky. And—guess what—after the mess is cleaned up, they'll do it again, tomorrow and the next day and the next, to the last holiday of recorded time.

Jollity, goddess cheerful and great,
Give us every excuse to celebrate.

Playing Card Divination
by Lily Gardner

Is someone near to you unreliable? Do you need to be cautious of scandal or business troubles? Are you unsure generally about the future? If you're looking for simple answers to everyday questions, playing cards are a good divination tool.

History of Cards

Playing cards were first seen in Europe in the thirteenth century. People started using cards to tell fortunes by the sixteenth century. The first book on divination with playing cards, an art known as cartomancy, was written by Francesco Marcolini in 1541. By the eighteenth century, there were many packs of cards and different systems in place. and cartomancers were in great demand. Peasants and aristocrats alike sought answers from the cards. It was common knowledge that Napoleon Bonaparte consulted Madame Lenormand, a famous card reader, who predicted his victories and his ruin.

Although a deck of playing cards closely resembles a tarot deck, no one has been able to determine which came first. As with the tarot deck, playing cards have court cards with kings, queens, and jacks. Also like tarot, playing cards are divided into four suits. The clubs correspond with the tarot wands, the spades with swords, the hearts with cups, and the diamonds with pentacles. One theory states that the clubs/Wands suit symbolizes the peasant class; spades/Swords are the aristocracy, hearts/Cup the clergy; and diamonds/Pentacles the merchant class.

If the suits in playing cards mirror medieval society, the number of cards in a deck and its divisions mirror the way we measure the year. A deck of playing cards has fifty two cards just as the year has fifty two weeks. There are four suits which correspond to the four seasons of the year, the four elements, and the four winds. Each suit contains thirteen cards which corresponds to the lunar months in the year. The cards are either red or black, symbolizing day and night.

Interpreting the Cards

There are various methods of divination using playing cards. Here is one system for interpreting the meaning of individual cards (suggestions for spreads for readings follows):

Diamonds

King: A man, materialistic, practical, down-to-earth.

Queen: A woman, materialistic, practical, down-to-earth.

Jack: A relative, fair and false.

Ten: Journey; a change that brings wealth.

Nine: Opportunities and surprises having to do with business.

Eight: Late marriage, unexpected money.

Seven: A gift.

Six: A reconciliation; caution, don't remarry.

Five: Successful business meeting.

Four: Fat sorrow; someone dies and leaves you money.

Three: Legal or domestic battles.

Two: Love affair heats up.

Ace: A wedding ring.

Hearts

King: A man affectionate, generous, impetuous, creative.

Queen: A woman affectionate, generous, impetuous, creative.

Jack: A young friend, trustworthy.

Ten: Happiness, good fortune.

Nine: The wish card; your wishes come true.

Eight: Invitations, but also partings.

Seven: Someone is unreliable.

Six: Unexpected good fortune.

Five: Jealousy, indecision.

Four: Changes, travel.

Three: Possible poverty or shame.

Two: Success, friendship.

Ace: Happiness, love, friendship.

Spades

King: A man, powerful, intelligent, melancholy, crafty.

Queen: A woman powerful, intelligent, melancholy, crafty.

Jack: A young man, well-meaning.

Ten: Grief, sickness, death.

Nine: Bad luck, quarrels, delays.

Eight: Disappointments and opposition.

Seven: Lean sorrow.

Six: An improvement in one's life.

Five: Anxiety, setbacks, obstacles.

Four: Jealousy, business troubles.

Three: Infidelity.

Two: Scandal, gossip, deceit.

Ace: Conflicts, difficult love affair.

Clubs

King: A man, honest, open, enthusiastic.

Queen: A woman honest, open, enthusiastic.

Jack: A reliable friend.

Ten: A gift.

Nine: New romance.

Eight: Caution against recklessness.

Seven: Prosperity.

Six: Business success.

Five: Help from friend or mate.

Four: Bad luck.

Three: Good marriage.

Two: Disappointment.

Ace: Harmony, property, love, achievement.

Choosing an Indicator

An indicator is the face card that represents the seeker. Women are usually represented by the queens, men by the kings, and young people by the jacks. Choose the character traits that best fit the seeker's sense of self, as explained in the guide to individual cards above. Typically, the indicator card is placed back in the deck. If this card appears in the reading, it generally means that the seeker has control of the issue that is currently being discussed.

Face Cards

Face cards of the same suit indicate a close relationship. The opposite suit indicates a negative affinity. Clubs are the opposite of spades. Hearts are the opposite of diamonds.

Each face card faces right or left. The direction the face card is looking can give the seeker some valuable clues. For example, let's say the king of spades is looking at the six of clubs. This likely indicates a man in the seeker's life will enjoy success in business. If the king of spades is the seeker's indicator, then he will likely enjoy much success.

Spreads

The following spreads can be used in reading cards.

The Linear Spread

The Linear Spread gives a quick answer to challenges and indicates the skills one might need if facing the challenge. To start, from left to right lay six cards out in a row. The first card represents the self. The second card represents the seeker's environment. The third card represents the challenge. The fourth card represents the character traits it takes to meet the challenge. The fifth card is the outcome card based on current circumstances. The sixth card represents the final outcome, the aftermath from the fifth card.

The Chakra Spread

The Chakra Spread is a seven-card spread that represents the chakras. This spread is laid in a straight column starting at the bottom. The second card is placed above the first and so on through seven.

The first card represents the root chakra and relates to grounding and self-preservation. What makes the seeker feel at home, most like his or herself, is addressed here.

The second card represents the *Hara* chakra. This card addresses a person's sexuality, desire, and the sensual part of his or her experience.

The third card represents the solar plexus. This chakra addresses our will, sense of personal power, and energy.

The fourth card corresponds with the heart chakra. This chakra relates to love and compassion. It also is the integrator between the lower chakras of body and the upper chakras of mind and spirit.

The fifth card relates to the throat chakra and relates to creativity and communication.

The sixth card relates to the third eye chakra. It relates to our intuition, our dream world, our imaginative life.

The seventh card corresponds with the crown chakra. This chakra addresses our state of enlightment and wisdom.

The Romany Spread

The Romany Spread has been used by Gypsy, or Rom, fortune-tellers for over two hundred years. For this spread, choose an indicator, then place it back in the deck. The spread consists of three rows of seven cards that face the reader. The cards are laid out left to right beginning with the top row. The top row represents the seeker's past. The next seven cards for the middle row represent the seeker's present situation. The bottom row of seven cards represents the seeker's future.

If the indicator shows up in the spread, the question follows: Is the seeker living in the past, the present, or is he or she focused toward the future? Where the card appears in the spread determines the answer to these questions.

Happy Seeking

While tarot decks deal with the seeker's inner life, the readings you'll receive from playing cards address the mundane life. Keep this in mind as you being your searches and investigations into the wisdom of the cards. In the end, always remember, as with any divination tool, it is important that you do not take what is given you in a fatalistic way. The visions and notions you are granted by the cards are mere suggestions of what might happen to you, given the present set of circumstances. No matter what the cards seem to say, we always have the ability to make choices and change.

For Further Study

Benham, Gurney. *Playing Cards: History of the Pack and Explanations of its Many Secrets.* Spring Books, no date given.

Orient, Grand. *A Handbook of Cartomancy: Fortune-Telling and Occult Divination.* William Rider and Son, 1909.

Valiente, Doreen. *Natural Magic.* Phoenix Publishing, 1975.

Articles for Spring

The Sacred Trees of Ancient Greece

by deTraci Regula

When we think of ancient Greece, our minds conjure up images of tall columns of marble on beautiful temples, and ancient cities built around paved plazas. It's easy to forget that the people of the Greek countryside in ancient times celebrated more natural magics. The rural folk in the mountains and on the islands didn't need marble columns. They had the original magical column growing all around them—trees.

Ancient Greek Tree Lore

In ancient Greece, many deities and divinities were associated with trees and certain temple sites were built around living reminders of the divine presence. For instance, Zeus's oaks foretold the future at Dodona, and Apollo and Artemis shared with Isis the sacred palm trees of the island of Delos. At the oracle at Delphi, chewing the leaves of the bay tree inspired Pythonesses. One of the nymphs, Daphne, was said to have taken permanent refuge from unwanted attentions by transforming into a laurel tree. To Artemis, goddess of the hunt, all of the trees of the wood were her domain. Meanwhile, gray-eyed Athena took her epithet from the downy silver undersides of the leaves of her special tree, the olive, whose useful oil lit the lamps of Greece, soothed its sore muscles, and preserved and cooked its food. Some olive trees were considered sacred to the state of Greece itself, and destroying even a dead olive tree stump could be considered a crime.

In general, the trees of the ancient Greek landscape were so well inhabited with divinities that woodcutters had to take special precautions lest they accidentally fell a sacred tree. That is, dryads were nymphs who inhabited trees, and they were often kept com-

106

pany by the naiads, or water-nymphs, who were not averse to sitting in a tree occasionally. The most dangerous moments to offend a tree nymph are at midday, in the moments of eerie quiet that descend over Greece when the Sun is at its highest, and at midnight, the more familiar hour of evil. Prohibitions forbade draining trees of their resins or gums on certain days. The first few days of August, called *dromais,* are full of these prohibitions—though few of them are observed today.

Few modern Greeks would claim that a tree is sacred, at least not to outsiders. But the reverence paid to remarkable trees, which grow large or thrive in unexpected places, still continues. These traditions have lingered longest on the Dodecanese islands, such as Carpathos, where much ancient lore survives in the mountain villages.

At the Hotel Stavris on the island of Crete, a tamarisk tree, which grows on the edge of the patio next to the parking lot, is described in more loving and proud terms than any of the rooms or other amenities. It has plunged its roots eighty feet into the rock, where it seeks out brackish water; like the Cretans, it is said to belong to both the mountains and the shore. It is anthropomorphized and provided with human characteristics—described as "tenacious" and "fierce as a Cretan!" Its leaves repel insects; its shade is soothing to guests. Even though its roots cracked the walls of the local telephone office, the tree was not to be hurt; they simply relocated the telephone office.

This may have something to do with the fact that the much praised tree grows in an area settled by the ancient Dorians, the tree-lovingest of all Greek. In fact, the inhabitants of the area still show the characteristic blond hair and blue eyes of that ancient tribe. More than just ancient genes have been preserved—so has the reverence for the sacred trees.

Isian Religion Today

by Denise Dumars

The Academy Award–winning film *Gladiator* begins at the time of the Roman conquest of Germania. In his accounts of this military campaign, Tacitus writes that deep in the European forest the Romans found a tribe of Germans called the Suebi who were worshipping Isis in a boat. The Romans were astonished—how had these northern "barbarians" even learned of Isis, let alone come to worship her? How, indeed.

Isis and the Gods of Egypt in a New Light

The worship of the Egyptian goddess Isis first crossed the Mediterranean in the ancient Greek and Roman eras. In time, Isis became entrenched as a powerful symbol of female divinity throughout Europe and the Middle East. The gods of old Europe had been those of a mainly non-literate people. Ancient Egyptian religion presented itself with copious amounts of documentation—in the form of hieroglyphics. Today, with hieroglyphics translated, and with accounts by Plutarch and Lucius Apuleius, we have a wealth of knowledge about Isis and her role in the Egyptian pantheon.

It is easy to see how Isis came to prominence. In the mythology, she is very nearly all things to all people. She is a nurturing mother, a loving wife, a grieving widow, a wise ruler, a master of the magical and healing arts, and a protector and helper of women. Her aspects are so numerous that she is called "She of Ten Thousand Names." Westerners have been enchanted by the colorful representations of Isis from the time of Napoleon to the discovery of King Tutankhamen's tomb this century. Magical orders in the early twentieth century often have made

use of Isis in their magic. Even the Irish poet William But-
ler Yeats belonged to a sect of the Golden Dawn that worshipped Isis along with the old Irish deities.

Many of the traditions of modern Isian religion were
born in Ireland. Novelist Olivia Robertson and her
brother, clergyman Lawrence Durdin-Robertson, were
brought as children from Surrey in England to reside in
Clonegal Castle in Enniscorthy, Ireland. The family was
related to Robert Graves, the author of *The White Goddess*.
Lady Olivia studied in London to be a medium and
healer, and in 1975 her book, *The Call of Isis,* was first published. Lady Olivia and her brother founded the Fellowship of Isis in 1976, which has chapters all over the world.

Jonathan Cott learned of the revival of the Isian faith
in researching his book, *The Search for Omm Sety,* about a
British woman who believed she was a reincarnated Egyptian. His groundbreaking book, *Isis and Osiris,* was the
first journalistic study of this religion, and as such this
book provides a wealth of information about modern
Isian religion. Another book, deTraci Regula's *The Mysteries of Isis* brought many Wiccans and other neo-Pagans
to the worship of Isis. The book itself is an initiation into
Isian religion, as each chapter represents an hour in the
day of an Isian temple.

Modern Isian Worship

Some Isian groups are women-only and worship only the
goddesses of Egypt. Most, however, welcome both men
and women and honor both the goddesses and gods. A
typical Isian ceremony may look something like this: In a
suburban American dwelling, men and women of differing ethnic backgrounds, professions, and generations
prepare for a ceremony dressed in Egyptian white or
linen garb and wearing images of Isis, the ankh and lotus,
or other Egyptians gods and symbols. They have brought

traditional Middle Eastern foods to share after the ritual. A priestess or priest, or sometimes both, stand before an altar dedicated to Isis and to any other deities being called upon during the ritual. Such rituals may include asperging participants with salt water, or smudging participants with *kyphi*, a traditional Egyptian incense. The priest or priestess initiates an inner journey of meditation, and participants make offerings to the gods, such as milk, lotus buns, wine, and flowers, and burn petitions to Isis in a cauldron. Participants may then be anointed with lotus oil, and they make music with drums, chants, and the Egyptian rattle called the *sistrum*. Other rites may be unique to each group.

Overall, Isians are everyday people. Isians may or may not consider themselves Pagan or belong to any other organized religion. Most Isians, it seems, find the peace and serenity of Isis a wonderful complement to their busy lives and other worship activities.

For Further Study

Almond, Jocelyn, and Keith Seddon. *An Egyptian Book of Shadows.* Thorsons, 1999.

Cott, Jonathan. *Isis and Osiris.* Doubleday, 1994.

Ellis, Normandi. *Awakening Osiris.* Phanes Press, 1988.

Lesko, Barbara. *The Great Goddesses of Egypt.* Univ. of Oklahoma Press, 1999.

Regula, deTraci. *The Mysteries of Isis.* Llewellyn Publications, 1995.

Stirring Up Some Love Magic

by Karri Ann Allrich

Cooking is a sensual experience, to be sure. Every devoted kitchen goddess does understand the pleasure of sautéing freshly cut garlic in olive oil, or simmering home-made sauces on the stove. Delicious aromas fill the house with promise, and tastes and textures delight the tongue.

Still, while some people are born to cook, others are, well, not. But here's the good news: Even if you're domestically challenged, there are plenty of simple foods and edibles that can be tossed

together to bring pleasure to both the cook and the recipient. All you need are the right ingredients, a properly stocked pantry shelf, and a touch of magic.

Sharing Magic Food

Food is meant to be shared and savored. As such, it makes a natural medium for love magic. Love magic is not about making someone fall in love with you. It's about the art of invitation, sharing a sensual experience, and delighting in the present moment. Sharing a meal together becomes a natural form of communication, a way to invoke our sensual selves. Still, there are a few important notions to keep in mind when planning a meal intended to seduce.

The first thing to consider is ambiance. You should, even before thinking about cooking, clear your space of any lingering negative energy by opening windows and sweeping your rooms widdershins (counterclockwise) to dispel stagnant and trapped energies. You want your space to feel calm and welcoming. Burn a white sage or rosemary bundle and allow the sacred smoke to cleanse and clear your home. Gather your romantic effects—soft lighting, flickering candles, and mood music go a long way to creating an environment conducive to the pursuit of love. If serving at the table, get out your best crockery and flatware—in general, go the extra mile whenever possible. When choosing scented candles for the kitchen or the table, warm and edible scents like vanilla and cinnamon are better than floral-based scents. Natural fruit or spice-based fragrances won't clash with the aromas and flavors of your cooking.

Along with setting the mood, the subtle art of presentation is also important. The eyes absorb pleasure as well. Prepare food that has eye appeal, paying attention to colors, textures, and, most of all, freshness. Try starting with a crunchy green salad accented with ripened pear slices, fire-roasted red peppers, toasted walnuts, and crumbles of soft goat cheese. Follow with a generous bowl of buttered linguini, smothered with a colorful array of roasted vegetables and dusted with shavings of good Parmesan cheese and chopped sweet basil leaves. Salad with pasta is a superb example of an easy, romantic meal with visual and tactile allure. Still, whatever you choose to make, garnish each serving plate with a flourish of freshly chopped herbs or a sprinkling of spices.

Choosing recipes that are crafted from fresh seasonal ingredients is simply sexy. Foods in season contain so much more vitality, energy, and depth of flavor than something poured from a jar or stored in trucks and transported from warmer climates. When it comes to making magic, fresher is better. Learn to enjoy your time at the produce market. Linger amidst the colors, textures, and scents. Tune in to the changing cycle of seasonal fruits and vegetables. Getting in touch with the specific pleasures of each season in the year helps us understand the nourishing cycles of the Earth. It encourages us to live in the moment and celebrate the bounty.

For the purposes of love magic, food that is a little bit messy, saucy, and best eaten with the fingers is a good choice. Fondues are wonderful. Pastas are very sexy, especially spaghetti, linguini, and fettuccini. Think fun and light. You don't want to overload your digestion if you're hoping for a little romance after dessert. As you cook, stir deosil (clockwise) while focusing your intentions on love and blessing each ingredient with good will. Invite Venus, the goddess of love, to your table, and ask her blessings for a beautiful evening filled with romance. In fact, with Venus in mind, I've gathered together some of her favorite ingredients and appropriate food choices for a supremely seductive dinner.

A Romantic Dinner

With pasta, you can create a romantic dinner without much hassle. From a simple garlic and olive oil sauce to sautéed shrimp with baby peas and lemon, pastas are a favorite Goddess staple. Therefore, always keep a variety of pastas on hand, and you have a wonderful base for all kinds of fresh seasonal foods. Or if you enjoy rice, try northern Italy's Arborio variety. Used in risotto, and stirred clockwise for twenty-five minutes, Arborio rice is a perfect base for any love ingredient. Feel free to add your magical herbs, spices, cooked seafood, roasted vegetables, and cheeses.

Tomatoes are Venus' favorite love food, so keep plenty of cans of organic crushed and whole tomatoes on hand for your meal. Use them for a basic quick red sauce, and season with love-enhancing basil, passion-inducing garlic, and marjoram for a dash of harmony.

Olive oil, too, is a must for cooking. Olives are a gift from the goddess Athena, bringing clarity and fair judgment to your table (useful traits to invoke in the gentle art of love). Other pantry staples might include a good balsamic vinegar for enhancing sauces, roasted vegetables, salads, and bread-dipping olive oils. There is something powerfully seductive about it.

To increase the fire element in your cooking, and ignite passion and desire, always keep fresh heads of garlic in your kitchen. Garlic also protects, which is a welcome magical energy for many situations. Other favorite love foods include almonds, chestnuts, oysters, and asparagus. One crucial tip for cooking asparagus, though: It is not sexy when overcooked, so treat it gently and cook it briefly, in a scant amount of water and olive oil, until it is just barely tender-crisp.

Capers are long renowned for inviting lust and passion. And they add a salty accent to any Italian- or Mediterranean-inspired dish. Chili peppers are hot and add the fire element to your cooking; use them for enticing passion and heat in a relationship. Here is one of my favorite love recipes: linguini pasta tossed in a simple sauce of warmed extra virgin olive oil spiked with chili pepper flakes and crushed garlic. After seven years together, it's still my soul mate's favorite.

Fruit is associated with the Goddess and with intentions of love. Apples, apricots, blueberries, cherries, grapes, figs, mangoes, papayas, and strawberries are all sensual love foods, especially when shared, eaten with your fingers, or dipped into melted chocolate, whipped cream, or simple brown sugar. Be creative. Lemons are linked to love, and oranges to happiness and fidelity. Use their juices and grated zest accordingly.

For your seasonings, keep sea salt on hand for purification and protection. Always add a pinch to boiling pasta water to boost the flavor. Pepper is an irritant, so use wisely. Cinnamon invites warmth, love, and luck; use liberally whenever appropriate. Fresh cilantro leaves bring a lively accent to spicy foods, and this herb calls up passion. Dill strewn on fish or potato salad brings love and protection. Ginger invigorates and fans the flames of desire. Lavender invites higher love of a spiritual nature, while lemon balm brings peace and happiness to your table. Nutmeg, stored whole and freshly grated, brings luck, money, and love. Peppermint brings love and protection and adds a delightful twist to teas, summer pastas, rice, and salads. Thyme increase love, happiness, and money, as well as inviting dreams and enhancing divination. Experiment and enjoy.

As with all natural magic, I believe that the most important ingredient in love magic is the strength of your own self-worth. In loving yourself and clarifying that which you desire, you are well on your way to naturally inviting more love into your life, your kitchen, and your heart. So stock your pantry well in preparation, and start stirring up some culinary magic tonight.

Eucalypta Evergreening, Goddess of Herbalists

by Barbara Ardinger

Eucalypta Evergreening is the only goddess whose name is a verb. This is only right and proper, of course, for her plants are evergrowing and her priestesses everpreening. We can recognize Eucalypta Evergreening by her green hair flowing, the grass staining her clothing, and the mud between her toes oozing.

Eucalypta Evergreening dwells in the Temple of Matricaria, where she strolls every morning through the Gardens of Herba Santa and the surroundings meadows. Her land is called Zingiber, and she rules with a firm (if muddy) hand. She knows and watches over every flower fairy and nymph, every deva and dryad, every elf and hero of the greenwood and the glen.

Eucalypta Evergreening's herbalists are busier than short-order cooks. They gather for sabbats at their community gardens, which are called pharmacopiae, where stuff tends to collect—pruning shears, sickles, scythes, mortars and pestles, baskets and pots. To show their devotion to their grainy goddess, they constantly prepare their tinctures and essential oils, ointments, creams, decoctions, infusions, poltices, compresses, and liniments (plus the occasional spaghetti sauces and salad dressings). Of every possible humor, these herbalists pollinate and crossfertilize and practice both homeopathics and aromatic massage.

Eucalypta, goddess evergreening,
To herbalists all, thou art queen.
Offshoot, spring and spray, all are flourishing
Under thy care and nourishing.
Goddess vegetal, foliate, efflorescent,
Bring thy touch, all emerald iridescent.
To plantlife dost thou bring meaning,
Eucalypta, goddess evergreening.

Otherworldly Canines

by Roslyn Reid

Recently I adopted a Pembroke Welsh corgi. While researching the breed, I discovered some intriguing lore about them. According to a popular folk tale, the corgi is thought to be a "fairy steed" in the British Isles that transports the wee folk around on its back during moonlit nights. As proof of this, some point to the corgi's distinctive light-colored streaks on their backs, and call them "saddle marks."

Other folk stories about the corgi explain some of the quirks of this little dog, such as how it lost its tail by annoying the queen of the fairies. Though most of these stories might have been fabricated by corgi owners and breeders, I still was intrigued that this common dog was so often depicted in fable and lore as an otherworldly messenger, or *psy-*

chopomp (a Greek word which literally translates as "soul sender," used to describe an entity which moves easily between this world and the next). Certainly we are all acquainted with the stereotype of cats as Witches' familiars. But dogs—an animal which couldn't be less mysterious if it tried?

One need only to pick up J.C. Cooper's *Illustrated Encyclopaedia of Traditional Symbols* to discover more about the significance of the dog in many cultures. Actually, quite a few ancient peoples thought dogs were spiritual messengers. Some included dogs in funeral processions, and the Aztecs and Greeks sacrificed dogs for this reason.

The role of dogs as spiritual messenger dates back about 5,000 years to ancient India, where the Moon was considered death's gate and was guarded by the goddess Sarama with her two dogs. Yama, the Hindu god of death, has a dog, which also appears in Buddhist tradition as the Lion Dog. Most of us are more familiar with the figure of a later deity, Anubis, the jackal-hound who escorted the ancient Egyptians to their next world. Anubis is one of the oldest known deities, having been imported from Asia where he was called Up-Uat, or "Opener of the Way."

Dogs are depicted as being so comfortable in working between the worlds that the suggestion to use a dog for pulling a mandrake root from the ground can be found a twelfth-century herbal manuscript. One would tie a hungry dog to the mandrake, throw meat to the dog just out of its reach, then beat a hasty retreat. This would cause it to lunge at the meat, yanking up the root. In lore, just so you know, the scream of an extracted mandrake root was said to kill a human, so such animal intermediaries were highly prized.

Walker suggests dogs were associated with death because they are carrion eaters, much the same as jackals and vultures. To this very day there is a Semitic tradition that the approach of the death goddess can only be seen by dogs, who then sound the alarm by howling. The familiar image of dogs howling at the moon can also be found in many tarot decks, in the Moon card. Paul Huson writes in *The Devil's Picturebook* that the gates to the underworld were customarily guarded by two hounds, and he considers this image a remnant of the goddess Diana's pack of hunting dogs, who guarded those gates in Greece.

As to why the corgi is so commonly thought to be such a intermediary, consider the dog depicted on the Gundestrup cauldron, one of the most well-known relics of the ancient Celts. The artisan who fashioned this cauldron apparently thought it appropriate that this door to death should be guarded by a dog, and possibly by one of the Celtic Hounds of Annwn. Annwn, or Annwfn, is a Welsh term designating the otherworld; and in Welsh, its hounds are known as Cwn Annwn. According to famous British folklorist Richard Kieckhefer, in Wales these dogs are considered the hounds of Pwyll, Lord of Sleep. Once our dog myths reach the British Isles, they branch out into many different iterations. For example, in the remote Faroe Isles, the elves and fairies have their own herds of cattle, which they pasture with the help of dogs, just as regular farmers do. According to nineteenth-century religious historian Paul Christian, these islands have a legend that says a glimpse of an unearthly calf or dog is a sign of the protection which the fairies bring to the farm.

In legend and folklore, the Welsh Cwn Annwn usually appear as small red-gray or red-eared dogs, which of course sounds very much like a corgi. These particular canines in fact have many different names in the British Isles—yell hounds, cwn cyrff (corpse dogs), ratchets, and Gabriel hounds (as captured in fiction by gothic writer Mary Stewart). But despite the names, these dogs have the same purpose—to guide souls to the otherworld.

In the end, after our lengthy journey through myth and legend, John and Caitlin Matthews categorize the dog as one of the oldest animals of traditional Celtic teachings, and call them "those whose memory is longest of all and who can penetrate the depths of time."

This seems to be where the corgi fairy steed legend gets its wings. Indeed, perhaps it is not by accident that the Pembroke Welsh Corgi Club of America is known by the acronym PWCCA—*pwca* is a Welsh word for the spirits which clean up all the leftover crops in the garden on Samhain, after harvest is over. So if you notice something unusual about the way your corgi is wandering around the yard at dusk some evening, it might just pay to take a closer look at its back—perhaps you can catch a glimpse into the otherworld.

Mermaids

by Anna Franklin

Mermaids are legendary creatures that have the upper bodies of lovely women and the tails of fish. They may occasionally be seen sunning themselves on rocks as they gaze into mirrors and comb their long hair. Like the Greek Sirens, they have sweet voices and sing to lure human lovers into the depths of the waves, or to summon storms that wreck ships. The many beliefs and legends that surround mermaids says something about the long-lasting allure of these beautiful creatures.

The early Christian Church took a dim view of mermaids—they were demons who tempted the righteous. In Irish legend, St. Patrick banished old Pagan women from the earth by turning them into mermaids. The mermaid of Iona was offered redemption if she gave up her sea home, but this she was unable to do, and her tears became the gray-green pebbles of the island's shore.

Like other fairies, mermaids are said to have no souls but they can gain one by marrying a human. They make good wives and caring mothers, and for this reason many men have sought them. The Clan McVeagh in Sutherland, in Scotland, claim descent from a union of a mermaid and a fisherman. To capture a mermaid, it is first necessary to secure her magic cap, belt, or comb, and to hide it. If she finds these objects she will return to the sea, as this is her greatest desire. In one Scottish tale, Johnny Croy got round this by contracting a seven-year marriage with a mermaid. They duly sailed away to sea after the seven years, together with six of their children, having to leave the seventh behind because Johnny's mother had taken the precaution of branding it with a cross.

The Legend of the Mermaid's Gifts

Mermaids also have the power to grant gifts. One day Lutey of Cury was beachcombing near the Lizard in Cornwall when he found a mermaid stranded in a rock pool. She asked him to return her to the sea and he agreed. In gratitude she granted him three wishes, and he chose the power of breaking Witches' spells, the power to force familiars to do good for others, and that these powers should be passed on to his descendants. She also rewarded his kindness with two other gifts: that his family should never want, and that he could call her whenever he wanted by aid of her magic comb. He then gently carried her down to the sea, but as she was true to her nature she tried to bewitch him into entering the water with her. A dog's barking at the last minute was the only thing that broke the spell. She slid away, saying that she loved him and would return in nine years. She was true to her word, and after nine years Lutey was fishing with his son and the mermaid rose from the sea. Lutey told his son it was time to keep his promise, and he, seemingly happily, sank beneath the waves with the mermaid.

Mermen and Mermaids

It follows that if there are mermaids, there must be mermen. Gervase of Tilbury, in 1211, said there were many mermen about the coasts of Britain. They had been spotted over the years and were said to be ugly—with a wild appearance, green hair, snub noses, and large mouths. In 1723, Denmark set up a Royal Commission to disprove the existence of mermaids, but to their surprise they encountered a merman near the Faeroe Isles with deep-set eyes and a black beard.

In Ireland, they are called *merrow* or *moruadh,* Gaelic for "sea maidens." These mer-people are human above the waist and fish below. The males have green teeth and hair, pig eyes, and red noses, but they are jovial and friendly. The females are beautiful and gentle but have webbed fingers. They wear feathered red caps, or *cohullen druith,* and if these are stolen they cannot return to the sea. Female merrows have been known to fall in love with the fishermen they come across, and a woman of Bantry was said to be the child of such a marriage; she was covered all over in fish scales. Fishermen are afraid of merrows, because to see them means a storm is coming. Both male and female merrows sometimes come ashore in the form of small, hornless cows.

Belief in mermaids was still widespread in coastal areas of Britain in the nineteenth century, and as recently as 1947 an eighty-year-old fisherman from the Isle of Muck claimed he had seen a mermaid near the shore, combing her hair.

The word mermaid itself may derive from the French *mer,* or "sea," or it may be a corruption of meremaid, or merrymaid. It is possible that the concept of mermaids derives from ancient fish-tailed goddesses such as Atargatis, the Semitic Moon and love goddess. She is known in Greece as Derketo, and was the precursor to such deities as Aphrodite who was "foam born" in the sea. Aphrodite is the goddess of love, fertility, and fair sailing, often accompanied by her sacred dolphins, tritons, and tritonids. Like mermaids she is depicted with a mirror and comb, the Greek names of which signify the female vulva. In early astrology, her mirror represented the planet Venus.

Like the goddesses, mermaids are connected with love and the Moon. While all that happens under the light of the Sun is apparent, what happens during the night, under the mysterious light of the Moon, is hidden. It is most often associated with the feminine, with women's menstrual cycles, and the waxing and waning of the womb. The Moon, or the Moon goddess, rules moisture and the tides; dew falls richest on moonlit nights. The Moon is strange and enigmatic, itself often regarded as a fairy-land or a realm of the dead, inhabited by spirits. Small wonder that it is associated with magic, fairies, and spirits.

The Green Man and His Ways

by Abby Willowroot

Deep in the ancient forests and fields of Europe, the Green Man has long roamed, free and splendid. The ways of the Green Man are the ways of wild nature and the seasons of the Earth. He is present wherever crops are grown and harvested. He is there when animals mate and give birth. He is there when the seasons change and the Sun shines. The Green Man was well-known to the people Europe. Recognition of and reverence for him, and for the energy of vegetation and nature, was universal.

During the Middle Ages, stone masons carved the Green Man's likeness into the walls and arches of the finest cathedrals; there are thousands of Green Man heads carved across Europe. By the time of the Renaissance, European indigenous religions were under constant attack by the newly powerful Catholic Church. This was also an attack on the Green Man and his magic. Still, the cathedral presence of the Green Man was a constant source of strength to the people. The Green Man's image silently echoed the spirit of nature. His vigorous masculine energy was at once mysterious and familiar. As the dying and returning god of vegetation, he was similar to Jesus. In this way the people of the Middle Ages blended their traditional folk beliefs with the new religion of Christian Catholicism.

The Green Man's wisdom is that of the eternal truths, cycles, and passages. We all are born, grow, age, and die, each in our own time. It is this deep and sacred truth that is echoed in the figure of the Green Man. The Green Man is a magical bridge between nature and us. Human in form, he is also vegetable and animal at the same time. His mysteries are the secrets of all growing things. He is present in all natural foods—vegetables, salads, broccoli, corn, and the grains and fruits of the Earth. He lives in all crops and in all things green and growing.

The Green Man is as much a part of us as we are of him. His energy fills the trees that make the oxygen we breathe. The Green Man gives us the breath of life. At harvest, he surrenders his essence at the height of his magnificence. Though he dies as a plant, he is born anew in the cells and tissues of animals and humans. Here he nourishes us and grows, until in time, we cease to be and his energy is released again into the earth. There it springs forth again as crops or plants in the never-ending cycle of death and rebirth.

A Green Man Ritual

Practicing the ways of the Green Man means living in harmony with nature and living according to the seasons. It means looking for the blessings and gifts that are unique to each time of the year. Without winter, there is no spring; without summer there is no harvest. Rituals of the Green Man can be done for many purposes—to heal the environment, to restore balance, or to ensure abundance and the success of new ventures. Green Man rituals should be performed with green, white or light blue, and yellow candles. Green candles are for growth, health, and vegetation. White or blue candles represent air. Yellow candles shine with the light of the Sun and its vital energy and warmth.

Symbols used in Green Man rituals may include: a growing plant, a branch, fruit, dried grains, a small bowl of earth, leaves, berries, and acorns or other nuts.

A Green Man Invocation

I call to you now, spirit of nature, strong and free
Come and teach me, I am ready to honor you
I celebrate your gifts; I am ready to learn your truths,
As my ancestors did before me.
I see your power and your pain, beneath the green mantle
Of the scars on your body and the great sadness in your eyes.
You are no longer abandoned, we hear you again;
We are ready, to honor your ways.
Reveal yourself, Green Man,
Weave you spells of green magic.
Teach me and I will listen for your voice;
I will celebrate your sacred wisdom ways.

It is best to do a Green Man ritual outside, and if possible in a wooded place. Take your shoes off, sink your toes into the cool earth, and feel the energy of the Green Man move up through your body. Before you begin your ritual, take a few moments to listen to the trees, notice how they rustle, creak, and groan as the wind passes through them. Breathe in the oxygen they have produced for you, and know this is the miracle of the Green Man's magic.

In earlier times peasants knew the ways of the fields and forest, and gave back to the Earth with the sacrifice of the Green Man. Today we still have opportunities to make sacrifices and give back to the Earth, but the sacrifices we are making are those of care, awareness, and moderation. Recycling and conservation are contemporary Green Man sacrifices.

Today the Green Man is reemerging into our consciousness. His presence brings balance and energy to the reclaiming of our ancient heritage. For men, the Green Man is especially important, as he is a guide to accessing balanced male power. In our time, the Green Man is emerging with a clear, strong voice, guiding us toward a healthier and more stable balance with nature.

Ostara Symbolism

by Sedwin

Ostara is the Latin name for the Anglo-Saxon goddess of spring, Eostre. Her counterpart in ancient Greece was Eos, and she was known in Rome as Aurora. It was Eostre who brought the dawn each day, as well as the dawn of the year when the Earth woke from her winter sleep.

Vernal Equinox

The Vernal Equinox, a time of balance, when day and night are equal, was traditionally a day to celebrate both Earth and Sun. At this time of year, our ancestors honored the balance of all things: female and male, spiritual and physical. In Celtic Cornwall and Wales, this day was called Lady Day and marked the return of the Goddess after her winter hibernation. Lady Day was eventually Christianized and became a day (March 25) to celebrate the Virgin Mary. Variations on the idea of celebrating the return of the Goddess existed in many parts of ancient Europe, and on Crete gave rise to the story of Demeter and Persephone.

Renewal and rebirth has been an underlying springtime theme for many millennia in many cultures. For example, the Sumerian Dumuzi, beloved by Inanna, and their Babylonian counterparts, Tammuz and Ishtar, and in Egypt Osiris husband of Isis, all were resurrected after meeting violent ends. This theme was repeated in Rome with Attis and Cybele, and in the Icelandic Valhalla of Balder and Frigg, as well as with Jesus Christ. In folklore, the resurrection theme survived into modern times in rural Europe as the Green Man and Queen of the May.

As beliefs, myths, and religions replaced one another, and dates were altered by the change from the Julian to the

Gregorian calendar, themes and symbols became inter-twined. Ostara evolved into Easter, the date of which is determined by the first Full Moon following the equinox. The three days Jesus spent in the tomb, or underworld, echo the three days of the dark New Moon of winter, when all life sleeps.

Symbols Today

Many of our present-day symbols have a long history. Because of the ancient creation myth where the universe was thought to have been formed from a cosmic egg, eggs symbolized sacred life and were decorated to honor Gaia, or Mother Earth. In the Middle Ages decorated eggs were used as an Easter tithe to parish priests.

Even today, eggs are used more than ever in special food for this time of year. In Italy, whole eggs are baked into braided bread. In Russia and other eastern European coun-tries, eggs are an ingredient in preparing babka and pashka. Using eggs in breads honors both the sun god and Demeter, the goddess of grain.

The Easter bunny is much older than its current-day commercialized descendant. Saxon legend tells us that a humble rabbit decorated eggs and presented them to Eostre to honor her. Both eggs and rabbits are symbols of fertility. Up until medieval times it was a custom to place eggs around the fields in early spring to invoke their powers of fertility and enhance crop yield. As for rabbits, it's no surprise why they were associated with fertility. In Wales, the rabbit was considered lucky by tin miners because they burrowed into the earth. And the rabbit was thought some-what mysterious because it seemed to dwell in two worlds—the physical world and the underworld. As rabbits returned from the underworld after winter hibernation, they seemed to bring with them the renewal of the Earth.

Other symbols of this time of year include the Easter basket. The origin of the basket itself may be closely linked to eggs, because it is believed that people of early civilizations were inspired to weave baskets by watching birds build the nests in which they laid their eggs. And this time of year wouldn't be complete without a profusion of yellow—yellow flowers, simnel cake, saffron loaf, and eggs dyed yellow to symbolize the growing strength of the returning Sun.

In our busy world, it's important to pause and appreciate the new life that is unfolding all around us. The Earth is renewing herself, and the signs of reawakening are everywhere. This season brings freshness into our lives as we begin to shed heavy winter clothes and feel the warmth of the sunlight on our skin.

It is time to reverse the turn inward that we made at Winter Solstice, and to plan our path into summer with fresh challenges to help us grow. This time of planting is also for planting spiritual seeds.

For Further Study

Jones, Julia, and Barbara Deer. *A Calendar of Feasts: Cattern Cakes and Lace.* Dorling Kindersley Limited, 1987.

Ferguson, Diana. *The Magical Year: A Pagan Perspective on the Natural World.* Labyrinth Publishing, 1996.

McCoy, Edain. *Witta: An Irsh Pagan Tradition.* Llewellyn Publications, 1993.

Making Your Own Talismanic Jewelry

by Mary Magpie

For Pagans, talismanic jewelry is a special and personal tool and object of beauty. Such an item can be intricate, like a hand-crafted silver ring, or very simple, like a holey stone threaded on to a cord and worn on the neck. Most of us are not skilled in silver or goldsmithing, but with a little effort we can still make our own talismanic jewels that have at least a small degree of originality.

Some Jewelry-Making Tips

To start, you should know that craft stores and mail-order businesses sell jewelry findings, or the settings and other equipment required for making your own jewelry. Often these consist of rings, brooches, pendants and so on that only require the fitting of a suitable gemstone, which they usually also sell. Sometimes they include instructions on how to assemble elements to make beautiful jewelry. Once you have the components it is just a matter of putting the two together.

Usually, you will need just some basic equipment. I have made a lot of talismans using just two pairs of needle-nosed pliers and a "pusher," which is like a screwdriver with the end neatly cut off. This is used to push claws and bezels around jewels. Claws are only suitable for holding faceted stones. Bezels are the thin bands or tiny raised walls of metal around a setting that hold a gem in place; they are used for cabochons and other nonfaceted gemstones.

For claws, add just a tiny drop of superglue to the back of the stone to make it secure. Press your first claw down, then move to the one opposite. Next, do another pair of opposite claws until the gem is securely set, working around all the claws again to make sure they are firm. Be careful not to press too hard; some gems are brittle and will break.

For bezels, use a dab of superglue as well. Press the bezel down over the edge of the gem in one place, then move to the opposite side and repeat. Now work around the gem, pressing the bezel in place to secure the stone.

Some people simply glue their gemstones into place, but that can be risky, depending on the quality of the glue. If you decide on glue either for extra security or instead of setting the gem properly, use only as much as you need and use the best and most suitable adhesive you can find. Read the packaging to check that you have the right substance. Generally it is safest to work in a well-ventilated area as many glues contain solvents that can be dangerous to you. These solvents can also damage delicate stones, so check before you use.

For making pendants and earrings, the components are equally available. A good way of fixing irregularly shaped items, such as pebbles or tumbled gems, is to attach a bell cap to the top with very strong glue, then thread this on a cord or chain. Remember to check the glue periodically as it is not permanent.

If you have trouble holding onto your gemstone while working, use a little piece of blue-tack or something similar to grip it. Some people use chewing gum, though this can leave a residue, so I don't recommend it. Turquoise is particularly easy to mark, so handle this gemstone as little as possible.

If you are making a pendant you will probably need to add a jump ring to link it to a chain. This is the tiny loop of metal that connects chains to clasps, and pendants to chains, and they are very difficult to put on. The best way to do so is to open the ring out slightly using two pairs of pliers, slip it over the ring in your pendant, then close it securely. Jump rings tend to be the weakest link in any chain and it can be a good idea to get these soldered securely. Unless you are experienced in soldering precious metals, though, I advise you take your piece to a jeweller to have this

done properly. The cost is usually fairly low, and is far better than ruining all your hard work.

In the end, you may choose to make a simple no-sew talismanic bag by cutting out a circle of thin leather or other natural material. It needs to be large enough to enclose your talisman with some material left to spare. Place the talisman in the center, and draw up the edges. Tie a piece of cotton or silk thread around the bundle to securely seal it. Now attach a cord long enough to go comfortably around your neck or wrist. The best cords are made from natural materials.

Please note that you should take care if children are around, as they will probably have no difficulty in pulling your talisman apart and may choke on the small parts.

When you are done with all of these steps, your talisman is ready to wear. If you want to, program it for your purpose. Otherwise, just let its magic come into your life.

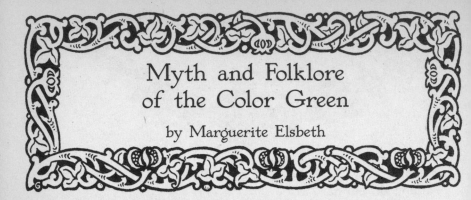

Myth and Folklore of the Color Green

by Marguerite Elsbeth

It was not that long ago that the color green was banned by early Christians because of its use in Pagan ceremonies, though it came back into favor as a fertility symbol by the late Middle Ages. It's a good thing for current-day nature worshippers that the green prohibition eventually ceased, for the color is significant in the healing magic of most earth-based spiritual practices.

Green is the color of life. The word "green" springs from the Teutonic language, and literally means "to grow." Perhaps this came about because green is associated with springtime. It brings an echo of nature to mind, as it is the predominant color we see after winter. When mixed with blue, green reminds us of waters, fields, and forests, and when combined with tan or beige, green says "organic." Green is the color of freshness and renewal, and as such it naturally radiates feelings of youthful energy, healing, and wellness whenever we look at it.

Green Arcana

Green falls in between blue and yellow on the visible color spectrum. It is a calming color, with both a warming and cooling effect. F-Sharp, the musical note associated with green, is a mild sedative and depressant. It promotes the physical relaxation necessary for mental workers, and is beneficial for creative and inventive activities. It also affects balance and poise in action.

Green is associated with the third chakra, called the throat center, or pharyngeal plexus, that is located in the area of the throat. It relates to the planet Venus, and the elements of earth, air, and water in the west, and to ether in the east. When viewed in this way, green is associated with joy, ecstasy, and bliss. The green throat center controls the thyroid and parathyroid glands, the kidneys, the thalamus, the sensory organs, the lumbar region of the spine, and the skin.

The month of May is colored spring green, and its birthstone is the emerald, an Earth Mother gem and a stone of nature that heightens ecological consciousness. August is colored deep green. Its birthstone is the peridot that signifies happiness in marriage and is both a receiver and transmitter of healing energy.

Are You a Green Being?

East Indian mystics see green as the marriage of balance and harmony, the color ray that bridges our karma because it provides a healing link between our emotional actions and reactions. Indeed, green has everything to do with sharing and balance. If we see green in our dreams it means we need adaptability, reconciliation, healing, and harmony within ourselves or in our dealings with others.

People who are attracted to green usually display an artistic, creative, harmonious, stable, enduring, and quiet personality—though too much of the green vibration may result in a capricious, wasteful, and indolent temperament. When green is a least favorite color, it may indicate a disposition that is lazy, wanton, overweight, subject to throat infections, and on occasion, envy.

Gaea

Green is an important symbol of the gods and goddesses worshipped by earth-based spiritual traditions. One major ancient mythic figure is the Green Man, a Pagan god of fertility, death, and rebirth, and also the Earth Father complement to the Gaea, the Earth Mother. Gaea is the Greco-Roman goddess who emerged out of chaos, and gave birth as she slept to Uranus, the sky god. He showered fertile rain upon her secret clefts as he gazed down fondly upon her from the mountains, and she bore grass, flowers, trees, and an astounding array of birds and beasts. The lush rain of Uranus also made the rivers flow, and swelled hollow earthen places into lakes and seas.

Gaea, the Earth Mother, has a tarot card all her own called the Empress. In this card she is usually depicted as the goddess of love, beauty, growth, and fruitfulness. She is a pregnant matron symbolizing the Great Mother principle in nature. She represents the activity of the subconscious mind, creative imagination, reproduction, and growth. And naturally, she is dressed in bright, verdant green colors.

Green Grounding

For a ritual grounding that will utilize the natural magic of the color green, lie flat on the earth in a grassy area. Close your eyes and relax. Feel yourself being pulled down by the gravity of the planet Earth beneath you. Imagine all bad feelings seeping deep into the ground; see all negativity burn up in the Earth's molten core. Now, feel vital energy coming to you from the grass and trees. Allow this green energy of renewal to revitalize your entire being. Thank the green Earth.

Green Trivia

Green is the most restful color for the human eye.

Time moves faster in a green room.

Green has great healing power, and can soothe pain.

People who work in green environments have fewer stomach aches.

Green is beneficial around teething infants.

Suicides dropped 34 percent when London's Blackfriar Bridge was painted green.

The color of avocado green is synonymous with the 60s and 70s in the minds of those who can remember that time period.

Green represents money and good luck in the U.S.

For Further Study

Gage, John. *Color and Culture: Practice and Meaning from Antiquity to Abstraction.* University of California Press, 1999.

Diviner of the Hills

by Jim Weaver

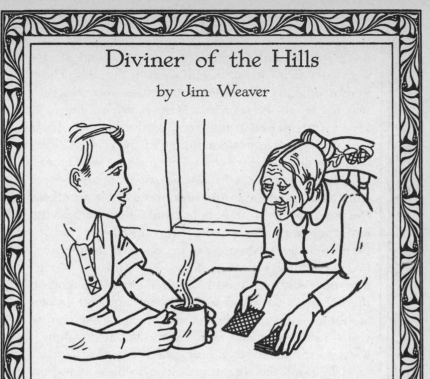

The magic of spring comes softly to the Appalachian hills of southeastern Ohio. The misty green of new leaves spreads up the hills and across the tops of the ridges. Then, the dogwood and redbud trees begin to bloom, and their flowers soon star the hills and hollows with white and pink blossoms. And in the woodland, the wild trilliums form thick carpets of white on the forest floor.

I was born in these hills. And in these hills on a spring day over thirty years ago, I met the person who planted the seed of magic in my life.

A Tradition of Country Magic

As a boy, I knew that this region of the country was rich with folklore and magic. For instance, stories of hauntings and other strange occurrences were common in this isolated hill country. Among the more popular stories were tales of the diviners who lived in the hills. These were people who were said to have the "second sight"; that is, the gift of prophecy. These diviners normally kept to themselves, living deep in the hollows. Their favorite divining tools were ordinary playing cards. Many communities, it seemed, had their resident Wise One.

Although it was seldom discussed openly, people from all walks of life would make regular visits to these "fortunetellers." Most people would never admit the faith they had in these seers. I certainly never thought I'd become one of them. I was in college at the time and had gone through a rough period in my life. My parents were newly divorced, and I had final exams looming on the horizon. I was depressed, and perhaps a bit desperate for guidance, so at my mother's urging I agreed to visit a "card reader" she knew over in the next county. It was a woman the locals simply called Ma.

I followed the directions given to me, driving my mother's Buick deeper and deeper into the back hills. I drove past long-abandoned coal mining towns covered with tangles of trumpet vine and ivy. I bounced along on dirt roads, past woods so thick and overgrown that tree branches brushed against the windows of the car. Here and there I could see the gnarled branches of lilac bushes, marking the remnants of forgotten homesteads.

Finally, I spied a weather-beaten farmhouse sitting back from the road, rising above waist-high weeds. I pulled into the rutted drive and came to a stop in front of a sagging porch. I had arrived at Ma's place.

At the sound of my knock a raspy voice replied: "Come in." I entered cautiously.

Ma was sitting in a rocker at the kitchen table. To ward off the cool spring weather, her tiny shoulders were covered by a yellow shawl. It seemed she must have lived only in this one room. Her iron bed, covered with antique quilts, sat along one wall. Across the room was a pot-bellied stove. To catch her tobacco, which she chewed, a brass spittoon sat at her feet. The kitchen table is where she did her "readins."

She motioned me to sit across from her. As she tucked a wisp of gray hair behind her ear, she handed me a worn and faded deck of playing cards saying: "Go ahead son, cut 'em."

Then she picked up the deck and laid out only seven cards, face-up, straight across, from left to right. I never gave her any information about myself. She never really looked at the cards as her frail hands placed them on the table. Instead, she looked at me, or perhaps past me—I couldn't be certain. Immediately she began to tell me about myself. Her comments were dramatically on target. Her future predictions were quite specific and accurate; they came to pass within the week.

She never demanded payment of any kind. "Did I help you?" she'd simply ask. She would accept small sums of money—whatever you chose to give. Many who sought her help were poor country folk who would pay her back by doing her chores or bringing her meals.

In general, Ma's card-reading style was simple. Her greatest power, however, was in the psychic impressions she received as she looked at you. This was her true ability—to see a person and so capture that person's image in her mind that she immediately knew what was going on in the person's life. That is the true knack of a seer.

Ma was probably self-taught. She had no degrees. Nor was she ever boastful about her powers. She was a simple country woman, who without realizing it, dedicated her life to the power of positive magic.

Developing Seeing Skills

You can develop this skill too, given enough time and practice. This is my suggestion: Next time you do a reading, have your seeker shuffle and cut whatever type of cards you're using; then, pick up the deck and lay out the first seven cards from the top of the deck. Go from left to right, faceup. Start reading each card as you lay it out. Try not to stare at the card too long. Instead, look at the person you're reading for. You'll begin to see impressions in your mind's eye.

Continue in this way until you've laid out the seventh card, then look at the entire spread. Is there a theme? If so, what is it? Keep practicing, and you'll find this method will come very naturally after a while. I've found this spread is good for covering a short span of time, perhaps seven to ten days.

Ma has long since passed on. She never knew how much she inspired me, but each time I work with the cards, I have her to thank. She embodied the wisdom of the Crone, and taught me to look to the Old Ones—for they have much to teach us, if we watch and listen. After knowing her, I was inspired to learn more about the world of folk magic.

I was blessed to have known her.

Star Light, Star Bright

by Elizabeth Barrette

...Eggs, butter, cheese, bread
stick, stock,
stone dead
O-U-T

Every culture has its own folklore. What most people don't realize is that children have a folklore all their own; they share a diverse collection of rhymes, songs, and customs from coast to coast.

Among these we find many with magical implications, including rhymes for divination, for making wishes, for counting things, for changing the weather, for attracting good luck or averting bad luck, and much more. The alternative spirituality movement has also given us some new ones that are currently catching on with Pagan kids. Sing one at a gathering, and you may be surprised to find six kids carrying it home in six different ways.

Magical Children's Rhymes

Like all folklore, children's rhymes exist in multiple versions. Many of the ones written down in books differ slightly from the ones I recall from my own childhood, and both may differ from the ones you know. Folklorists sometimes collect as many versions as they can find of a single rhyme, which helps identify its main idea but proves that there is rarely one "true" or original form to folklore. See how many you can find by asking your friends.

In general, children's magical rhymes vary widely in style, but certain features do show up frequently. First, most of them are short, ranging from two to twelve lines. Second, they almost always rhyme. These two factors make them easy to remember and spread. Third, they often include nonsense, anywhere from a single word to the whole verse (possibly they are "magic words," or an example of children's general fondness for secrets). Finally, most rhymes relate to a very specific circumstance and must be said in a certain way, sometimes with matching gestures, in order to work.

Children's Divinations

Want a peek at the future? Numerous rhymes use natural events to predict other things happening in your life. This sweet little couplet, also sometimes used as a wishing rhyme, suggests that you'll meet a friend:

> *I see the Moon, the Moon sees me;*
> *The Moon sees somebody I want to see.*

Older children like to play games for guessing such things as their future occupation—who they'll marry, and so forth. Here's a rhyme that combines those ideas; children play it to determine their own job or their spouse's job. It works by chanting the words while counting out buttons; when you get to the end of the available buttons, the word said on the last button is the answer:

> *Rich man,*
> *Poor man,*
> *Beggar man,*
> *Thief,*
> *Doctor,*
> *Lawyer,*
> *Merchant,*
> *Chief.*

Wishing Rhymes

Children enjoy making wishes. There are dozens, if not hundreds, of jingles that focus on getting wishes. Usually the verse itself includes instructions for how to make wishes come true. The most famous is probably this one:

> *Star light, star bright,*
> *First star I see tonight,*

I wish I may, I wish I might,
Have the wish I wish tonight.

This one is unusual for a wishing rhyme in that it gives the user so much control. All you have to do for an opportunity to make a wish is wait outside for the first star to appear. This rhyme below offers even more control:

Touch blue,
And your wish
Will come true.

Most wishing rhymes, however, require you to wait for some less-than-common event outside your own influence. This reflects the magical principle that rarity can bring power. Here's a typical example:

See a pin and pick it up
All the day you'll have good luck.

The version I learned was actually in reference to a penny rather than a pin, but both versions seem pretty popular.

Counting Rhymes

These rhymes provide a reasonably fair way of eliminating players from consideration, or of choosing one person from a group for some role. Most kids can't count well enough to tell from the beginning who will wind up being chosen if the rhyme has a consistent number of syllables; but a few rhymes include a random factor that makes it a little more fair. Some rhymes eliminate, others select. These are among the silliest of rhymes, often nothing but loosely related gibberish, as with the following:

Eenie Meenie Cafateenie,
Ala bama boo.
Ootchie kootchie ala mootchie
I choose you.

Of course, this is a common elimination rhyme, with lots of variations. A more famous version goes like this:

Eenie, meenie, miny, moe,
Catch a tiger by the toe.
If he hollers, make him pay
Fifty dollars every day.
My mother says to pick the very best one—
Y-O-U spells you and you are not it.

Another version of this rhyme involves counting out the days of the week, or spelling out the name of the day it is when you're using the rhyme. *American Children's Folklore* cites counting-out rhymes as some of the oldest and most universally recorded examples of children's folklore. My favorite tidbit of information was the "Knock on Wood" rhyme; its roots are thought to go back to an ancient Druidic version around the first century B.C., and it was believed to be a means of choosing a human sacrifice:

Eena, meena, mona, mite
Basca, lora, hora, bite,
Hugga, bucca, bau;
Eggs, butter, cheese, bread,
Stick, stock, stone dead—O-U-T!

By the way, children adore gross and creepy imagery. Often, therefore, children take a perfectly innocuous ditty and make it rude.

Weather Rhymes

Everyone worrries about the weather. Will it rain, will it snow? Will the sun shine today? Many rhymes aim to predict the weather based on the behavior of animals or other natural phenomena. Here's a winter rhyme about birds and snow:

Swallows fly high: clear blue sky;
Swallows fly low: there will come snow.

This couplet also has versions predicting rain instead of snow. Some verses aim to change the weather rather than predicting it. Probably the most famous weather rhyme is:

Rain, rain, go away
Come again another day!

A chorus of this invariably breaks out when a thunder-shower interferes with a parade, ballgame, or other event. Notice, though, that the charm includes an invitation for the rain to come back; it's important never to banish anything without such a safety catch, for fear of causing a drought or other problem. Finally there are weather rhymes which simply celebrate, like this catchy tune:

Welcome back to the rain, rain, rain,
We're glad the water's coming down again,
The seeds are born in the storm,
Welcome back to the rain.

Although of comparatively recent invention, this ditty is catching on. I've heard Pagan kids singing this one at gatherings, not just in the official children's programming but also on their own.

Miscellaneous Rhymes

Plenty of rhymes don't fall into a clear category. Some are one-of-a-kind, while others belong to obscure groups where it's hard to assemble several for comparison. This sassy example probably comes closer to the original spirit of Halloween—or All Hallows' Eve—than more polite modern customs do:

Trick or treat,
Smell my feet,
Give me something good to eat.
If you don't,
I don't care.
I'll pull down your underwear.

Killing a ladybug, a beneficial insect, can bring bad luck. If one of these cute pink beetles lands on you, shoo her away with this incantation. Like many children's rhymes, it boasts grotesque imagery, even though the actual intent in this case is harmless.

Ladybug, ladybug,
Fly away home;

Your house is on fire,
Your children will burn.

Finally there are warning rhymes, which don't do anything besides suggest that you avoid a particular action and its consequence. Children are especially fond of chanting these at each other after someone has just done the unwise thing named in the rhyme. The most prevalent is a couplet taken from a longer rhyme:

Step on a crack,
Break your mother's back.

The "crack" in the original was symbolic of a grave opening, and predates such modern innovations as pavement and linoleum tile which make it almost impossible to avoid stepping on cracks.

For Further Study

Bronner, Simon J. *American Children's Folklore.* August House Publishers, 1988.
A guide to diverse types of children's folklore.

Starhawk, Diane Baker, and Anne Hill. *Circle Round: Raising Children in Goddess Traditions.* Bantam, 1998.
A beautiful collection of activities, stories, songs, and much more for Pagan families.

Sherman, Josepha, and T. K. F. Weiskopf. *Greasy Grimy Gopher Guts: The Subversive Folklore of Childhood.* August House Publishers, 1995.
More children's folklore, with an emphasis on the gross kind.

Potter, Carole. *Knock on Wood: An Encyclopedia of Superstition.* Longmeadow Press, 1983.
A handy reference on folklore and superstitions for all ages.

Training Pets for Ritual Work

by Cerridwen Iris Shea

If you have pets, the time will come when they become curious about your rituals—sticking their noses in your ritual implements, sniffing around your feet. Instead of fighting this curiosity, you can make use of your pets in your rituals. Training them for the rituals is the best way to make sure that noses, whiskers, and tails don't go up in flame—or worse.

My Pet Rituals

My feline housemates grew up around ritual. When she was tiny, Elsa used to sleep on my altar pentacle; in fact, it was her favorite place in the home. As she got larger, she didn't realize that she couldn't quite fit, and was quite shocked when she knocked items off the altar. Fortunately, she's now quite good about leaving sacred objects alone.

It's important that your pets get familiar with your ritual items. Most animals are naturally curious. If they haven't seen a tool before, they will want to know all about it. When I bring a new item into the house, I usually leave it out, or when I unwrap it I leave it somewhere where my pets can explore it. They sniff it, move it around a bit, and perhaps rub against it, marking it. Of course, with four cats, if one of them marks something, the other three must follow and copy her in quick succession.

Once they've thoroughly explored an item, I can set it on my altar to charge. Since my animals are familiar with everything on my altar, they leave it alone, mostly.

Probably the most important ritual item to teach pets about is your candle. Anything with a flame can be hazardous not just to the pet, but to the entire house. Obviously, you do not leave candles unattended. Occasionally, I will leave jar candles burning on my stove altar while I'm in another part of the house, but only for a few minutes. While I often use tapers in small holders for ritual or short spellwork, any long-term spellwork is done with jar candles. It's just safer all the way around.

To introduce your pets to candles, let them come near the candle. Usually they approach cautiously, and then, as they feel the heat, they back away. If you think the pet is getting too close, say "No!" and firmly push the pet out of the way. You don't want the pet to associate something negative with candles, you just don't want them coming too close when the candles are lit. In other words, don't scold the pet when he or she approaches an unlit candle. Otherwise, you will find chewed up or broken candles all over the place.

In general, you should allow your pet to get comfortable with your ritual setup before you actually start a ritual. It is quite distracting to have an animal who feels uncertain in a ritual while you're trying to concentrate, and it's almost impossible to raise energy that way. I recommend setting up the altar one day when you do not plan to have a ritual. Allow your pet to explore the ritual area in a relaxed way.

Something I always do with a new pet is to hold a welcoming ritual specifically for the pet. This is a low-stress, cast circle where I welcome the pet, ask blessings, and let the pet to get used to a ritual circle.

There are many ways a pet can participate in ritual. My cats usually sit in the circle and watch everything that is going on. Often, they can see much more than I can. They rarely participate in my circles around Samhain when I tend the dead—too many unfamiliar souls for them to feel comfortable. But in one of my regular ritual circles, they sit and watch, or fall asleep. During meditation, they often sit over my heart chakra or solar plexus and purr, heightening the relaxation. When the cats participate in circle, I always make sure that I have some treats within the space—when the bread is passed around, the cats get a treat. When we feast, they get a snack.

A friend of mine has one male cat and one female cat. The female cat sleeps in another room during the ritual, but comes out and joins us for the feast. The male cat usually sits just inside the circle and watches everything that goes on. During meditations, he makes the rounds, checking on each of us. If someone takes longer than usual to return from meditation, he gently nuzzles her along. If someone gets emotional, he is there to offer comfort. Another friend of mine has a bird who "sings" along with the chants—not only does this add a unique kind of energy, but it promotes quite a bit of laughter.

Yet another friend of mine trained her dog to be a guardian, especially during outdoor rituals. Instead of keeping the dog within circle, letting him put his head in people's laps, or letting people play with him, she sets him off to one side of the circle, just outside the boundary. He watches her cast the circle, and then watches what goes on within and without the circle. If someone approaches, he gives a warning bark—not aggressive, just factual. If the person persists, he will gently but firmly try to guide that person away. He's a big dog —a Husky mix—and usually people will do as he asks. At the end of the circle, he comes in for the feast and gets his treats. It only took him two or three rituals to catch on that this was his job in ritual. He's quite wonderful, and I feel safer with him around.

If your pet shows no interest in joining ritual, don't force the pet. Let the animal get interested on his or her own. Let the animal decide when the time is right to join in. Show a lot of patience and a lot of love.

If an animal shows signs of discomfort or senses something you can't, pay attention. The animal's senses are much more highly tuned than yours. Double-check your circle and your protection, and reinforce where necessary.

Pets can add much love, joy, laughter, and focus to a ritual. If you have pets, I encourage you to let them get accustomed to your ritual work and include them in it. You will be surprised at the leaps, and tangents, your magic takes.

A Magical Herbal Book

by Laurel Nightspring Reufner

Years ago, when I first started studying Paganism, I decided to make my own Book of Shadows. It would include my favorite spells and rituals, and would be made by hand, complete with sundry arcane herbs glued right into the binding. Since that time, I've come a long way in bookmaking and can now share with you how to avoid some of the errors of my earlier ways. What follows then are the directions for making your very own hardbound, handsewn journal, into which you can include a variety of magical herbs right in the binding. The herbal information at the end of this article will also guide you in making an herbal covered binder.

Getting Started

The materials you need for your book are easy to find. They are specific to this particular project, but with some thought you can easily adapt other materials into the design of your books. It's all depends on your own creativity.

Paper: 21 sheets, 8½ by 11 inches

Matboard or sturdy cardboard: 2 pieces, 5½ by 9 inches

Cloth or paper for the cover, 11 by 14½ inches

Paper for end leaves: 2 pieces, 8½ by 11 inches

Powdered herbs: one teaspoon or so of several varieties

Glue: either white glue or pva adhesive

A small dish to hold glue

A stiff brush for spreading the glue

An awl, or sharp needle (such as a darning needle)

Various tools—ruler, quilting needle, craft knife, bulldog clip, scrap paper, wax paper, a pencil

Making the Book

Before you start, read these directions all the way through. They may not make that much sense right now, but it'll help to know the whole process when you're actually putting your book together. To start, fold each sheet of your twenty-one sheets of paper in half, across the length, so you have a piece of paper that measures 5½ by 8½. Tuck the folded pages into one another, leaving two signatures, or sections, of pages composed of eleven and ten sections respectively. This will give you a total of eighty pages in your finished book, plus two extra sheets to glue the signatures onto the cover.

Now, stack your signatures so that the folded edges are aligned and facing you, and clip them together with the bulldog clip. Measure in one inch from the top edge, and, using a pencil, draw a vertical line down both signatures. Measure in one inch more from this mark and repeat. Do the same thing on from the bottom edge, making marks one and two inches in.

Remove the bulldog clip, and open out the signatures so they are unfolded. Using the pencil marks as guides, take the awl or a sturdy needle and punch holes all the way through each signature. When you're done, fold the signatures back up, stack them atop one another once more, and clip. It's time to sew the signatures together. Using a piece of quilting thread between 25 and 30 inches in length, thread your needle. Beginning on the outside of the righthand side of the top signature spine, push the needle through the hole you made in the last step. Pull the thread through to the inside, leaving about five inches dangling out the back. You'll use that to tie the thread off in a moment. From the inside of the signature, push the needle through the next hole—the second hole from the right—and pull the thread all the way to the outside, making sure it's taut against the fold of the paper. Hold on to the tail you left for tying off the thread as you're pulling it tight, or you'll have to start over again.

Go on to the next hole—the third one in line—and push the needle in from the outside, pulling it taut once more. Bring the needle out the fourth and final hole in the signature. You should now have the needle on the outside once more, ready to sew through the bottom signature of your book. If you need to, tighten up the thread along the spine, take a deep breath, and push the needle into the first hole (from the left this time) of the bottom signature. All you do then is repeat the same process used in sewing the first signature, only going in the opposite direction. (Instead of going right-to-left, as in the first signature, you go left-to-right.)

Once you've reached the end of the spine you should have two lengths of thread dangling, one above the other. If necessary, tighten up the thread along the spine, making sure it is snug on the lefthand side where the thread goes from the top signature to the bottom one. After everything is all snug, take the two thread tails and tie them off together. You've just sewn your book.

The next step is to measure and mark where the book's spine will be on the cover paper. Lightly fold it in half, being careful not to crease it. You just want to find the midway point, not completely fold it in half. The page block spine is about one-half inch wide, and the total width of the boards is also about one-half inch wide, meaning you'll need to leave about an inch in the middle of the cover to make room for the spine. Lay your ruler beside the long edge of the cover paper and measure one-half inch to either side of the fold line, making tick marks at those points. Do the same thing at the bottom edge and then connect the marks. The space between the lines is the spine.

It might be a good idea to lay your boards out on the cover paper and lightly mark where they'll be glued down. The guidelines you drew in the last step mark one boundary. Lay your boards along those lines, centering them top to bottom on the paper, and lightly draw guidelines with the pencil. Pour some of the glue into your small dish. This will make it easier to load the brush with glue. Quickly and evenly spread the glue over one of the boards. Flip the board over, and lay it down on the cover paper, paying attention to where your guidelines are all located. Repeat the process with the other board.

We now need to trim the corners so the cover won't bulge when glued down onto the board. Using the craft knife cut off all four corners of the cover paper, coming to between ¼- and ⅛-inch of the corners of the boards. Spread more glue along the upper edge of the board (or the upper edge of the paper, if you want), and fold it over onto the board, smoothing it down as you go. Repeat the same process with the bottom edge, and then move on to the sides. Use a rag or paper towel to wipe off any excess glue. Tear off a piece of wax paper measuring at least the width of your cover, lay it down on a flat surface, and then place the glued board combination face down on the wax paper. Pile on a few books to help flatten it and then leave the assembly to dry for a little while.

When the cover is dry, or almost completely dry, cut off about two-thirds of the first and last pages in your signature block. These will be glued down to the boards in order to attach the pages to the cover. Pour out some more glue, if needed, and then brush glue over one of the pages you just trimmed. Aligning the spine of the signature with the edge of the board, glue the trimmed page down onto the board, pressing it smooth as you go. Wipe off any excess glue and tuck a piece of wax paper between the pages that are intact and the page you just glued to the board. Repeat for the back of the page block. It's starting to look like a real journal now, isn't it?

Set your book aside for a little while so it will dry, then go on to the next and last step—adding your magical herbs. Once you are satisfied the glue has dried enough, open your book to the front, and spread on a coat of glue and lightly sprinkle half of your herb mixture over the glued area. Brush glue out onto one of the end leaves. Place the end leaf over the herb area and smooth it out. End leaves are centered over the boards and help hide the edges from where the cover paper was folded over and glued down. Slip in a piece of wax paper to keep things that aren't supposed to stick together protected. Then repeat the process with the other side of the journal and the remaining herbs. That's all there is to it.

Choosing and Preparing the Herbs

Trust me on this one, when preparing your herbs for the book, you want to make sure they are dry before you grind them to a fine powder. The more finely ground, the better—otherwise you'll have wart-like bumps all over your cover.

Of course a major aspect of this whole exercise is choosing which herbs to use. I would say that it depends on the purpose for which the book is created. Keep in mind that some herbs are rather strongly scented—that is, unless you absolutely love the smell of garlic, don't use it. What follows are some suggestions, which will hopefully lead you to ideas of your own. These are not written in stone. Always choose your herbs based on what you like and on pure whim. While making a book can be serious business, it should also be fun.

Herbal Energies for Your Herbal Book

A book dedicated to things spiritual and magical might make use of cedar, bergamot, sandalwood, dragon's blood, white sage, gardenia, sweetgrass, or tobacco.

A generic little spellbook would benefit from bergamot, patchouli, carnation, dragon's blood, vervain, basil, or cinquefoil. Further, any herb that makes you feel more spiritual or magical will work wonderfully in your book.

If you want some magical balance to your book, try using herbs associated with the four elements (plus one): earth, air, fire, water, and spirit.

Air: anise, caraway, lemon verbena, white sage, lavender

Fire: bay, cedar, calendula, dragon's blood, sunflower

Water: geranium, heather, vanilla, cardamom, mallow

Earth: magnolia, patchouli, vervain, horehound, mugwort

Spirit: gum Arabic, sandalwood, gardenia, African violet, copal

Will your little book contain a collection of love sonnets or maybe some love spells? You might consider adding basil, lemon verbena, chamomile, roses, patchouli, or vanilla bean to the binding. Especially appropriate for such a collection would be parsley, sage, rosemary, and thyme, as mentioned in the folksong "Scarborough Fair." These are ingredients in a medieval love charm.

And what is love without beauty? For a collection of beauty recipes and spells try lemon peel, maidenhair, heather, yerba santa, flax, or catnip. I'd only use the catnip if the book would be safe from the attentions of a cat. Otherwise you might find your binding shredded and the cat asleep on the pages, purring away.

A book dedicated to healing might contain sage, lemon balm, fennel, calendula, cinnamon, or walnut. Any of the mint varieties could also be used. And rose geranium has an uplifting effect. Other traits to include in such a collection would be balance and strength. Clover, honeysuckle, lilac, and meadowsweet are all good for balance; pennyroyal, oak, carnation, and bay help promote strength.

Another possible way to choose your herbs is to base your choices on the wheel of the zodiac. You can choose herbs based on your Sun sign, Moon sign, or perhaps your ascendant. Or you could decide on a more balanced approach and pick an herb for each of the zodiacal signs. Here's a quick list to assist you:

Ares: geranium, honeysuckle, marjoram, nettle, rosemary

Taurus: apple, Cyprus, lovage, poppy, violets

Gemini: lavender, tansy, vervain, walnut, oak

Cancer: daisy, honeysuckle, hyssop, jasmine, lemon balm

Leo: borage, chamomile, citrus, eyebright, sunflowers

Virgo: barley, fennel, pansy, wheat

Libra: apple, ash, cherry, rose, violet

Scorpio: basil, bryony, chrysanthemum, palms, wormwood

Sagittarius: beech, birch, dandelion, elm, feverfew, holly

Capricorn: carnation, comfrey, cypress, ivy, poplar

Aquarius: fruit trees, orchids, heather

Pisces: jonquil, seaweed, fig, willow

Some Notes on Herbal Books

If you are working on honing your psychic talents, be it through meditation, scrying, tarot working, or whatever else, a small journal is an excellent way to keep track of your progress. Some herbs to aid you in your goal could include angelica, bay, yarrow, honeysuckle, nutmeg, and anise. You might also want to consider some of the herbs listed in the previous section. Many of these could serve a similar function in psychic development.

Dream journaling is another way folks are developing their mental abilities and better understandng themselves. Lavender, rosemary, heliotrope, mimosa, and passionflower are all excellent choices to assist in this. And if you can stand the smell, valerian, mugwort, and hops possess dream-inducing qualities. Any of the recipes out there for dream pillows work equally well in your herbal book.

Books make great gifts to those who like to write, sketch, or otherwise create. Some good herbs to include in these bindings would be passionflower, rosemary, basil, bay, or patchouli. Your favorite inspirational scent would also be a good choice.

A good suggestion is to make a book for someone going off to school. Some excellent herbs for increasing a person's mental faculties are peppermint, caraway, mustard seed, dragon's blood, and yarrow. Citrus scents are wonderful mental pick-me-ups. And as Ophelia reminded Hamlet: "There's rosemary, that's for remembrance."

Your book can also include botanical paper that are made with marigolds or banana leaves. There are several different types on the market; try looking in art or craft stores. And if you can make your own paper, your choices would be limited only by your imagination.

Other ideas for your book include placing dried and pressed leaves within the binding. Or try using them as bookmarks. You could also glue, or otherwise affix, dried leaves, flowers, and seed-pods to the front cover as decoration. Some herbs you might choose to use for these purposes include bay leaves, rose petals, sunflower petals, whole star anise, or whole pressed pansies.

I hope you have fun making your own book, and that you have even more fun designing and decorating it. Given the variety of the plant world, the possibilities are endless.

For Further Study

Many of the herbal attributes in this article come from my personal correspondence charts, culled from a variety of books, online resources, and personal experience. With that in mind, here are some resources for herbal attribution, as well as for making handmade books. All of these would make great references for further work.

Cunningham, Scott. *The Complete Book of Incense, Oils, & Brews.* Llewellyn Publications, 1999. Several of the recipes in this book can be adapted for an herbal book. It also includes useful details on how to create your own herbal recipes.

Cunningham, Scott. *Scott Cunningham's Encyclopedia of Magical Herbs.* Llewellyn Publications, 1985. This book contains wonderful lists—located in the back of the book— as well as interesting lore on hundreds of herbs.

The Complete Works of William Shakespeare. Various Publishers. The Bard often made reference to many of the botanicals in use during the Elizabethan era. You can also check out Shakespeare (and do a word search for herbs) on the Web at http://www.shakespeare.com.

Golden, Alisa. *Creating Handmade Books*. Sterling Publishing Co., 1998.
This book is a must have if you want learn more about making your own books.

How to Make Magic Wands

by Lily Gardner

Wands have served as tools since humans could break a branch off a tree and point. They are as old as magic itself.

As a wand extends from your arm, magically speaking, it extends from your will. It can be used to direct energy and amplify power, or it can help you cast your circle, draw magical symbols, or stir a cauldron.

The traditional wand is a simple branch of oak, willow, or hazelwood cut the length of your arm from the crook of your elbow to the end of your middle finger. The wand is best cut on Wednesday, the day of Mercury. Although the simple branch is traditional, many Witches possess wands made from an array of woods and crystals that reflect either their personal energy or the intent the wand is being used for.

Personal Energy

There are hundreds of ways to design a wand that reflects personal energy. Here are a few ideas.

Fashion a wand using your astrological sign. Suppose Cancer is your birth sign. Make your wand from willow, a tree favored by the Moon, Cancer's planet. Paint the wand silver or gray, Cancer's colors, or paint the Cancer glyph on your wand with silver paint. Insert Cancer stones, such as pearl or moonstones. Because Cancer is a water sign, you might wrap your wand in watery colors of blue and green or attach charms of fish and crabs.

You could fashion your wand from your Chinese birth year. Suppose you were born in the year of the rabbit. The rabbit is associated with the Chinese element of wood, so any wood that appeals to you will work. Green is the color of the rabbit, so wrap your wand with green leather strips or ribbon. It is said that you will be especially lucky if you use the color green in combination with red. Wrap a band of rabbit fur around your wand, or hang rabbit fetishes from the ribbons.

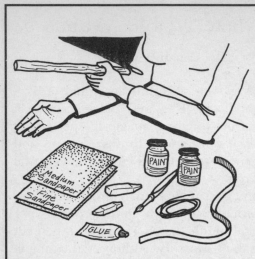

Say the frog is your totem animal. Consider making your wand from fir wood. Both the fir and the frog symbolize rebirth. Paint your wand frog-green. The Norse rune, Inguz, would be an appropriate symbol to paint, as it represents fertility and the Moon. Frogs rule over creativity, so stones of tiger's-eye will add power to your wand.

Fashion a wand to invoke your patron goddess or god, using wood, crystals, and colors that are sacred to them. Many Witches make wands with stones representing the chakras. To do this, you will need seven crystals to represent the seven chakras. At the base of your wand, use a smoky quartz to represent the root chakra; carnelian or tiger's-eye to represent the second, or Hara, chakra; citrine or topaz for the third chakra, or solar plexus; aventurine, bloodstone, or rose quartz for the fourth chakra, the heart; aquamarine or sodalite for the fifth chakra, the throat; lapis or sugilite for the sixth chakra, the third eye; and amethyst for the crown chakra. To further empower your wand, wrap it with gold braid or silk to represent the kundalini serpent that begins at the base of the spine. The kundalini is the foundation of consciousness and our life force.

Intent

The beauty of making a wand for a specific goal is the spell actually begins the moment you start gathering materials and preparing for it. Simply hold your magical goal firmly in your mind and heart as you go about fashioning a wand, and the wand is sure to have tremendous power by the time you're ready to use it.

Gather a straight tree branch from the ground or from a tree itself. If you take a live branch, remember to ask permission from the tree and its owner before removing it. Assuming you have the tree's permission, leave an offering of copper, tobacco, or crystals. Next, take your wand home and sand it starting with a medium-grade sandpaper, such as number 120. Finish with a number 180 sandpaper for fine sanding. If you focus your intention on its magical use, you will empower  your wand. When it's sanded, you can hollow out one end with a small knife and glue in a quartz crystal tip. Quartz crystals help focus energy. Some Witches tip their wands with acorns or pine cones.

Fasten a ribbon or cord with glue just beneath the wand tip. Before you actually wrap your wand, finish decorating it with the crystals and symbols you've chosen. You'll want to wrap your wand tightly at each end and more loosely in the middle. Tip the ends of your cord with fetishes or charms and have them dangle off the end of the wand.

The final step is to dedicate the wand. Many Witches put a drop of their own blood on the wand. It is said that menstrual blood is very powerful. Consecrate it by passing it through the smoke of burning incense and the flame of a burning candle to empower your wand. Drop a few drops of holy water on your wand and sprinkle a few grains of salt on your wand to strengthen and deepen its magic. If you have a name in mind for your wand, name it now. Finally, hold the wand against your solar plexus, the chakra of will, and empower your wand.

Wands are powerful tools. Made with good intention from the work of your own hand, they can work mighty magic.

Once in a Blue Moon

by Emely Flak

We all often hear the expression "once in a blue Moon" for events that are deemed rather rare. But do we ever stop to wonder what exactly is a blue Moon, and what is the frequency of its occurrence?

The blue Moon phenomenon is not as mysterious a phenomenon as you might think, and in fact it is not actually even an astronomical event. Over time, the expression "once in a blue Moon" has undergone a couple of transformations before meaning what we understand it to be today.

Historically speaking, the term "blue Moon" has been used to describe natural events when, because of a natural disaster, the Moon has actually appeared blue in color. In Newfoundland in 1951, for example, forest fires in Alberta caused smoke particles to fill the sky. As a result, the Moon had a blue haze around it. Because an environmental influence on the Moon's appearance is rather rare, this led to the belief that this blue-colored Moon was indeed an unusual and infrequent happening.

The 1937, the *Maine Farmer's Almanac* documented another definition; the Almanac described a blue Moon as the thirteenth Full Moon in a tropical year. Unlike a calendar year, a tropical year spans one winter solstice to the next one. Most tropical years feature twelve Full Moons, making the additional Full Moon an infrequent event.

Today, we understand the blue Moon to be the second Full Moon that takes place in one calendar month. The Moon is not blue or any way different from any other Full Moon. Nor is this a particularly rare phenomenon. On average, a blue Moon occurs every 2.75 years, or in other words, every two years and nine months or so.

Note: This frequency is calculated on a lunar cycle taking 29.5 days; since the average calendar month is 30.5 days, the blue Moon occurrence therefore occurs fairly infrequently, but it is not rare. This calculation also suggests that in the month of February, we will never see a blue Moon, because February is always less than 29 days, therefore never exceeding a lunar cycle. In fact, in some nonleap years, in the month of February there is no Full Moon at all. Overall, this means that in a period of one hundred years, we can expect to see approximately forty-one blue Moons.

The Metonic Cycle

Named after the Greek astronomer, Meton, the Metonic cycle is used to calculate the frequency and schedule of blue Moons. In 432 B.C., Meton established that the dates and phases of the lunar cycles repeat exactly after nineteen years. This was determined on the Gregorian calendar that we currently use. Over a period of nineteen years, or in one Metonic cycle, there are 235 lunar months and 228 calendar months. This means that in this period of nineteen years, we will see seven blue Moons. In one Metonic cycle, there will also be at least one time when will witness two blue Moons in one calendar year. This event last took place 1999, when we saw two full Moons in the months of January and March. The next blue Moon occurs on July 31, 2004.

In all, the blue Moon has little significance in a Pagan or Wiccan context. Paganism was widespread for thousands of years before the Gregorian calendar was established, meaning that a second Full Moon in a calendar month has no spiritual relevance in a nature-centered religion. Next time you hear someone say "once in a blue Moon," you will be able to test his or her knowledge of this cliché. Take the opportunity to explain the meaning and frequency of a blue Moon. You will probably surprise them with the actual frequency of the event, as many people believe it is something is not likely to happen for years, if at all.

Changing Your Patron Diety

by Jenna Tigerheart

Most of us work with various different deities at different phases of our lives. Perhaps you've had a child and find yourself switched from a maiden role, to a more parental one; by necessity you'll now be working with a different deity (a more, shall we say, parental one).

Any major life change can bring us to a new deity. So the question is: How do you go about saying "Goodbye!" to the old deity and "Welcome!" to the new one? The following is a ritual for just this purpose. To start, you need one item to symbolize the departing deity, one item to symbolize the new deity, quarter candles, and a bowl of sand or sea salt. On the Full Moon, after you cast your circle, hold up the item symbolizing the departing deity and say the following words:

> *Goddess, you have led me well and guided me in your way.*
> *I thank you for your care in bringing me to today.*
> *Time has come for paths to change; our ways must diverge.*
> *Your lessons I will remember; I move forward without fear.*

Place the item into the bowl of sand or sea salt, and let it remain there until the New Moon. If the item is burnable, burn it before your concluding ritual. If not, bury it. On the New Moon, cast your circle, hold up the item, and say these words:

> *Goddess, I invite you into my life to lead me from today.*
> *My life is changing its direction to enter a new phase.*
> *With this transformation I need guidance new.*
> *With all your gifts and talents, I ask this of you.*

Place the symbolic item on to your altar, and raise some energy to honor the new deity.

Keris in Malaysia

by S Y Zenith

The *keris* is a double-edged Malay dagger with a wavy blade. The art of making a keris encompasses the finest Malay arts of black-smith-ing, woodcarving, and silversmithing techniques that have survived through the millennia.

The Making of the Keris

The keris, which is sometimes spelled as "kris," is a classic emblem of the Malay race; it has been a national weapon for over six hundred years, and so has much significance in local history and culture. The keris is highly revered by all Malays. They regard it as an object of mystery and mysticism, and there are many old legends of warriors who made use of this weapon's magical qualities.

A keris is distinguished from other forms of daggers by its sinuous blade that widens abruptly just below the hilt. Its edges and tip are sharp, and most blades have damascened patterns known as *pamor* on them. These patterns are said to enhance the knife's supernatural powers and protects its owner from harm and misfortune.

The creation of a keris demands great skill and meticulous attention. The most famous such ironsmiths come from long established lines of craftsmen in the eastern Malaysian states of Terengganu and Kelantan. Traditionally, the art of keris-making is inherited from ancestors. The skills required for crafting the keris were once kept secret from outsiders, and keris-makers of old enjoyed aristocratic patronage.

There are various methods for making a keris. The blades usually comprise between two to seven thin layers of different types of iron or metals. A legendary 15th-century hero, Hang Tuah, in the court of the Malacca Sultanate, was said to posses a keris with more than twenty-one layers of metal. Some keris blades are made of iron, but most are alloyed with another metal such as nickel, which is pounded over and over until the desired damasked effect is achieved. To create the wavy edges of a blade, the metal is repeatedly heated and the edges are then hammered into shape against the side of an anvil.

The Magic of the Keris

The keris is largely considered by most Malays to possess supernatural or spiritual power. Superior weapons believed to have protective qualities are solemnly revered and accorded certain rites and rituals to appease the spiritual element inhabiting the weapon. It is believed by many Malays that ill-treatment or neglect of their keris may cause the guardian spirit to depart to its home in the spirit realm. This would render the keris powerless.

A keris is judged superior according to the quality of alloys used. It is also considered important that a keris be compatible with its owner. According to one belief, one must ensure that the length of the blade corresponds to the distance between the nipples of its owner. In general, antique keris are considered more potent. These are usually family heirlooms handed down through the generations.

A keris would not be complete without a hilt and sheath also created by skilled craftsmen—the woodcarver and the silversmith. Some of hilts and scabbards are crafted from ivory, horn, finely chiseled gold and silver, or intricately carved wood. The most magnificent hilts and sheaths are in the regalia of the Malay royalty—sultans and their families, those of noble birth, ministers of state, and individuals of prestige or authority. As a rule, all such personages wear elaborate keris during all state ceremonies and other important occasions.

Royal keris are usually embellished with intricately engraved traditional motifs in gold and silver. It is said that the sultan of Perak has in his possession the famous Taming Sari Keris, which the legendary hero Hang Tuah is said to have brought back to Malacca. This particular keris is beautifully studded with precious gemstones on the hilt and sheath. The common Malay citizen wears the keris as an adornment in his waistband during formal occasions.

The Keris Today

Used as ornament and for the sake of decorum, the keris remains part of modern mainstream Malay life, with its deeply ingrained superstition and spiritual symbolism. In fact, the keris continues to be one of the most treasured possessions of many, including the nation's traditional faith healers, medicine men, mediums, witch-doctors, and other keepers of esoteric knowledge of older traditions. These men use the keris during ceremonies ranging from healings, banishings, and spirit exorcisings. While the method of ritual use depends on the individual practitioner, the keris is almost always central to the ceremonies.

Once a warrior's lethal weapon, the keris will continue to be thought of with great reverence by Malays.

For Further Study

Skeat, Walter William. *Malay Magic.* Frank Cass & Co. Ltd. First published 1900, rReprinted 1965.

Fairies of the Animals

by Edain McCoy

When considering the folklore of fairy beings, we tend to think in terms of fairies and their connection to the land and its foliage. But there are many fairies who appear in animals forms that we never much consider. After all, animals are part of nature too, and they maintain much closer ties to the unseen world than we humans do.

For instance, among the folklore of the Native Americans of northeastern America is a dwarfish fairy known as the *gandayak*. This creature lives in lakes and streams and cares for fish, sometimes even helping fish escape capture by fisherman. In exchange for this, fish carry the gandayaks on their way through the water.

Fairies who love and care for horses, and who protect stables, have been known throughout Europe; the most well-known such fairy is the *vasily* of eastern Russia. A dwarf fairy, the vasily makes its bed in hay hidden in old barns. They do not like humans, though no record exists of them harming anyone. The Russian people believe that if they hear sleigh bells ringing when no sleigh is around, this means that the vasily are caring for nearby horses.

Many reports of trooping fairies who ride diminutive horses have been recorded in European folklore. Others, like Scotland's *shopiltees*, ride seahorses, or appear in a seashore guise. The *valkyries* of Germanic legend also ride horses through the night skies, and the Swiss *painajainen* and Italian *linchettos* are small horses who run about the Alps.

The beautiful and ultrafeminine *vilas* of Poland tend to stay hidden in forests because of their great beauty, but they have a great love for dogs. Many rescue teams in the mountains believe their dogs have been lead to humans in need by vilas. Dogs in general have an affinity with the fairy world, and some fairies appear in the guise of dogs. One of the most famous is *Cu Sith*, whose appearance foretells a death. Those who have seen him say his eyes are yellow and his paws are invariably wet. The *selkies* of northern Celtic lands appear in the guise of seals. These fairies are said to be able to shed their seal skins and appear in the form of beautiful humans, but it is believed that interacting with them can cause us to be caught in their world.

Another fairy that appears as a seal is the *kelpie* of Cornwall and Wales, also known as an *uisges* in Ireland. These creatures have bulbous noses, the mane of a horse, and the webbed feet of a duck. Their purpose seems uncertain as they are not receptive to human contact; some legends claim they cannibalize their own kind, while other legends claim they are protectors of water fowl. In Ireland, there lives the *pooka*, a mischievous half-goat, half-horse fairy who delights in frightening humans while claiming unharvested food for his own. In Greece lives the satyr, a half-human, half-goat being whose behavior is one of randiness and sexual license.

Animals seem to be able to see fairies with ease. Birds are known to warn fairies of impending trouble, which is perhaps the origin of our saying "A little bird told me." Gnomes ride on the backs of foxes and wolves, and some small flower fairies are transported by birds or on the backs of lightning bugs.

About the only animal who does not have a reputation for getting along with fairies is the cat. Many European folktales tell us that a cat will drive fairies away, just as they do mice.

Money Powder Spell

by Eileen Holland

This powder smells wonderfully rich, and it will bring what riches you desire your way. Focus on financial magic, growth, increase, and opportunity as you make it; remember to specify that it work in a way that harms none. Money Powder is a magickal boost, not a substitute for hard work, steady employment, or sustained effort.

Money Powder Recipe

1   part star anise, freshly ground

1   part fenugreek powder

½   part white mustard seeds

¼   part gold glitter

1   green stone

1   green candle

   Ginger incense

Star anise is a dark-brown, star-shaped, anise-scented seed pod that can be found in oriental markets. Freshly ground aniseed might be substituted in a pinch. There is no substitute for fenugreek powder, which is called *helba* in Arabic and can be found in gourmet shops and Middle Eastern markets. White mustard seeds are actually golden-colored. Dark brown mustard seeds or powdered mustard could be substituted, but the white seeds look and work best because of their golden color. Actual gold dust could be substituted for the gold glitter, but if you could afford gold dust you would probably have no need for this spell. Money Powder is best made while the Moon is waxing, or when the Sun is in Taurus. To empower the powder, put a green stone in it. Aventurine is a great choice, but any will

do. Burn a green candle and ginger or ginseng incense while you make the powder. Mix the ash from the burned incense into the powder. Store Money Powder in a tightly sealed glass container. Here are some suggestions for its use:

Sprinkle the powder in your wallet and mailbox, and on your doorstep to attract money to you. If your problem is overspending, focus on holding on to your money while you sprinkle the powder. Give the powder as a gift for a friend who is having a hard time.

Open the bottle and smell the powder while focusing on your financial need or goal. Pour a little into your palm, and rub it into your hand toward yourself as you visualize money coming to you and staying with you. Sprinkle a trail of the powder toward your home, shop, office, or other enterprise. Imagine the money flowing in.

Rub the powder between your hands before making phone calls to clients, buyers, brokers, debtors, potential employers, and so on.

Make a trail of the powder leading up to the doorway of a company you hope to do business with, or have applied to for a job. Or, make a trail of the powder leading away from their door, in the direction of your home or office. Focus on making a positive financial connection.

Drop a pinch of the powder into any letters that relate to money or employment before you mail them.

Use the powder in baths, spells, charms, rituals, and any workings designed to manifest prosperity, increase abundance, or meet a specific financial need or goal.

Moving Energy for Magic

by Ann Moura

In Green Witchcraft, magic works through the individual, bringing together Earth and cosmic energy, then sending it to perform a task. This all happens within the medium of a person's body.

Body heat indicates energy. We should be aware then, as heat is most easily transmitted or lost through the top of the head, the soles of the feet, and the palms of the hands, that these points are then the primary access points in our bodies for energy. That is, universal energies come through the top of the head, and are generally accessed for balancing and cleansing of the chakras, and for spiritual connection with the cosmic aspect of the divine. Earth energies are drawn up through the feet for directing into spell work. The following are some suggestions for making the best use to the body to direct and make use of universal energies.

Directing Energies through the Body

The soles of the feet and the palms of the hands are energy points that relate to the elementals in their sequence of earth, air, fire, and water. The left foot is the stability of earth; the right foot is the movement through air; the right hand is the action of fire, and left hand is the intuitive flow of water. The symbol of the pentagram is formed when you include the head as a representation of a connection to the cosmic energy. It is here that the brain acts as a great battery, generating mental impulses of energy. The hands are the primary tools for moving energy, even when holding ritual items such as the athame or wand. Thus, the right hand is used to draw in elemental fire for energizing and empowering your magic, while the left hand is used to draw in elemental water to soothe, protect, and urge matters to completion. Energies from other people are easily accessed in ritual through the crown of the head, making this a source of migraines, fuzzy-headedness, and headaches when there is an overload of negative energies. The brain tries to equalize the flow throughout the body, but instead becomes overworked, requiring you to ground and center, manipulate cleansing energy, or use crystals to realign your own energies and purge the unwanted energies.

Grounding and centering prior to performing magical work brings an inner calm and pulls Earth energy inside you through your feet to rise and intertwine with your personal energy. Without this crucial practice, you will siphon off your own energy, leaving yourself depleted by the end of your ritual or spell. For help in visualizing this energy movement, you may want to view the source of Earth energy as coming from the living planet Gaia, or coming from the molten center core of the planet, the magma. When you cast the circle, envision it as a sphere that contains the energy raised in and around you. It is open when your spell is completed, and its residual energy is released back into the Earth through your palms by touching the ground.

There are different ways to raise and gather energy to activate spells. This includes dancing around the circle (deosil for positive energy, widdershins for negative energy), chanting a short rhyme in a rising crescendo, or altering your breathing pattern with a sweeping intake followed by a rapid exhalation directly onto the spell materials. The whole procedure, from raising to focusing, directing, and sending the energy, should be one fluid motion. The soles of the feet as they move in dance are maintaining the Earth connection, drawing up manifesting power and balancing

strength, as well as blending the spiritual, psychic, and mental energies of air to be passed into physicality through spell work. The hands motion in unison to invoke the elementals and the divine, to call upon devas and spirit energies, and to bestow and receive blessings. Gestures also aid with visualizing the motion of energy in spells and other magical work. The hands draw the raised energy, direct it into a spell item, or point and send it where it needs to go. Energy is focused into a palpable ball between the palms of the hands, then thrust into a spell object through the fingers or the palms. By giving the hands a single emphatic shake with the fingers pointed, energy may be propelled in a particular direction. A deep cleansing breath brings closure to the process, along with affirmations such as, "It is done!" and, "So mote it be!"

Sending and receiving blessings creates an energy loop between your hands and the power of the divine. To practice this connection, do the following sequence of motions once for unity, twice for balance, or three times for completion. Hold your hands palms up with arms outstretched in front of you, then gather energy from the air by turning the palms inward. Drawing the palms close to your chest with arms crossed, so blending these energies with your personal energy. To release the energy, lower and uncross the arms, and thrust the hands forward again with a pushing motion that places the palms outward with the heels down and fingertips up.

To draw in cleansing energy from the divine, begin by holding your arms and hands in a triangle encompassing your head. Place the heels of the palms above your head nearly touching at the center, and angle your hands back with fingers bent inward (like a bowl). Bring the hands down along the sides of the head, with the palms still upward, until level with the shoulders, while you envision a white light rushing through your body, gathering unwanted energies back into your hands. Turn the palms downward and bring your arms parallel to your sides. Continue the downward push to bring the palms into contact with the ground, thus releasing the purged energies. This type of energy movement is especially useful for clearing your head and revitalizing your system after working too hard or being in unpleasant company.

After all of these ritual movements of energy, you should feel an emptiness where the magic was performed, and sense the vibration of energy left behind. But in the end you need to make sure the spell casting energies is no longer be part of you. Give a blessing to the Earth for aiding in the magical work as you release the residue energy into the ground, then take some refreshment to restore normal awareness.

Almanac Section

Calendar

Time Changes

Lunar Phases

Moon Signs

Full Moons

Sabbats

World Holidays

Incense of the Day

Color of the Day

Almanac Listings

In these listings you will find the date, day, lunar phase, Moon sign, color and incense for the day, and festivals from around the world.

The Date

The date is used in numerological calculations that govern magical rites.

The Day

Each day is ruled by a planet that possesses specific magical influences:

MONDAY (MOON): Peace, sleep, healing, compassion, friends, psychic awareness, purification, and fertility.

TUESDAY (MARS): Passion, sex, courage, aggression, and protection.

WEDNESDAY (MERCURY): The conscious mind, study, travel, divination, and wisdom.

THURSDAY (JUPITER): Expansion, money, prosperity, and generosity.

FRIDAY (VENUS): Love, friendship, reconciliation, and beauty.

SATURDAY (SATURN): Longevity, exorcism, endings, homes, and houses.

SUNDAY (SUN): Healing, spirituality, success, strength, and protection.

The Lunar Phase

The lunar phase is important in determining the best times for magic.

THE WAXING MOON (from the New Moon to the Full) is the ideal time for magic to draw things toward you.

THE FULL MOON is the time of greatest power.

THE WANING MOON (from the Full Moon to the New) is a time for study, meditation, and little magical work (except magic designed to banish harmful energies).

The Moon's Sign

The Moon continuously "moves" through the zodiac, from Aries to Pisces. Each sign possesses its own significance:

ARIES: Good for starting things, but lacks staying power. Things occur rapidly, but quickly pass. People tend to be argumentatitve and assertive.

TAURUS: Things begun now last the longest, tend to increase in value, and become hard to alter. Brings out appreciation for beauty and sensory experience.

GEMINI: Things begun now are easily changed by outside influence. Time for shortcuts, communication, games, and fun.

CANCER: Stimulates emotional rapport between people. Pinpoints need, supports growth and nurturance. Tends to domestic concerns.

LEO: Draws emphasis to the self, to central ideas or institutions, away from connections with others and emotional needs. People tend to be melodramatic.

VIRGO: Favors accomplishment of details and commands from higher up. Focuses on health, hygiene, and daily schedules.

LIBRA: Favors cooperation, social activities, beautification of surroundings, balance, and partnership.

SCORPIO: Increases awareness of psychic power. Precipitates psychic crises and ends connections thoroughly. People tend to brood and become secretive.

SAGITTARIUS: Encourages flights of imagination and confidence. This is an adventurous, philosophical, and athletic Moon sign. Favors expansion and growth.

CAPRICORN: Develops strong structure. Focus on traditions, responsibilities, and obligations. A good time to set boundaries and rules.

AQUARIUS: Rebellious energy. Time to break habits and make abrupt change. Personal freedom and individuality is the focus.

PISCES: The focus is on dreaming, nostalgia, intuition, and psychic impressions. A good time for spiritual or philanthropic activities.

Color and Incense

The color and incense for the day are based on information from *Personal Alchemy* by Amber Wolfe, and relate to the planet that rules each day. This information can be taken into consideration along with other factors when planning works of magic or when blending magic into mundane life. Please note that the incense selections are not hard-and-fast. If you can not find or do not like the incense listed for the day, choose a similar scent that appeals to you.

Festivals and Holidays

Festivals are listed throughout the year. The exact dates of many of these ancient festivals are difficult to determine; prevailing data has been used.

Time Changes

The times and dates of all astrological phenomena in this almanac are based on **Eastern Standard Time (EST).** They have NOT been adjusted for Daylight

Saving Time. If you live outside of EST, you will need to make the following changes:

PACIFIC STANDARD TIME: Subtract three hours.

MOUNTAIN STANDARD TIME: Subtract two hours.

CENTRAL STANDARD TIME: Subtract one hour.

ALASKA/HAWAII: Subtract five hours.

DAYLIGHT SAVING TIME: Add an hour. Daylight Saving Time runs from April 6 to October 26, 2003.

2003 Sabbats and Full Moons

January 18	Full Moon 5:48 am
February 2	Imbolc
February 16	Full Moon 6:51 pm
March 18	Full Moon 5:35 am
March 20	Ostara (Spring Equinox)
April 16	Full Moon 2:36 pm
May 1	Beltane
May 15	Full Moon 10:36 pm
June 14	Full Moon 6:16 am
June 21	Litha (Summer Solstice)
July 13	Full Moon 2:21 pm
August 1	Lammas
August 11	Full Moon 11:48 pm
September 10	Full Moon 11:36 am
September 23	Mabon (Fall Equinox)
October 10	Full Moon 2:27 am
October 31	Samhain
November 8	Full Moon 8:13 pm
December 8	Full Moon 3:37 pm
December 22	Yule (Winter Solstice)

Capricorn

♑

1 Wednesday
New Year's Day • Kwanzaa ends   Moon Sign: Sagittarius
Waning Moon   Moon enters Capricorn 6:42 pm
Moon Phase: Fourth Quarter   Incense: Eucalyptus
Color: Brown

☽ Thursday
First Writing (Japanese)   Moon Sign: Capricorn
Waning Moon   Incense: Chrysanthemum
Moon Phase: New Moon 3:23 pm
Color: Green

3 Friday
St. Genevieve's Day   Moon Sign: Carpicorn
Waxing Moon   Moon enters Aquarius 10:56 pm
Moon Phase: First Quarter   Incense: Nutmeg
Color: White

4 Saturday
Frost Fairs on the Thames   Moon Sign: Aquarius
Waxing Moon   Incense: Lavender
Moon Phase: First Quarter
Color: Gray

5 Sunday
Epiphany Eve   Moon Sign: Aquarius
Waxing Moon   Incense: Poplar
Moon Phase: First Quarter
Color: Yellow

6 Monday
Epiphany   Moon Sign: Aquarius
Waxing Moon   Moon enters Pisces 5:57 am
Moon Phase: First Quarter   Incense: Maple
Color: Silver

7 Tuesday
Rizdvo (Ukrainian)   Moon Sign: Pisces
Waxing Moon   Incense: Gardenia
Moon Phase: First Quarter
Color: Gray

8 Wednesday
Midwives' Day   Moon Sign: Pisces
Waxing Moon   Moon enters Aries 4:15 pm
Moon Phase: First Quarter   Incense: Cedar
Color: White

---

9 Thursday
Feast of the Black Nazarene (Filipino)   Moon Sign: Aries
Waxing Moon   Incense: Evergreen
Moon Phase: First Quarter
Color: Turquoise

◐ Friday
Business God's Day (Japanese)   Moon Sign: Aries
Waxing Moon   Incense: Ginger
Moon Phase: Second Quarter 8:15 am
Color: Rose

---

11 Saturday
Carmentalia (Roman)   Moon Sign: Aries
Waxing Moon   Moon enters Taurus 4:48 am
Moon Phase: Second Quarter   Incense: Jasmine
Color: Brown

---

12 Sunday
Revolution Day (Tanzanian)   Moon Sign: Taurus
Waxing Moon   Incense: Cinnamon
Moon Phase: Second Quarter
Color: Peach

---

13 Monday
Twentieth Day (Norwegian)   Moon Sign: Taurus
Waxing Moon   Moon enters Gemini 5:08 pm
Moon Phase: Second Quarter   Incense: Lilac
Color: Gray

---

14 Tuesday
Feast of the Ass (French)   Moon Sign: Gemini
Waxing Moon   Incense: Honeysuckle
Moon Phase: Second Quarter
Color: White

15 Wednesday
Martin Luther King, Jr.'s Birthday (actual)   Moon Sign: Gemini
Waxing Moon   Incense: Maple
Moon Phase: Second Quarter
Color: Yellow

16 Thursday
Apprentices' Day   Moon Sign: Gemini
Waxing Moon   Moon enters Cancer 2:56 am
Moon Phase: Second Quarter   Incense: Vanilla
Color: Green

17 Friday
St. Anthony's Day (Mexican)   Moon Sign: Cancer
Waxing Moon   Incense: Parsley
Moon Phase: Second Quarter
Color: Peach

☺ Saturday
Assumption Day   Moon Sign: Cancer
Waxing Moon   Moon enters Leo 9:29 am
Moon Phase: Full Moon 5:48 am   Incense: Violet
Color: Blue

19 Sunday
Kitchen God Feast (Chinese)   Moon Sign: Leo
Waning Moon   Incense: Sage
Moon Phase: Third Quarter
Color: Gold

20 Monday
Martin Luther King, Jr.'s Birthday (observed)   Moon Sign: Leo
Waning Moon   Sun enters Aquarius 6:53 am
Moon Phase: Third Quarter   Moon enters Virgo 1:32 pm
Color: White   Incense: Coriander

21 Tuesday
St. Agnes Day   Moon Sign: Virgo
Waning Moon   Incense: Poplar
Moon Phase: Third Quarter
Color: Black

22 Wednesday
St. Vincent's Day
Waning Moon
Moon Phase: Third Quarter
Color: Brown

Moon Sign: Virgo
Moon enters Libra 4:23 pm
Incense: Pine

---

23 Thursday
St. Ildefonso's Day
Waning Moon
Moon Phase: Third Quarter
Color: Violet

Moon Sign: Libra
Incense: Sandalwood

---

24 Friday
Alasitas Fair (Bolivian)
Waning Moon
Moon Phase: Third Quarter
Color: Pink

Moon Sign: Libra
Moon enters Scorpio 7:09 pm
Incense: Rose

☾ Saturday
Burns' Night (Scottish)
Waning Moon
Moon Phase: Fourth Quarter 3:33 am
Color: Gray

Moon Sign: Scorpio
Incense: Cedar

---

26 Sunday
Republic Day (Indian)
Waxing Moon
Moon Phase: Fourth Quarter
Color: Orange

Moon Sign: Scorpio
Moon enters Sagittarius 10:26 pm
Incense: Basil

---

27 Monday
Vogelgruff (Swiss)
Waning Moon
Moon Phase: Fourth Quarter
Color: Lavender

Moon Sign: Sagittarius
Incense: Myrrh

---

28 Tuesday
St. Charlemagne's Day
Waning Moon
Moon Phase: Fourth Quarter
Color: Red

Moon Sign: Sagittarius
Incense: Juniper

Aquarius

≈

29 Wednesday
Australia Day   Moon Sign: Sagittarius
Waning Moon   Moon enters Capricorn 2:30 am
Moon Phase: Fourth Quarter   Incense: Neroli
Color: White

30 Thursday
Three Hierarchs' Day (Eastern Orthodox)   Moon Sign: Capricorn
Waning Moon   Incense: Carnation
Moon Phase: Fourth Quarter
Color: Green

31 Friday
Independence Day (Nauru)   Moon Sign: Capricorn
Waning Moon   Moon enters Aquarius 7:44 am
Moon Phase: Fourth Quarter   Incense: Dill
Color: Rose

Juniper Healing Lore

Juniper is a tree widely honored throughout the
world for its value in treating urinary tract problems. The berries have diuretic effects and can stimulate digestion while dissolving urinary and gall
stones. Juniper berries have been used for stomach
ailments, lung diseases, and colds. The leaves are
beneficial in treating colds, stomach disorders, con-
stipation, rheumatism, headaches, and nausea.
Juniper bark, powdered or boiled, soothes spider
bites and earache. Burned as an incense, juniper
relieves colds. One note of caution: juniper berries
and leaves should not be used during pregnancy or
by anyone with kidney problems.

—Kristin Madden

Saturday

Chinese New Year (ram)
Waning Moon
Moon Phase: New Moon 5:48 am
Color: Blue

Moon Sign: Aquarius
Incense: Patchouli

---

2 Sunday

Imbolc • Groundhog Day
Waxing Moon
Moon Phase: First Quarter
Color: Yellow

Moon Sign: Aquarius
Moon enters Pisces 2:55 pm
Incense: Coriander

---

3 Monday

St. Blaise's Day
Waxing Moon
Moon Phase: First Quarter
Color: White

Moon Sign: Pisces
Incense: Chyrsanthemum

---

4 Tuesday

Independence Day (Sri Lankan)
Waxing Moon
Moon Phase: First Quarter
Color: Gray

Moon Sign: Pisces
Incense: Chrysanthemum

---

5 Wednesday

Festival de la Alcaldesa (Italian)
Waxing Moon
Moon Phase: First Quarter
Color: Peach

Moon Sign: Pisces
Moon enters Aries 12:44 am
Incense: Sandalwood

---

6 Thursday

Bob Marley's Birthday (Jamaican)
Waxing Moon
Moon Phase: First Quarter
Color: Turquoise

Moon Sign: Aries
Incense: Carnation

---

7 Friday

Full Moon Poya (Sri Lankan)
Waxing Moon
Moon Phase: First Quarter
Color: Pink

Moon Sign: Aries
Moon enters Taurus 12:59 pm
Incense: Thyme

≈

8 Saturday
Mass for Broken Needles (Japanese)
Waxing Moon
Moon Phase: First Quarter
Color: Brown

Moon Sign: Taurus
Incense: Lilac

9 Sunday
St. Marion's Day (Lebanese)
Waxing Moon
Moon Phase: Second Quarter 6:11 am
Color: Peach

Moon Sign: Taurus
Incense: Clove

10 Monday
Gasparilla Day (Florida)
Waxing Moon
Moon Phase: Second Quarter
Color: Silver

Moon Sign: Taurus
Moon enters Gemini 1:45 am
Incense: Daffodil

11 Tuesday
Foundation Day (Japanese)
Waxing Moon
Moon Phase: Second Quarter
Color: White

Moon Sign: Gemini
Incense: Evergreen

12 Wednesday
Lincoln's Birthday (actual)
Waxing Moon
Moon Phase: Second Quarter
Color: Yellow

Moon Sign: Gemini
Moon enters Cancer 12:19 pm
Incense: Coriander

13 Thursday
Parentalia (Roman)
Waxing Moon
Moon Phase: Second Quarter
Color: White

Moon Sign: Cancer
Incense: Geranium

14 Friday
Valentine's Day
Waxing Moon
Moon Phase: Second Quarter
Color: Rose

Moon Sign: Cancer
Moon enters Leo 7:04 pm
Incense: Sandalwood

15 Saturday
Lupercalia (Roman)   Moon Sign: Leo
Waxing Moon   Incense: Juniper
Moon Phase: Second Quarter
Color: Gray

☺ Sunday
Maya Indian Lent (Mexican)   Moon Sign: Leo
Waxing Moon   Moon enters Virgo 10:22 pm
Moon Phase: Full Moon 6:51 pm   Incense: Poplar
Color: Gold

---

17 Monday
President's Day (observed)   Moon Sign: Virgo
Waning Moon   Incense: Rose
Moon Phase: Third Quarter
Color: Gray

---

18 Tuesday
Saint Bernadette's Second Vision   Moon Sign: Virgo
Waning Moon   Sun enters Pisces 9:00 pm
Moon Phase: Third Quarter   Moon enters Libra 11:48 pm
Color: Black   Incense: Sage

---

19 Wednesday
Pero Palo's Trial (Spanish)   Moon Sign: Libra
Waning Moon   Incense: Eucalyptus
Moon Phase: Third Quarter
Color: White

---

20 Thursday
Installation of the New Lama (Tibetan)   Moon Sign: Libra
Waning Moon   Incense: Musk
Moon Phase: Third Quarter
Color: Green

---

21 Friday
Feast of Lanterns (Chinese)   Moon Sign: Libra
Waning Moon   Moon enters Scorpio 1:09 am
Moon Phase: Third Quarter   Incense: Ylang ylang
Color: Peach

Pisces

♓

22 Saturday
Caristia (Roman)
Waning Moon
Moon Phase: Third Quarter
Color: Indigo

Moon Sign: Scorpio
Incense: Pine

☽ Sunday
Terminalia (Roman)
Waning Moon
Moon Phase: Fourth Quarter 11:46 am
Color: Orange

Moon Sign: Scorpio
Moon enters Sagittarius 3:46 am
Incense: Cinnamon

24 Monday
The Flight of Kings (Roman)
Waning Moon
Moon Phase: Fourth Quarter
Color: Lavender

Moon Sign: Sagittarius
Incense: Frankincense

25 Tuesday
National Day (Kuwaiti)
Waning Moon
Moon Phase: Fourth Quarter
Color: Red

Moon Sign: Sagittarius
Moon enters Capricorn 8:11 am
Incense: Musk

26 Wednesday
Zamboanga Festival (Filipino)
Waning Moon
Moon Phase: Fourth Quarter
Color: Brown

Moon Sign: Capricorn
Incense: Cedar

27 Thursday
Threepenny Day
Waning Moon
Moon Phase: Fourth Quarter
Color: Violet

Moon Sign: Capricorn
Moon enters Aquarius 2:24 pm
Incense: Jasmine

28 Friday
Kalevala Day (Finnish)
Waning Moon
Moon Phase: Fourth Quarter
Color: White

Moon Sign: Aquarius
Incense: Nutmeg

1 Saturday
Matronalia (Roman)
Waning Moon
Moon Phase: Fourth Quarter
Color: Gray

Moon Sign: Aquarius
Moon enters Pisces 10:26 pm
Incense: Lavender

2 Sunday
St. Chad's Day (English)
Waning Moon
Moon Phase: New Moon 9:35 pm
Color: Peach

Moon Sign: Pisces
Incense: Basil

3 Monday
Doll Festival (Japanese)
Waxing Moon
Moon Phase: First Quarter
Color: White

Moon Sign: Pisces
Incense: Peony

4 Tuesday
Mardi Gras
Waxing Moon
Moon Phase: First Quarter
Color: Red

Moon Sign: Pisces
Moon enters Aries 8:30 am
Incense: Gardenia

5 Wednesday
Ash Wednesday • Islamic New Year
Waxing Moon
Moon Phase: First Quarter
Color: Brown

Moon Sign: Aries
Incense: Maple

6 Thursday
Alamo Day
Waxing Moon
Moon Phase: First Quarter
Color: Turquoise

Moon Sign: Aries
Moon enters Taurus 8:36 pm
Incense: Vanilla

7 Friday
Festival of Rama (Hindu)
Waxing Moon
Moon Phase: First Quarter
Color: Rose

Moon Sign: Taurus
Incense: Ginger

Pisces ♓

8 Saturday
International Women's Day
Waxing Moon
Moon Phase: First Quarter
Color: Brown

Moon Sign: Taurus
Incense: Patchouli

9 Sunday
Forty Saints' Day (Romanian)
Waxing Moon
Moon Phase: First Quarter
Color: Gold

Moon Sign: Taurus
Moon enters Gemini 9:38 am
Incense: Parsley

10 Monday
Tibet Day
Waxing Moon
Moon Phase: First Quarter
Color: Silver

Moon Sign: Gemini
Incense: Lilac

☽ Tuesday
Feast of Gauri (Hindu)
Waxing Moon
Moon Phase: Second Quarter 2:15 am
Color: White

Moon Sign: Gemini
Moon enters Cancer 9:12 pm
Incense: Poplar

12 Wednesday
Receiving the Water (Buddhist)
Waxing Moon
Moon Phase: Second Quarter
Color: Peach

Moon Sign: Cancer
Incense: Pine

13 Thursday
Purification Feast (Balinese)
Waxing Moon
Moon Phase: Second Quarter
Color: Green

Moon Sign: Cancer
Incense: Sandalwood

14 Friday
Mamuralia (Roman)
Waxing Moon
Moon Phase: Second Quarter
Color: Pink

Moon Sign: Cancer
Moon enters Leo 5:06 am
Incense: Rose

15 Saturday
Phallus Festival (Japanese)
Waxing Moon
Moon Phase: Second Quarter
Color: Blue

Moon Sign: Leo
Incense: Lilac

16 Sunday
St. Urho's Day (Finnish)
Waxing Moon
Moon Phase: Second Quarter
Color: Yellow

Moon Sign: Leo
Moon enters Virgo 8:52 am
Incense: Cinnamon

17 Monday
St. Patrick's Day
Waxing Moon
Moon Phase: Second Quarter
Color: White

Moon Sign: Virgo
Incense: Chrysanthemum

☺ Tuesday
Purim
Waxing Moon
Moon Phase: Full Moon 5:35 am
Color: Gray

Moon Sign: Virgo
Moon enters Libra 9:43 am
Incense: Juniper

19 Wednesday
St. Joseph's Day (Sicilian)
Waning Moon
Moon Phase: Third Quarter
Color: White

Moon Sign: Libra
Incense: Neroli

20 Thursday
Ostara • Spring Equinox • Int'l Astrology Day
Waning Moon
Moon Phase: Third Quarter
Color: Violet

Moon Sign: Libra
Sun enters Aries 8:00 pm
Moon enters Scorpio 9:38 pm
Incense: Carnation

21 Friday
Juarez Day (Mexican)
Waning Moon
Moon Phase: Third Quarter
Color: White

Moon Sign: Scorpio
Incense: Dill

22 Saturday

Hilaria (Roman)
Waning Moon
Moon Phase: Third Quarter
Color: Indigo

Moon Sign: Scorpio
Moon enters Sagittarius 10:33 am
Incense: Pine

23 Sunday

Pakistan Day
Waning Moon
Moon Phase: Third Quarter
Color: Orange

Moon Sign: Sagittarius
Incense: Sage

24 Monday

Day of Blood (Roman)
Waning Moon
Moon Phase: Fourth Quarter 8:51 pm
Color: Lavender

Moon Sign: Sagittarius
Moon enters Capricorn 1:48 pm
Incense: Myrrh

25 Tuesday

Tichborne Dole (English)
Waning Moon
Moon Phase: Fourth Quarter
Color: Black

Moon Sign: Capricorn
Incense: Honeysuckle

26 Wednesday

Prince Kuhio Day (Hawaiian)
Waning Moon
Moon Phase: Fourth Quarter
Color: Yellow

Moon Sign: Capricorn
Moon enters Aquarius 7:51 pm
Incense: Coriander

27 Thursday

Smell the Breezes Day (Egyptian)
Waning Moon
Moon Phase: Fourth Quarter
Color: White

Moon Sign: Aquarius
Incense: Evergreen

28 Friday

Oranges and Lemons Service (English)
Waning Moon
Moon Phase: Fourth Quarter
Color: Peach

Moon Sign: Aquarius
Incense: Almond

29 Saturday
St. Eustace's Day   Moon Sign: Aquarius
Waning Moon   Moon enters Pisces 4:26 am
Moon Phase: Fourth Quarter   Incense: Lavender
Color: Gray

30 Sunday
Seward's Day (Alaskan)   Moon Sign: Pisces
Waning Moon   Incense: Basil
Moon Phase: Fourth Quarter
Color: Peach

31 Monday
The Borrowed Days (European)   Moon Sign: Pisces
Waning Moon   Moon enters Aries 3:04 pm
Moon Phase: Fourth Quarter   Incense: Daffodil
Color: Silver

Day of the Week Lore

How many of us know how the days of our week
derived their names? With this knowledge we can
attune our magical intent to the respective vibrations
of each day's name. Understanding the origins of
each day of the week helps us appreciate why Wiccan spells and rituals are carried out on certain
days. Be advised, however, the English names of the
days do not always identify the ruling planet. Students
of French, Italian, or Latin can more quickly recognise
the matching word stems.

Monday–The Day of the Moon

As the name suggests Monday is the Moon Day. In the
French word, *lundi*, we can see the link to lunar cycles.
This is a day to harness the moon's energy and focus
on issues related to women's health, fertility, and the
domestic scene.

—Emely Flak

☽ **Tuesday**
April Fools' Day
Waning Moon
Moon Phase: New Moon 2:19 pm
Color: Red

Moon Sign: Aries
Incense: Musk

2 **Wednesday**
The Battle of Flowers (French)
Waxing Moon
Moon Phase: First Quarter
Color: Peach

Moon Sign: Aries
Incense: Sandalwood

3 **Thursday**
Thirteenth Day Out (Iranian)
Waxing Moon
Moon Phase: First Quarter
Color: Turquoise

Moon Sign: Aries
Moon enters Taurus 3:20 am
Incense: Carnation

4 **Friday**
National Day (Senegalese)
Waxing Moon
Moon Phase: First Quarter
Color: Rose

Moon Sign: Taurus
Incense: Thyme

5 **Saturday**
Tomb-Sweeping Day (Chinese)
Waxing Moon
Moon Phase: First Quarter
Color: Brown

Moon Sign: Taurus
Moon enters Gemini 4:24 pm
Incense: Jasmine

6 **Sunday**
Daylight Saving Time begins at 2:00 am
Waxing Moon
Moon Phase: First Quarter
Color: Yellow

Moon Sign: Gemini
Incense: Coriander

7 **Monday**
Festival of Pure Brightness (Chinese)
Waxing Moon
Moon Phase: First Quarter
Color: White

Moon Sign: Gemini
Incense: Rose

8 Tuesday
Buddha's Birthday   Moon Sign: Gemini
Waxing Moon   Moon enters Cancer 4:36 am
Moon Phase: First Quarter   Incense: Gardenia
Color: Gray

◖ Wednesday
Valour Day (Philippine)   Moon Sign: Cancer
Waxing Moon   Incense: Eucalyptus
Moon Phase: Second Quarter 6:40 pm
Color: White

10 Thursday
The Tenth of April (English)   Moon Sign: Cancer
Waxing Moon   Moon enters Leo 1:54 pm
Moon Phase: Second Quarter   Incense: Geranium
Color: Green

11 Friday
Heroes' Day (Costa Rican)   Moon Sign: Leo
Waxing Moon   Incense: Ylang ylang
Moon Phase: Second Quarter
Color: Pink

12 Saturday
Cerealia (Roman)   Moon Sign: Leo
Waxing Moon   Moon enters Virgo 7:07 pm
Moon Phase: Second Quarter   Incense: Violet
Color: Indigo

13 Sunday
Palm Sunday   Moon Sign: Virgo
Waxing Moon   Incense: Clove
Moon Phase: Second Quarter
Color: Peach

14 Monday
Sanno Festival (Japanese)   Moon Sign: Virgo
Waxing Moon   Moon enters Libra 8:42 pm
Moon Phase: Second Quarter   Incense: Frankincense
Color: Gray

Aries

♈

15 Tuesday
Plowing Festival (Chinese)
Waxing Moon
Moon Phase: Second Quarter
Color: White

Moon Sign: Libra
Incense: Ginger

☺ **Wednesday**
Zurich Spring Festival (Swiss)
Waxing Moon
Moon Phase: Full Moon 2:36 pm
Color: Yellow

Moon Sign: Libra
Moon enters Scorpio 8:16 pm
Incense: Cedar

---

17 Thursday
Passover begins
Waning Moon
Moon Phase: Third Quarter
Color: Violet

Moon Sign: Scorpio
Incense: Musk

---

18 Friday
Good Friday
Waning Moon
Moon Phase: Third Quarter
Color: White

Moon Sign: Scorpio
Moon enters Sagittarius 7:51 pm
Incense: Nutmeg

---

19 Saturday
Women's Celebration (Balinese)
Waning Moon
Moon Phase: Third Quarter
Color: Blue

Moon Sign: Sagittarius
Incense: Patchouli

---

20 Sunday
Easter
Waning Moon
Moon Phase: Third Quarter
Color: Gold

Moon Sign: Sagittarius
Sun enters Taurus 7:03 am
Moon enters Capricorn 9:20 pm
Incense: Poplar

---

21 Monday
Tiradentes Day (Brazilian)
Waning Moon
Moon Phase: Third Quarter
Color: Silver

Moon Sign: Capricorn
Incense: Peony

22 Tuesday
Earth Day   Moon Sign: Capricorn
Waning Moon   Incense: Pine
Moon Phase: Third Quarter
Color: Black

◖ Wednesday
Passover ends   Moon Sign: Capricorn
Waning Moon   Moon enters Aquarius 1:58 am
Moon Phase: Fourth Quarter 7:18 am   Incense: Maple
Color: Brown

24 Thursday
St. Mark's Eve   Moon Sign: Aquarius
Waning Moon   Incense: Sage
Moon Phase: Fourth Quarter
Color: White

25 Friday
Robigalia (Roman) • Orthodox Good Friday   Moon Sign: Aquarius
Waning Moon   Moon enters Pisces 10:02 am
Moon Phase: Fourth Quarter   Incense: Ginger
Color: Peach

26 Saturday
Arbor Day   Moon Sign: Pisces
Waning Moon   Incense: Lilac
Moon Phase: Fourth Quarter
Color: Gray

27 Sunday
Orthodox Easter   Moon Sign: Pisces
Waning Moon   Moon enters Aries 8:54 pm
Moon Phase: Fourth Quarter   Incense: Cinnamon
Color: Orange

28 Monday
Floralia (Roman)   Moon Sign: Aries
Waning Moon   Incense: Lavender
Moon Phase: Fourth Quarter
Color: Lavender

29 Tuesday
Green Day (Japanese)
Waning Moon
Moon Phase: Fourth Quarter
Color: Red

Moon Sign: Aries
Incense: Juniper

30 Wednesday
Walpurgis Night • May Eve
Waning Moon
Moon Phase: Fourth Quarter
Color: Yellow

Moon Sign: Aries
Moon enters Taurus 9:26 am
Incense: Pine

Tuesday and Wednesday Lore

Tuesday, the Day of Honor

The name of Tuesday comes from the warrior god Tui, or Tiw, of Teutonic mythology. The French word, *mardi*, corresponds to Mars, the Roman God of War. Tuesday is a time to focus on masculine vibrations for invocations relating to hunting, competition, or sporting prowess. This day of Mars is also good for goal setting, motivation, and courage.

Wednesday, the Day of Wisdom

Wednesday is named after Odin, or Woden, the great Anglo Saxon god of war and wisdom. The French word for Wednesday, *mercredi*, more clearly shows its link to Mercury, the Roman god of science, commerce, and travel. Meditation and focus on learning, study, travel, and communication are best performed on Wednesday, the day of Mercury.

—Emely Flak

Thursday
Beltane • May Day
Waning Moon
Moon Phase: New Moon 7:15 am
Color: Green

Moon Sign: Taurus
Incense: Jasmine

---

2 Friday
Big Kite Flying (Japanese)
Waxing Moon
Moon Phase: First Quarter
Color: Peach

Moon Sign: Taurus
Moon enters Gemini 10:27 pm
Incense: Rose

---

3 Saturday
Holy Cross Day
Waxing Moon
Moon Phase: First Quarter
Color: Gray

Moon Sign: Gemini
Incense: Juniper

---

4 Sunday
Bona Dea (Roman)
Waxing Moon
Moon Phase: First Quarter
Color: Yellow

Moon Sign: Gemini
Incense: Sage

---

5 Monday
Cinco de Mayo (Mexican)
Waxing Moon
Moon Phase: First Quarter
Color: Gray

Moon Sign: Gemini
Moon enters Cancer 10:42 am
Incense: Coriander

---

6 Tuesday
Martyrs' Day (Lebanese)
Waxing Moon
Moon Phase: First Quarter
Color: White

Moon Sign: Cancer
Incense: Honeysuckle

---

7 Wednesday
Pilgrimage of St. Nicholas (Italian)
Waxing Moon
Moon Phase: First Quarter
Color: Peach

Moon Sign: Cancer
Moon enters Leo 8:46 pm
Incense: Neroli

8 Thursday
Liberation Day (French)
Waxing Moon
Moon Phase: First Quarter
Color: Turquoise

Moon Sign: Leo
Incense: Vanilla

Friday
Lemuria (Roman)
Waxing Moon
Moon Phase: Second Quarter 6:53 am
Color: Rose

Moon Sign: Leo
Incense: Dill

10 Saturday
First Day of Bird Week (Japanese)
Waxing Moon
Moon Phase: Second Quarter
Color: Indigo

Moon Sign: Leo
Moon enters Virgo 3:31 am
Incense: Pine

11 Sunday
Mother's Day
Waxing Moon
Moon Phase: Second Quarter
Color: Gold

Moon Sign: Virgo
Incense: Basil

12 Monday
Florence Nightingale's Birthday
Waxing Moon
Moon Phase: Second Quarter
Color: White

Moon Sign: Virgo
Moon enters Libra 6:42 am
Incense: Chrysanthemum

13 Tuesday
Pilgrimage to Fatima (Portuguese)
Waxing Moon
Moon Phase: Second Quarter
Color: Gray

Moon Sign: Libra
Incense: Evergreen

14 Wednesday
Carabao Festival (Spanish)
Waxing Moon
Moon Phase: Second Quarter
Color: Yellow

Moon Sign: Libra
Moon enters Scorpio 7:14 am
Incense: Eucalyptus

☻ Thursday
Lunar Eclipse   Moon Sign: Scorpio
Waxing Moon   Incense: Sandalwood
Moon Phase: Full Moon 10:36 pm
Color: White

---

16 Friday
St. Honoratus' Day   Moon Sign: Scorpio
Waning Moon   Moon enters Sagittarius 6:43 am
Moon Phase: Third Quarter   Incense: Thyme
Color: Pink

---

17 Saturday
Norwegian Independence Day   Moon Sign: Sagittarius
Waning Moon   Incense: Lavender
Moon Phase: Third Quarter
Color: Brown

---

18 Sunday
Las Piedras Day (Uruguayan)   Moon Sign: Sagittarius
Waning Moon   Moon enters Capricorn 7:03 am
Moon Phase: Third Quarter   Incense: Coriander
Color: Peach

---

19 Monday
Pilgrimage to Treguier (French)   Moon Sign: Capricorn
Waning Moon   Incense: Myrrh
Moon Phase: Third Quarter
Color: Silver

---

20 Tuesday
Mecklenburg Independence Day   Moon Sign: Capricorn
Waning Moon   Moon enters Aquarius 10:01 am
Moon Phase: Third Quarter   Incense: Sage
Color: Black

---

21 Wednesday
Victoria Day (Canadian)   Moon Sign: Aquarius
Waning Moon   Sun enters Gemini 6:12 am
Moon Phase: Third Quarter   Incense: Cedar
Color: White

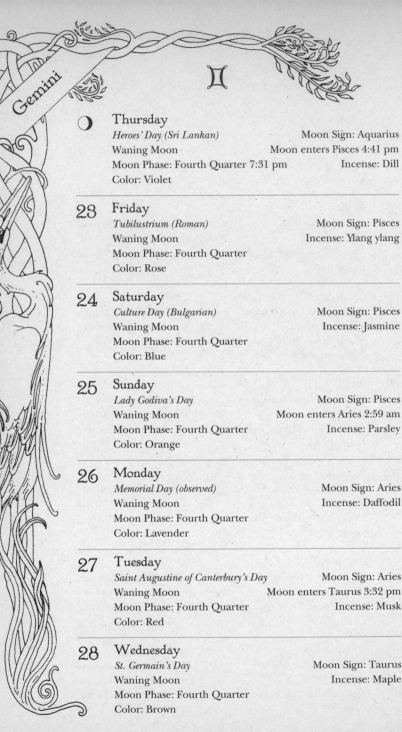

♊

Thursday
Heroes' Day (Sri Lankan)
Waning Moon
Moon Phase: Fourth Quarter 7:31 pm
Color: Violet

Moon Sign: Aquarius
Moon enters Pisces 4:41 pm
Incense: Dill

23 Friday
Tubilustrium (Roman)
Waning Moon
Moon Phase: Fourth Quarter
Color: Rose

Moon Sign: Pisces
Incense: Ylang ylang

24 Saturday
Culture Day (Bulgarian)
Waning Moon
Moon Phase: Fourth Quarter
Color: Blue

Moon Sign: Pisces
Incense: Jasmine

25 Sunday
Lady Godiva's Day
Waning Moon
Moon Phase: Fourth Quarter
Color: Orange

Moon Sign: Pisces
Moon enters Aries 2:59 am
Incense: Parsley

26 Monday
Memorial Day (observed)
Waning Moon
Moon Phase: Fourth Quarter
Color: Lavender

Moon Sign: Aries
Incense: Daffodil

27 Tuesday
Saint Augustine of Canterbury's Day
Waning Moon
Moon Phase: Fourth Quarter
Color: Red

Moon Sign: Aries
Moon enters Taurus 3:32 pm
Incense: Musk

28 Wednesday
St. Germain's Day
Waning Moon
Moon Phase: Fourth Quarter
Color: Brown

Moon Sign: Taurus
Incense: Maple

29 Thursday
Royal Oak Day (English)
Waning Moon
Moon Phase: Fourth Quarter
Color: Green

Moon Sign: Taurus
Incense: Carnation

Friday
Memorial Day (actual) • *Solar eclipse*
Waning Moon
Moon Phase: New Moon 11:20 pm
Color: White

Moon Sign: Taurus
Moon enters Gemini 4:32 am
Incense: Almond

31 Saturday
Republic Day (South African)
Waxing Moon
Moon Phase: First Quarter
Color: Gray

Moon Sign: Gemini
Incense: Violet

Bear Lore

Humans have had a great connection to bear through the ages. Bear has elicited fear, attraction, worship, and respect in cultures around the world. Countless legends exist explaining how clans descended from the union of a bear and a human ancestor. In many stories, the bear is believed to be half-human already. Bear is a healer, an otherworldly guide, and a psychopomp. Bear bestows power and protection to warriors, while embodying the gentle fierceness of the Great Mother. Ursa Major links us with the starry heavens just as the earthly bear links us with the inner Earth and our inner selves.

—Kristin Madden

♊

1 Sunday
National Day (Tunisian)
Waxing Moon
Moon Phase: First Quarter
Color: Yellow

Moon Sign: Gemini
Moon enters Cancer 4:27 pm
Incense: Clove

---

2 Monday
Rice Harvest Festival (Malaysian)
Waxing Moon
Moon Phase: First Quarter
Color: Silver

Moon Sign: Cancer
Incense: Rose

---

3 Tuesday
Memorial to Broken Dolls (Japanese)
Waxing Moon
Moon Phase: First Quarter
Color: White

Moon Sign: Cancer
Incense: Gardenia

---

4 Wednesday
Full Moon Day (Burmese)
Waxing Moon
Moon Phase: First Quarter
Color: Peach

Moon Sign: Cancer
Moon enters Leo 2:25 am
Incense: Pine

---

5 Thursday
Constitution Day (Danish)
Waxing Moon
Moon Phase: First Quarter
Color: Turquoise

Moon Sign: Leo
Incense: Geranium

---

6 Friday
Shavuot
Waxing Moon
Moon Phase: First Quarter
Color: Rose

Moon Sign: Leo
Moon enters Virgo 9:51 am
Incense: Nutmeg

☽ Saturday
St. Robert of Newminster's Day
Waxing Moon
Moon Phase: Second Quarter 3:28 pm
Color: Brown

Moon Sign: Virgo
Incense: Cedar

8 Sunday
Pentecost
Waxing Moon
Moon Phase: Second Quarter
Color: Peach

Moon Sign: Virgo
Moon enters Libra 2:30 pm
Incense: Cinnamon

---

9 Monday
Vestalia (Roman)
Waxing Moon
Moon Phase: Second Quarter
Color: Lavender

Moon Sign: Libra
Incense: Frankincense

---

10 Tuesday
Time-Observance Day (Chinese)
Waxing Moon
Moon Phase: Second Quarter
Color: Black

Moon Sign: Libra
Moon enters Scorpio 4:39 pm
Incense: Ginger

---

11 Wednesday
Kamehameha Day (Hawaiian)
Waxing Moon
Moon Phase: Second Quarter
Color: Brown

Moon Sign: Scorpio
Incense: Neroli

---

12 Thursday
Independence Day (Filipino)
Waxing Moon
Moon Phase: Second Quarter
Color: Violet

Moon Sign: Scorpio
Moon enters Sagittarius 5:12 pm
Incense: Musk

---

13 Friday
St. Anthony of Padua's Day
Waxing Moon
Moon Phase: Second Quarter
Color: Pink

Moon Sign: Sagittarius
Incense: Rose

☻ Saturday
Flag Day
Waxing Moon
Moon Phase: Full Moon 6:16 am
Color: Blue

Moon Sign: Sagittarius
Moon enters Capricorn 5:38 pm
Incense: Patchouli

Gemini ♊

15 Sunday
Father's Day
Waning Moon
Moon Phase: Third Quarter
Color: Gold

Moon Sign: Capricorn
Incense: Basil

---

16 Monday
Bloomsday (Irish)
Waning Moon
Moon Phase: Third Quarter
Color: Silver

Moon Sign: Capricorn
Moon enters Aquarius 7:41 pm
Incense: Peony

---

17 Tuesday
Bunker Hill Day
Waning Moon
Moon Phase: Third Quarter
Color: Gray

Moon Sign: Aquarius
Incense: Poplar

---

18 Wednesday
Independence Day (Egyptian)
Waning Moon
Moon Phase: Third Quarter
Color: White

Moon Sign: Aquarius
Incense: Coriander

---

19 Thursday
Juneteenth
Waning Moon
Moon Phase: Third Quarter
Color: Green

Moon Sign: Aquarius
Moon enters Pisces 12:57 am
Incense: Sage

---

20 Friday
Flag Day (Argentinian)
Waning Moon
Moon Phase: Third Quarter
Color: Peach

Moon Sign: Pisces
Incense: Dill

☾ Saturday
Litha • Summer Solstice
Waning Moon
Moon Phase: Fourth Quarter 9:45 am
Color: Indigo

Moon Sign: Pisces
Moon enters Aries 10:06 am
Sun enters Cancer 2:10 pm
Incense: Maple

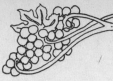

22 Sunday
Rose Festival (English)
Waning Moon
Moon Phase: Fourth Quarter
Color: Orange

Moon Sign: Aries
Incense: Parsley

---

23 Monday
St. John's Eve
Waning Moon
Moon Phase: Fourth Quarter
Color: White

Moon Sign: Aries
Moon enters Taurus 10:15 pm
Incense: Lavender

---

24 Tuesday
St. John's Day
Waning Moon
Moon Phase: Fourth Quarter
Color: Red

Moon Sign: Taurus
Incense: Juniper

---

25 Wednesday
Fiesta of Santa Orosia (Spanish)
Waning Moon
Moon Phase: Fourth Quarter
Color: Yellow

Moon Sign: Taurus
Incense: Sandalwood

---

26 Thursday
Pied Piper Day (German)
Waning Moon
Moon Phase: Fourth Quarter
Color: White

Moon Sign: Taurus
Moon enters Gemini 11:13 am
Incense: Carnation

---

27 Friday
Day of the Seven Sleepers (Islamic)
Waning Moon
Moon Phase: Fourth Quarter
Color: Pink

Moon Sign: Gemini
Incense: Thyme

---

28 Saturday
Paul Bunyan Day
Waning Moon
Moon Phase: Fourth Quarter
Color: Gray

Moon Sign: Gemini
Moon enters Cancer 10:52 pm
Incense: Lilac

Cancer

♋

♑ Sunday
Saint Peter and Paul's Day   Moon Sign: Cancer
Waning Moon   Incense: Cinnamon
Moon Phase: New Moon 1:39 pm
Color: Peach

---

30 Monday
The Burning of the Three Firs (French)   Moon Sign: Cancer
Waxing Moon   Incense: Chrysanthemum
Moon Phase: First Quarter
Color: Lavender

~✻~

Drum Purification Ceremony

• Beat the drum slightly faster than a heartbeat until you slip into a light trance.

• Offer its sound to each of the four directions. Then offer it to the sky and the earth. Then return to the center again, and offer the sound to the creator.

• Drum along your entire body, stopping at each chakra so the sound can harmonize your energy systems and clear unwanted vibrations.

• Hold the drum out to center once more as an offering of thanks to the creator. Increase the pace of your drumbeat to four times more quickly than you heartbeat, and then end with one strong beat.

—Kristin Madden

July

1 Tuesday
Climbing Mount Fuji (Japanese)
Waxing Moon
Moon Phase: First Quarter
Color: White

Moon Sign: Cancer
Moon enters Leo 8:13 am
Incense: Honeysuckle

2 Wednesday
Heroes' Day (Zambian)
Waxing Moon
Moon Phase: First Quarter
Color: Yellow

Moon Sign: Leo
Incense: Eucalyptus

3 Thursday
Indian Sun Dance (Native American)
Waxing Moon
Moon Phase: First Quarter
Color: Turquoise

Moon Sign: Leo
Moon enters Virgo 3:16 pm
Incense: Geranium

4 Friday
Independence Day
Waxing Moon
Moon Phase: First Quarter
Color: Pink

Moon Sign: Virgo
Incense: Sandalwood

5 Saturday
Tynwald (Nordic)
Waxing Moon
Moon Phase: First Quarter
Color: Brown

Moon Sign: Virgo
Moon enters Libra 8:20 pm
Incense: Juniper

6 Sunday
Khao Phansa Day (Thai)
Waxing Moon
Moon Phase: Second Quarter 9:32 pm
Color: Yellow

Moon Sign: Libra
Incense: Sage

7 Monday
Weaver's Festival (Japanese)
Waxing Moon
Moon Phase: Second Quarter
Color: White

Moon Sign: Libra
Moon enters Scorpio 11:43 pm
Incense: Myrrh

8 Tuesday
St. Elizabeth's Day (Portuguese)
Waxing Moon
Moon Phase: Second Quarter
Color: Red

Moon Sign: Scorpio
Incense: Evergreen

---

9 Wednesday
Battle of Sempach Day (Swiss)
Waxing Moon
Moon Phase: Second Quarter
Color: Brown

Moon Sign: Scorpio
Incense: Cedar

---

10 Thursday
Lady Godiva Day (English)
Waxing Moon
Moon Phase: Second Quarter
Color: Violet

Moon Sign: Scorpio
Moon enters Sagittarius 1:48 am
Incense: Musk

---

11 Friday
Revolution Day (Mongolian)
Waxing Moon
Moon Phase: Second Quarter
Color: Peach

Moon Sign: Sagittarius
Incense: Ylang ylang

---

12 Saturday
Lobster Carnival (Nova Scotian)
Waxing Moon
Moon Phase: Second Quarter
Color: Blue

Moon Sign: Sagittarius
Moon enters Capricorn 3:21 am
Incense: Pine

☺ Sunday
Festival of the Three Cows (Spanish)
Waxing Moon
Moon Phase: Full Moon 2:21 pm
Color: Gold

Moon Sign: Capricorn
Incense: Clove

---

14 Monday
Bastille Day (French)
Waning Moon
Moon Phase: Third Quarter
Color: Gray

Moon Sign: Capricorn
Moon enters Aquarius 5:38 am
Incense: Rose

15 Tuesday
St. Swithin's Day   Moon Sign: Aquarius
Waning Moon   Incense: Sage
Moon Phase: Third Quarter
Color: Black

---

16 Wednesday
Our Lady of Carmel   Moon Sign: Aquarius
Waning Moon   Moon enters Pisces 10:14 am
Moon Phase: Third Quarter   Incense: Maple
Color: White

---

17 Thursday
Rivera Day (Puerto Rican)   Moon Sign: Pisces
Waning Moon   Incense: Jasmine
Moon Phase: Third Quarter
Color: Green

---

18 Friday
Gion Matsuri Festival (Japanese)   Moon Sign: Pisces
Waning Moon   Moon enters Aries 6:20 pm
Moon Phase: Third Quarter   Incense: Nutmeg
Color: Rose

---

19 Saturday
Flitch Day (English)   Moon Sign: Aries
Waning Moon   Incense: Lavender
Moon Phase: Third Quarter
Color: Indigo

---

20 Sunday
Binding of Wreaths (Lithuanian)   Moon Sign: Aries
Waning Moon   Incense: Basil
Moon Phase: Third Quarter
Color: Orange

☾ Monday
National Day (Belgian)   Moon Sign: Aries
Waning Moon   Moon enters Taurus 5:48 am
Moon Phase: Fourth Quarter 2:01 am   Incense: Daffodil
Color: Lavender

22 Tuesday
St. Mary Magdalene's Day
Waning Moon
Moon Phase: Fourth Quarter
Color: Gray

Moon Sign: Taurus
Incense: Musk

---

23 Wednesday
Mysteries of Santa Cristina (Italian)
Waning Moon
Moon Phase: Fourth Quarter
Color: Peach

Moon Sign: Taurus
Sun enters Leo 1:04 am
Moon enters Gemini 6:42 pm
Incense: Pine

---

24 Thursday
Pioneer Day (Mormon)
Waning Moon
Moon Phase: Fourth Quarter
Color: White

Moon Sign: Gemini
Incense: Chrysanthemum

---

25 Friday
St. James' Day
Waning Moon
Moon Phase: Fourth Quarter
Color: Pink

Moon Sign: Gemini
Incense: Ginger

---

26 Saturday
St. Anne's Day
Waning Moon
Moon Phase: Fourth Quarter
Color: Gray

Moon Sign: Gemini
Moon enters Cancer 6:23 am
Incense: Violet

---

27 Sunday
Sleepyhead Day (Finnish)
Waning Moon
Moon Phase: Fourth Quarter
Color: Peach

Moon Sign: Cancer
Incense: Coriander

---

28 Monday
Independence Day (Peruvian)
Waning Moon
Moon Phase: Fourth Quarter
Color: Silver

Moon Sign: Cancer
Moon enters Leo 3:17 pm
Incense: Peony

☽ **Tuesday**
Pardon of the Birds (French)   Moon Sign: Leo
Waning Moon   Incense: Gardenia
Moon Phase: New Moon 1:53 am
Color: Red

30 **Wednesday**
Micmac Festival of St. Ann   Moon Sign: Leo
Waxing Moon   Moon enters Virgo 9:27 pm
Moon Phase: First Quarter   Incense: Neroli
Color: Yellow

31 **Thursday**
Weighing of the Aga Khan   Moon Sign: Virgo
Waxing Moon   Incense: Evergreen
Moon Phase: First Quarter
Color: Violet

Thursday and Friday Lore

Thursday, the Day of Strength

Thursday is dedicated to the Viking god of thunder, Thor. The planet Jupiter rules Thursday, as the French word for Thursday, *jeudi*, suggests. Thursday is the day to focus on wealth, success, luck, career development, legal matters, and material growth.

Friday, the Day of Love

Friday honors Odin's wife, the Norse goddess of love, Frigg. Another well-known goddess of love, Venus, from Roman mythology, is present in the French word for Friday, *vendredi*. Think today of love, and perform a ritual for romance. Just as Venus is the only planet named for a Goddess, Friday is the only day of the week named after a female.

—Emely Flak

Leo ♌

1 Friday
Lammas
Waxing Moon
Moon Phase: First Quarter
Color: White

Moon Sign: Virgo
Incense: Parsley

---

2 Saturday
Porcingula (Native American)
Waxing Moon
Moon Phase: First Quarter
Color: Gray

Moon Sign: Virgo
Moon enters Libra 1:48 am
Incense: Cedar

---

3 Sunday
Drimes (Greek)
Waxing Moon
Moon Phase: First Quarter
Color: Yellow

Moon Sign: Libra
Incense: Poplar

---

4 Monday
Cook Islands Constitution Celebration
Waxing Moon
Moon Phase: First Quarter
Color: White

Moon Sign: Libra
Moon enters Scorpio 5:12 am
Incense: Lavender

☽ Tuesday
Benediction of the Sea (French)
Waxing Moon
Moon Phase: Second Quarter 2:28 am
Color: Black

Moon Sign: Scorpio
Incense: Ginger

---

6 Wednesday
Hiroshima Peace Ceremony
Waxing Moon
Moon Phase: Second Quarter
Color: Brown

Moon Sign: Scorpio
Moon enters Sagittarius 8:11 am
Incense: Coriander

---

7 Thursday
Republic Day (Ivory Coast)
Waxing Moon
Moon Phase: Second Quarter
Color: Turquoise

Moon Sign: Sagittarius
Incense: Dill

8 Friday
Dog Days (Japanese)   Moon Sign: Sagittarius
Waxing Moon   Moon enters Capricorn 11:02 am
Moon Phase: Second Quarter   Incense: Rose
Color: Pink

---

9 Saturday
Nagasaki Peace Ceremony   Moon Sign: Capricorn
Waxing Moon   Incense: Patchouli
Moon Phase: Second Quarter
Color: Brown

---

10 Sunday
St. Lawrence's Day   Moon Sign: Capricorn
Waxing Moon   Moon enters Aquarius 2:23 pm
Moon Phase: Second Quarter   Incense: Cinnamon
Color: Peach

Monday
Puck Fair (Irish)   Moon Sign: Aquarius
Waxing Moon   Incense: Maple
Moon Phase: Full Moon 11:48 pm
Color: Gray

---

12 Tuesday
Fiesta of Santa Clara   Moon Sign: Aquarius
Waning Moon   Moon enters Pisces 7:19 pm
Moon Phase: Third Quarter   Incense: Juniper
Color: White

---

13 Wednesday
Women's Day (Tunisian)   Moon Sign: Pisces
Waning Moon   Incense: Sandalwood
Moon Phase: Third Quarter
Color: Peach

---

14 Thursday
Festival at Sassari   Moon Sign: Pisces
Waning Moon   Incense: Carnation
Moon Phase: Third Quarter
Color: Violet

15 Friday
Assumption Day
Waning Moon
Moon Phase: Third Quarter
Color: Rose

Moon Sign: Pisces
Moon enters Aries 3:00 am
Incense: Thyme

---

16 Saturday
Festival of Minstrels (European)
Waning Moon
Moon Phase: Third Quarter
Color: Blue

Moon Sign: Aries
Incense: Lilac

---

17 Sunday
Feast of the Hungry Ghosts (Chinese)
Waning Moon
Moon Phase: Third Quarter
Color: Orange

Moon Sign: Aries
Moon enters Taurus 1:52 pm
Incense: Sage

---

18 Monday
St. Helen's Day
Waning Moon
Moon Phase: Third Quarter
Color: Silver

Moon Sign: Taurus
Incense: Chyrsanthemum

☽ Tuesday
Rustic Vinalia (Roman)
Waning Moon
Moon Phase: Fourth Quarter 7:48 pm
Color: Gray

Moon Sign: Taurus
Incense: Honeysuckle

---

20 Wednesday
Constitution Day (Hungarian)
Waning Moon
Moon Phase: Fourth Quarter
Color: Brown

Moon Sign: Taurus
Moon enters Gemini 2:41 am
Incense: Eucalyptus

---

21 Thursday
Consualia (Roman)
Waning Moon
Moon Phase: Fourth Quarter
Color: White

Moon Sign: Gemini
Incense: Geranium

22 Friday
Feast of the Queenship of Mary (English)   Moon Sign: Gemini
Waning Moon   Moon enters Cancer 2:44 pm
Moon Phase: Fourth Quarter   Incense: Sandalwood
Color: Peach

23 Saturday
National Day (Romanian)   Moon Sign: Cancer
Waning Moon   Sun enters Virgo 8:08 am
Moon Phase: Fourth Quarter   Incense: Juniper
Color: Indigo

24 Sunday
St. Bartholomew's Day   Moon Sign: Cancer
Waning Moon   Moon enters Leo 11:48 pm
Moon Phase: Fourth Quarter   Incense: Clove
Color: Gold

25 Monday
Feast of the Green Corn (Native American)   Moon Sign: Leo
Waning Moon   Incense: Frankincense
Moon Phase: Fourth Quarter
Color: Lavender

26 Tuesday
Pardon of the Sea (French)   Moon Sign: Leo
Waning Moon   Incense: Evergreen
Moon Phase: Fourth Quarter
Color: Red

☽ Wednesday
Summer Break (English)   Moon Sign: Leo
Waning Moon   Moon enters Virgo 5:27 am
Moon Phase: New Moon 12:26 pm   Incense: Cedar
Color: White

28 Thursday
St. Augustine's Day   Moon Sign: Virgo
Waxing Moon   Incense: Musk
Moon Phase: First Quarter
Color: Green

29 Friday
St. John's Beheading
Waxing Moon
Moon Phase: First Quarter
Color: White

Moon Sign: Virgo
Moon enters Libra 8:41 am
Incense: Ylang ylang

30 Saturday
St. Rose of Lima Day (Peruvian)
Waxing Moon
Moon Phase: First Quarter
Color: Gray

Moon Sign: Libra
Incense: Pine

31 Sunday
Unto These Hills Pageant (Cherokee)
Waxing Moon
Moon Phase: First Quarter
Color: Yellow

Moon Sign: Libra
Moon enters Scorpio 11:00 am
Incense: Basil

Saturday and Sunday Lore

Saturday, the Day of Reckoning

Saturn, the Roman god of the harvest, rules this day of the Jewish Sabbath. The French word for Saturday, *samedi*, also suggests a link to Saturn. Saturday is seen as the day of reckoning—a time to summon energy for wisdom, legal matters, knowledge, and karma.

Sunday, the Day of the Sun

The day of the Sun is also the Christian sabbath, or day of the Lord—making Sunday a traditional day of rest, reflection, and worship. It is believed that babies born on this day are destined to be lucky. In general, Sunday is a day to inspire joy, peace, and happiness and to focus on growth, healing, and male health issues.

—Emely Flak

♍

1 Monday
Labor Day (observed)   Moon Sign: Scorpio
Waxing Moon   Incense: Myrrh
Moon Phase: First Quarter
Color: Gray

---

2 Tuesday
St. Mamas's Day   Moon Sign: Scorpio
Waxing Moon   Moon enters Sagittarius 1:32 pm
Moon Phase: First Quarter   Incense: Sage
Color: Black

☽ Wednesday
Founder's Day (San Marino)   Moon Sign: Sagittarius
Waxing Moon   Incense: Maple
Moon Phase: Second Quarter 7:34 am
Color: Peach

---

4 Thursday
Los Angeles' Birthday   Moon Sign: Sagittarius
Waxing Moon   Moon enters Capricorn 4:51 pm
Moon Phase: Second Quarter   Incense: Jasmine
Color: Turquoise

---

5 Friday
Roman Circus • First Labor Day (1882)   Moon Sign: Capricorn
Waxing Moon   Incense: Almond
Moon Phase: Second Quarter
Color: Rose

---

6 Saturday
Virgin of the Remedies (Mexican)   Moon Sign: Capricorn
Waxing Moon   Moon enters Aquarius 9:15 pm
Moon Phase: Second Quarter   Incense: Lavender
Color: Brown

---

7 Sunday
Festival of the Durga (Hindu)   Moon Sign: Aquarius
Waxing Moon   Incense: Coriander
Moon Phase: Second Quarter
Color: Orange

8 Monday
Birthday of the Virgin Mary
Waxing Moon
Moon Phase: Second Quarter
Color: Silver

Moon Sign: Aquarius
Incense: Rose

9 Tuesday
Chrysanthemum Festival (Japanese)
Waxing Moon
Moon Phase: Second Quarter
Color: White

Moon Sign: Aquarius
Moon enters Pisces 3:07 am
Incense: Musk

☺ Wednesday
Festival of the Poets (Japanese)
Waxing Moon
Moon Phase: Full Moon 11:36 am
Color: Yellow

Moon Sign: Pisces
Incense: Pine

11 Thursday
Coptic New Year
Waning Moon
Moon Phase: Third Quarter
Color: Green

Moon Sign: Pisces
Moon enters Aries 11:09 am
Incense: Chrysanthemum

12 Friday
National Day (Ethiopian)
Waning Moon
Moon Phase: Third Quarter
Color: Pink

Moon Sign: Aries
Incense: Nutmeg

13 Saturday
The Gods' Banquet (Roman)
Waning Moon
Moon Phase: Third Quarter
Color: Indigo

Moon Sign: Aries
Moon enters Taurus 9:50 pm
Incense: Jasmine

14 Sunday
Holy Cross Day
Waning Moon
Moon Phase: Third Quarter
Color: Gold

Moon Sign: Taurus
Incense: Parsley

15 Monday
Birthday of the Moon (Chinese)
Waning Moon
Moon Phase: Third Quarter
Color: Lavender

Moon Sign: Taurus
Incense: Daffodil

---

16 Tuesday
Independence Day (Mexican)
Waning Moon
Moon Phase: Third Quarter
Color: Gray

Moon Sign: Taurus
Moon enters Gemini 10:32 am
Incense: Gardenia

---

17 Wednesday
Von Steuben's Day
Waning Moon
Moon Phase: Third Quarter
Color: White

Moon Sign. Gemini
Incense: Neroli

◐ Thursday
Dr. Johnson's Birthday
Waning Moon
Moon Phase: Fourth Quarter 2:03 pm
Color: Violet

Moon Sign: Gemini
Moon enters Cancer 11:07 pm
Incense: Evergreen

---

19 Friday
St. Januarius' Day (Italian)
Waning Moon
Moon Phase: Fourth Quarter
Color: Peach

Moon Sign: Cancer
Incense: Ginger

---

20 Saturday
St. Eustace's Day
Waning Moon
Moon Phase: Fourth Quarter
Color: Blue

Moon Sign: Cancer
Incense: Violet

---

21 Sunday
Christ's Hospital Founder's Day (British)
Waning Moon
Moon Phase: Fourth Quarter
Color: Peach

Moon Sign: Cancer
Moon enters Leo 9:02 am
Incense: Poplar

≏

22 Monday
Saint Maurice's Day
Waning Moon
Moon Phase: Fourth Quarter
Color: White

Moon Sign: Leo
Incense: Peony

---

23 Tuesday
Mabon • Fall Equinox
Waning Moon
Moon Phase: Fourth Quarter
Color: Red

Moon Sign: Leo
Sun enters Libra 5:47 am
Moon enters Virgo 3:04 pm
Incense: Pine

---

24 Wednesday
Schwenkfelder Thanksgiving (German-American)
Waning Moon
Moon Phase: Fourth Quarter
Color: Brown

Moon Sign: Virgo
Incense: Coriander

☽ Thursday
Salute to the Sun (Chinese)
Waning Moon
Moon Phase: New Moon 10:09 pm
Color: White

Moon Sign: Virgo
Moon enters Libra 5:49 pm
Incense: Dill

---

26 Friday
Feast of Santa Justina (Mexican)
Waxing Moon
Moon Phase: First Quarter
Color: Pink

Moon Sign: Libra
Incense: Thyme

---

27 Saturday
Rosh Hashanah
Waxing Moon
Moon Phase: First Quarter
Color: Gray

Moon Sign: Libra
Moon enters Scorpio 6:52 pm
Incense: Cedar

---

28 Sunday
Confucius' Birthday
Waxing Moon
Moon Phase: First Quarter
Color: Yellow

Moon Sign: Scorpio
Incense: Cinnamon

≏

29 Monday
    Michaelmas   Moon Sign: Scorpio
    Waxing Moon   Moon enters Sagittarius 7:57 pm
    Moon Phase: First Quarter   Incense: Lavender
    Color: Silver

30 Tuesday
    St. Jerome's Day   Moon Sign: Sagittarius
    Waxing Moon   Incense: Juniper
    Moon Phase: First Quarter
    Color: Black

Scott Cunningham's Magical Principles

- Magic is natural.
- Harm none, not even yourself, through its use.
- Magic requires effort. You will receive what you put into it
- Magic should not be performed for pay.
- Magic should not be used in jest or to inflate your ego.
- Magic can be worked for your own gain, but only if it harms none.
- Magic is a divine act.
- Magic can be used for defense but should not be used for attack.
- Magic is knowledge of its way and laws and also of its effectiveness. Know that magic works!
- Magic is love. All magic should be performed out of love. The moment anger or hatred tinges your magic you have crossed the border into a dangerous world, one that will ultimately consume you.

♎

1 Wednesday
Armed Forces Day (South Korean)   Moon Sign: Sagittarius
Waxing Moon   Moon enters Capricorn 10:21 pm
Moon Phase: First Quarter   Incense: Sandalwood
Color: Peach

☾ 2 Thursday
Old Man's Day (Virgin Islands)   Moon Sign: Capricorn
Waxing Moon   Incense: Carnation
Moon Phase: Second Quarter 2:09 pm
Color: Violet

3 Friday
Moroccan New Year's Day   Moon Sign: Capricorn
Waxing Moon   Incense: Ylang ylang
Moon Phase: Second Quarter
Color: White

4 Saturday
St. Francis' Day   Moon Sign: Capricorn
Waxing Moon   Moon enters Aquarius 2:45 am
Moon Phase: Second Quarter   Incense: Patchouli
Color: Brown

5 Sunday
Republic Day (Portuguese)   Moon Sign: Aquarius
Waxing Moon   Incense: Sage
Moon Phase: Second Quarter
Color: Yellow

6 Monday
Yom Kippur   Moon Sign: Aquarius
Waxing Moon   Moon enters Pisces 9:20 am
Moon Phase: Second Quarter   Incense: Maple
Color: Silver

7 Tuesday
Kermesse (German)   Moon Sign: Pisces
Waxing Moon   Incense: Honeysuckle
Moon Phase: Second Quarter
Color: Black

8 Wednesday
Okunchi (Japanese)
Waxing Moon
Moon Phase: Second Quarter
Color: Brown

Moon Sign: Pisces
Moon enters Aries 6:07 pm
Incense: Eucalyptus

---

9 Thursday
Alphabet Day (South Korean)
Waxing Moon
Moon Phase: Second Quarter
Color: Turquoise

Moon Sign: Aries
Incense: Geranium

☺ Friday
Health Day (Japanese)
Waxing Moon
Moon Phase: Full Moon 2:27 am
Color: Peach

Moon Sign: Aries
Incense: Almond

---

11 Saturday
Sukkot begins
Waning Moon
Moon Phase: Third Quarter
Color: Blue

Moon Sign: Aries
Moon enters Taurus 5:05 am
Incense: Lilac

---

12 Sunday
National Day (Spanish)
Waning Moon
Moon Phase: Third Quarter
Color: Gold

Moon Sign: Taurus
Incense: Clove

---

13 Monday
Columbus Day (observed)
Waning Moon
Moon Phase: Third Quarter
Color: Silver

Moon Sign: Taurus
Moon enters Gemini 5:45 pm
Incense: Chrysanthemum

---

14 Tuesday
Battle Festival (Japan)
Waning Moon
Moon Phase: Third Quarter
Color: White

Moon Sign: Gemini
Incense: Evergreen

15 Wednesday
Deepavali (Hindu)
Waning Moon
Moon Phase: Third Quarter
Color: Yellow

Moon Sign: Gemini
Incense: Cedar

16 Thursday
The Lion Sermon (British)
Waning Moon
Moon Phase: Third Quarter
Color: White

Moon Sign: Gemini
Moon enters Cancer 6:41 am
Incense: Musk

17 Friday
Sukkot ends
Waning Moon
Moon Phase: Third Quarter
Color: Pink

Moon Sign: Cancer
Incense: Nutmeg

Saturday
Brooklyn Barbecue
Waning Moon
Moon Phase: Fourth Quarter 7:31 am
Color: Indigo

Moon Sign: Cancer
Moon enters Leo 5:41 pm
Incense: Juniper

19 Sunday
Our Lord of Miracles Procession (Peruvian)
Waning Moon
Moon Phase: Fourth Quarter
Color: Peach

Moon Sign: Leo
Incense: Basil

20 Monday
Colchester Oyster Feast
Waning Moon
Moon Phase: Fourth Quarter
Color: Lavender

Moon Sign: Leo
Incense: Frankincense

21 Tuesday
Feast of the Black Christ
Waning Moon
Moon Phase: Fourth Quarter
Color: Red

Moon Sign: Leo
Moon enters Virgo 1:01 am
Incense: Sage

♏

22 Wednesday
Goddess of Mercy Day (Chinese) Moon Sign: Virgo
Waning Moon Incense: Maple
Moon Phase: Fourth Quarter
Color: Brown

23 Thursday
Revolution Day (Hungarian) Moon Sign: Virgo
Waning Moon Sun enters Scorpio 3:08 pm
Moon Phase: Fourth Quarter Moon enters Libra 4:27 am
Color: Violet Incense: Jasmine

24 Friday
United Nations Day Moon Sign: Libra
Waning Moon Incense: Ginger
Moon Phase: Fourth Quarter
Color: Pink

☽ Saturday
St. Crispin's Day Moon Sign: Libra
Waning Moon Moon enters Scorpio 5:08 am
Moon Phase: New Moon 7:50 am Incense: Pine
Color: Gray

26 Sunday
Daylight Saving Time ends at 2:00 am Moon Sign: Scorpio
Waxing Moon Incense: Coriander
Moon Phase: First Quarter
Color: Orange

27 Monday
Ramadan begins Moon Sign: Scorpio
Waxing Moon Moon enters Sagittarius 4:55 am
Moon Phase: First Quarter Incense: Myrrh
Color: Gray

28 Tuesday
Ochi Day (Greek) Moon Sign: Sagittarius
Waxing Moon Incense: Musk
Moon Phase: First Quarter
Color: Black

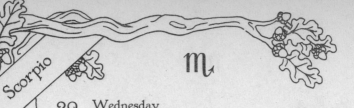

Scorpio ♏

29 Wednesday
Iroquois Feast of the Dead   Moon Sign: Sagittarius
Waxing Moon   Moon enters Capricorn 5:37 am
Moon Phase: First Quarter   Incense: Neroli
Color: Peach

30 Thursday
Meiji Festival (Japanese)   Moon Sign: Capricorn
Waxing Moon   Incense: Vanilla
Moon Phase: First Quarter
Color: White

◐ **Friday**
Halloween • Samhain   Moon Sign: Capricorn
Waxing Moon   Moon enters Aquarius 8:41 am
Moon Phase: Second Quarter 11:25 pm   Incense: Parsley
Color: Rose

‹ঞ২৯›

Hot Mulled Cider

This is a drink for the whole family. It brings to mind
cool autumn breezes and fall colors. Adults may
want to add a shot of dark rum to their cider.

½ cup   brown sugar
           dash nutmeg
1 tsp   whole allspice
     3   cinnamon sticks
1 tsp   whole cloves
¼ tsp   salt
     2   quarts apple cider

Combine the brown sugar, nutmeg, allspice, cinnamon, cloves, salt, and cider in large saucepan. Bring
to a boil; cover and simmer for 20 minutes. Strain to
remove spices.

—Kristin Madden

♏

1 Saturday
All Saints' Day
Waxing Moon
Moon Phase: Second Quarter
Color: Gray

Moon Sign: Aquarius
Incense: Lavender

2 Sunday
All Souls' Day
Waxing Moon
Moon Phase: Second Quarter
Color: Yellow

Moon Sign: Aquarius
Moon enters Pisces 2:52 pm
Incense: Poplar

3 Monday
St. Hubert's Day
Waxing Moon
Moon Phase: Second Quarter
Color: Lavender

Moon Sign: Pisces
Incense: Rose

4 Tuesday
Election Day
Waxing Moon
Moon Phase: Second Quarter
Color: Gray

Moon Sign: Pisces
Incense: Gardenia

5 Wednesday
Guy Fawkes Night (British)
Waxing Moon
Moon Phase: Second Quarter
Color: Peach

Moon Sign: Pisces
Moon enters Aries 12:02 am
Incense: Coriander

6 Thursday
Leonard's Ride (German)
Waxing Moon
Moon Phase: Second Quarter
Color: Turquoise

Moon Sign: Aries
Incense: Sandalwood

7 Friday
Mayan Day of the Dead
Waxing Moon
Moon Phase: Second Quarter
Color: Peach

Moon Sign: Aries
Moon enters Taurus 11:29 am
Incense: Dill

☺ **Saturday**
Lunar eclipse   Moon Sign: Taurus
Waxing Moon   Incense: Jasmine
Moon Phase: Full Moon 8:13 pm
Color: Brown

9 **Sunday**
Lord Mayor's Day (British)   Moon Sign: Taurus
Waning Moon   Incense: Cinnamon
Moon Phase: Third Quarter
Color: Gold

10 **Monday**
Martin Luther's Birthday   Moon Sign: Taurus
Waning Moon   Moon enters Gemini 12:14 am
Moon Phase: Third Quarter   Incense: Peony
Color: Gray

11 **Tuesday**
Veterans Day   Moon Sign: Gemini
Waning Moon   Incense: Ginger
Moon Phase: Third Quarter
Color: White

12 **Wednesday**
Tesuque Feast Day (Native American)   Moon Sign: Gemini
Waning Moon   Moon enters Cancer 1:10 pm
Moon Phase: Third Quarter   Incense: Eucalyptus
Color: Yellow

13 **Thursday**
Festival of Jupiter (Roman)   Moon Sign: Cancer
Waning Moon   Incense: Chrysanthemum
Moon Phase: Third Quarter
Color: Green

14 **Friday**
The Little Carnival (Greek)   Moon Sign: Cancer
Waning Moon   Incense: Thyme
Moon Phase: Third Quarter
Color: Pink

♏

15 Saturday
St. Leopold's Day
Waning Moon
Moon Phase: Third Quarter
Color: Blue

Moon Sign: Cancer
Moon enters Leo 12:48 am
Incense: Violet

☽ Sunday
St. Margaret of Scotland's Day
Waning Moon
Moon Phase: Fourth Quarter 11:15 pm
Color: Orange

Moon Sign: Leo
Incense: Sage

17 Monday
Queen Elizabeth's Day
Waning Moon
Moon Phase: Fourth Quarter
Color: Silver

Moon Sign: Leo
Moon enters Virgo 9:36 am
Incense: Lavender

18 Tuesday
St. Plato's Day
Waning Moon
Moon Phase: Fourth Quarter
Color: Black

Moon Sign: Virgo
Incense: Poplar

19 Wednesday
Garifuna Day (Belizian)
Waning Moon
Moon Phase: Fourth Quarter
Color: Brown

Moon Sign: Virgo
Moon enters Libra 2:42 pm
Incense: Cedar

20 Thursday
Commerce God Ceremony (Japanese)
Waning Moon
Moon Phase: Fourth Quarter
Color: White

Moon Sign: Libra
Incense: Evergreen

21 Friday
Repentance Day (German)
Waning Moon
Moon Phase: Fourth Quarter
Color: Rose

Moon Sign: Libra
Moon enters Scorpio 4:24 pm
Incense: Sandalwood

22 Saturday

St. Cecilia's Day
Waning Moon
Moon Phase: Fourth Quarter
Color: Indigo

Moon Sign: Scorpio
Sun enters Sagittarius 11:43 pm
Incense: Patchouli

☽ Sunday

Solar eclipse
Waning Moon
Moon Phase: New Moon 5:59 pm
Color: Gold

Moon Sign: Scorpio
Moon enters Sagittarius 4:02 pm
Incense: Clove

---

24 Monday

Feast of the Burning Lamps (Egyptian)
Waxing Moon
Moon Phase: First Quarter
Color: White

Moon Sign: Sagittarius
Incense: Maple

---

25 Tuesday

Ramadan ends
Waxing Moon
Moon Phase: First Quarter
Color: Red

Moon Sign: Sagittarius
Moon enters Capricorn 3:31 pm
Incense: Pine

---

26 Wednesday

Festival of Lights (Tibetan)
Waxing Moon
Moon Phase: First Quarter
Color: Yellow

Moon Sign: Capricorn
Incense: Neroli

---

27 Thursday

Thanksgiving Day
Waxing Moon
Moon Phase: First Quarter
Color: Violet

Moon Sign: Capricorn
Moon enters Aquarius 4:48 pm
Incense: Dill

---

28 Friday

Day of the New Dance (Tibetan)
Waxing Moon
Moon Phase: First Quarter
Color: White

Moon Sign: Aquarius
Incense: Ylang ylang

29 **Saturday**
Tubman's Birthday (Liberian)   Moon Sign: Aquarius
Waxing Moon   Moon enters Pisces 9:25 pm
Moon Phase: First Quarter   Incense: Lilac
Color: Gray

◗ **Sunday**
St. Andrew's Day   Moon Sign: Pisces
Waxing Moon   Incense: Basil
Moon Phase: Second Quarter 12:16 pm
Color: Peach

~❦~

The Return of the Sun God

In the wheel of the year, at the time of the Winter Solstice the Mother Goddess once again gives birth to the Sun God to bring warmth to the land. Also known as Yule, after the Germanic "yula," meaning the "wheel of the year," this time celebrates the cycle of nature and the rebirth of the sun. On the shortest day of the year the earth tilts its North axis once again towards the Sun. To appreciate the importance of this time when sun returns, we need to consider the cold, harsh conditions that prevailed in the Northern parts of the world. Yule was traditionally Scandinavian, Germanic, and Celtic in origins when in the fourth century B.C. Pope Julius I decided to replace the Pagan celebration with a Christian holiday. A Roman astronomer, who also happened to be a monk, was commissioned to establish a proposed day and year of birth for Jesus Christ. The agreed date of 25 December as Christmas Day falls within two to four days of the Winter Solstice.

—Emely Flak

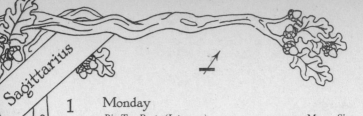

1 Monday
Big Tea Party (Japanese)
Waxing Moon
Moon Phase: Second Quarter
Color: Lavender

Moon Sign: Pisces
Incense: Frankincense

---

2 Tuesday
Republic Day (Laotian)
Waxing Moon
Moon Phase: Second Quarter
Color: White

Moon Sign: Pisces
Moon enters Aries 5:56 am
Incense: Juniper

---

3 Wednesday
St. Francis Xavier's Day
Waxing Moon
Moon Phase: Second Quarter
Color: Yellow

Moon Sign: Aries
Incense: Coriander

---

4 Thursday
St. Barbara's Day
Waxing Moon
Moon Phase: Second Quarter
Color: Violet

Moon Sign: Aries
Moon enters Taurus 5:30 pm
Incense: Carnation

---

5 Friday
Eve of St. Nicholas' Day
Waxing Moon
Moon Phase: Second Quarter
Color: Pink

Moon Sign: Taurus
Incense: Nutmeg

---

6 Saturday
St. Nicholas' Day
Waxing Moon
Moon Phase: Second Quarter
Color: Brown

Moon Sign: Taurus
Incense: Pine

---

7 Sunday
Burning the Devil (Guatemalan)
Waxing Moon
Moon Phase: Second Quarter
Color: Gold

Moon Sign: Taurus
Moon enters Gemini 6:26 am
Incense: Parsley

December

Monday
Feast of the Immaculate Conception
Waxing Moon
Moon Phase: Full Moon 3:37 pm
Color: White

Moon Sign: Gemini
Incense: Myrrh

---

9 **Tuesday**
St. Leocadia's Day
Waning Moon
Moon Phase: Third Quarter
Color: Gray

Moon Sign: Gemini
Moon enters Cancer 7:11 pm
Incense: Honeysuckle

---

10 **Wednesday**
Nobel Day
Waning Moon
Moon Phase: Third Quarter
Color: Peach

Moon Sign: Cancer
Incense: Sandalwood

---

11 **Thursday**
Pilgrimage at Tortugas
Waning Moon
Moon Phase: Third Quarter
Color: Green

Moon Sign: Cancer
Incense: Geranium

---

12 **Friday**
Fiesta of Our Lady of Guadalupe
Waning Moon
Moon Phase: Third Quarter
Color: Rose

Moon Sign: Cancer
Moon enters Leo 6:40 am
Incense: Ginger

---

13 **Saturday**
St. Lucy's Day (Swedish)
Waning Moon
Moon Phase: Third Quarter
Color: Blue

Moon Sign: Leo
Incense: Lavender

---

14 **Sunday**
Warriors' Memorial (Japanese)
Waning Moon
Moon Phase: Third Quarter
Color: Orange

Moon Sign: Leo
Moon enters Virgo 4:07 pm
Incense: Poplar

233

15 Monday
Consualia (Roman)
Waning Moon
Moon Phase: Third Quarter
Color: Gray

Moon Sign: Leo
Incense: Rose

---

16 Tuesday
Posadas (Mexican)
Waning Moon
Moon Phase: Fourth Quarter 12:42 pm
Color: Black

Moon Sign: Leo
Moon enters Libra 10:46 pm
Incense: Evergreen

---

17 Wednesday
Saturnalia (Roman)
Waning Moon
Moon Phase: Fourth Quarter
Color: White

Moon Sign: Libra
Incense: Eucalyptus

---

18 Thursday
Feast of the Virgin of Solitude
Waning Moon
Moon Phase: Fourth Quarter
Color: Turquoise

Moon Sign: Libra
Incense: Musk

---

19 Friday
Opalia (Roman)
Waning Moon
Moon Phase: Fourth Quarter
Color: Peach

Moon Sign: Libra
Moon enters Scorpio 2:20 am
Incense: Almond

---

20 Saturday
Hanukkah begins
Waning Moon
Moon Phase: Fourth Quarter
Color: Indigo

Moon Sign: Scorpio
Incense: Jasmine

---

21 Sunday
Independence Day (Kazakhstani)
Waning Moon
Moon Phase: Fourth Quarter
Color: Yellow

Moon Sign: Scorpio
Sun enters Sagittarius 3:16 am
Incense: Cinnamon

♑   December

22 Monday
Yule • Winter Solstice   Moon Sign: Sagittarius
Waning Moon   Sun enters Capricorn 2:04 am
Moon Phase: Fourth Quarter   Incense: Peony
Color: Lavender

  Tuesday
Larentalia (Roman)   Moon Sign: Sagittarius
Waning Moon   Moon enters Capricorn 2:55 am
Moon Phase: New Moon 4:43 am   Incense: Sage
Color: Red

24 Wednesday
Christmas Eve   Moon Sign: Capricorn
Waxing Moon   Incense: Cedar
Moon Phase: First Quarter
Color: Brown

25 Thursday
Christmas Day   Moon Sign: Capricorn
Waxing Moon   Moon enters Aquarius 3:13 am
Moon Phase: First Quarter   Incense: Vanilla
Color: Brown

26 Friday
Kwanzaa begins   Moon Sign: Aquarius
Waxing Moon   Incense: Dill
Moon Phase: First Quarter
Color: Pink

27 Saturday
Hannukah ends   Moon Sign: Aquarius
Waxing Moon   Moon enters Pisces 6:10 am
Moon Phase: First Quarter   Incense: Violet
Color: Gray

28 Sunday
Holy Innocents' Day   Moon Sign: Pisces
Waxing Moon   Incense: Sage
Moon Phase: First Quarter
Color: Peach

29 Monday
St. Thomas à Becket
Waxing Moon
Moon Phase: First Quarter
Color: Silver

Moon Sign: Pisces
Moon enters Aries 1:08 pm
Incense: Chyrsanthemum

30 Tuesday
Republic Day (Madagascar)
Waxing Moon
Moon Phase: Second Quarter 5:03 am
Color: White

Moon Sign: Aries
Incense: Gardenia

31 Wednesday
New Year's Eve
Waxing Moon
Moon Phase: Second Quarter
Color: Yellow

Moon Sign: Aries
Incense: Neroli

Yule Themes at Christmas

Many symbols and activities associated with the celebration of Christ's birth can be traced to the Pagan reverence for the Winter Solstice. As there is no hard evidence for the date of Jesus Christ's birth, we can assume that the Christians cleverly imposed their celebration at the time of a significant but appealing Pagan festival in their endeavours to convert the population of Europe. Today, the observance of Christmas has become a commercial affair, with enormous effort dedicated to consumption. Apart from Church services, little ritual remains to suggest any religious or spiritual activity or intent. Yet the celebration of this season's festival of light in the darkness of winter has survived.

—Emely Flak

Articles for Summer

Folklore of Roses

by Magenta Griffith

Much as the lotus plays a significant role in the folklore and art of the East, roses have long been important to Western cultures. For instance, roses have been sacred to many goddesses throughout history. In ancient times, the rose was the symbol of Aphrodite and Venus, the Greek and Roman goddesses of love. Later, the rose became the symbol of Mary, who was sometimes called the *Rose Mystica,* or the mystical rose.

According to the Greek poet Anacreon, when Aphrodite was born, rising from the sea, the sea foam that dripped off her body turned into white roses. This image is a representation of her purity and innocence. When she found her lover Adonis dying, the blood from his wound colored her flowers red.

Another Greek myth concerning roses tells of Rhodanthe, a shy maiden of Corinth known for her beauty, charm, and modesty. A devotee of Artemis, the chaste goddess of the hunt, Rhodanthe was nevertheless courted by many suitors. One day, she was tired of staying indoors to avoid her persistent paramours, and she went to the woods alone, where a would-be lover found her. She ran from him, but he chased her. Another lover came upon them, then another. She fled to a nearby temple and prayed to Artemis for rescue. Artemis turned her into a rose, blushing with embarrassment forever at her near-dishonorment.

During feasts in ancient Athens, the streets were strewn with rose petals. Youths of both sexes danced naked before the temple of Hymen, wearing crowns of roses to symbolize their innocence.

The Romans attribute the creation of the rose to Flora, the goddess of spring and flowers. When one of her nymphs died,

Flora turned her into a flower. She asked all the gods for help. Apollo gave the flower life, Bacchus gave nectar, and Pomona contributed a fruit. Thus was the rose created. Bees were attracted by the rose. When Cupid shot arrows at the bees, the arrows that missed the bees became the thorns.

To some Romans, roses symbolized the two sides of Venus. White roses were associated with purity and innocence; red roses with fiery lust. The Romans celebrated a rose festival every year on May 23, and many Romans believed that by planting roses on their graves they would appease the spirits of the dead. Rich patricians would plant entire gardens on their tombs and would leave money in their will to maintain the garden. The use of roses in burial ritual can be found throughout the former Roman Empire, including Wales, where white roses are still placed on graves of young children as a sign of their innocence.

The rose was sacred to Isis as well, and she is sometimes portrayed with a crown of roses. In Apuleus' classical epic tale, *The Golden Ass,* Lucius is turned into a donkey and wanders the Roman Empire. He has many adventures, all the while constantly praying to the gods and goddesses to change him back into human form. Finally, Isis comes to him in a dream. She tells him, in an oft-quoted passage, that, "She is Nature, the Mother of all, the queen of the gods. She is called by many names, but that her true name is Isis." If he will promise to worship her, she will restore him to his true form. She tells him to go to the sacred ceremony of Isis that will be held the next day, and instructs him to eat the sacred roses that her priest carries in the procession. Lucius did as he was instructed, and was immediately turned back into a man. In the end, he became an initiate of the mysteries of Isis in gratitude.

Symbolism of Roses

Roses, since they conceal a hidden inner core, have been thought of as a symbol of secrecy by many cultures. The rose was the flower of Harpocrates, the young Horus, who is the god of silence. This god is usually pictured as a young boy with his finger to his lips. He stumbled upon Venus when she was engaged in one of her amorous liaisons. Cupid gave Harpocrates a rose in return for his silence. Thus, the custom in the Middle Ages of putting a rose on the ceiling of a meeting room. Anything said there was considered *sub rosa,* or under the rose, and therefore not to be repeated. Roses were often painted on the ceilings of meeting rooms, which led to rose motifs becoming popular as ceiling decoration.

A white rose is said to represent innocence; a pink rose, first love; and a red rose, true and lasting love. The red rose is also a symbol of beauty and devotion.

The rose represents the feminine in alchemy, and corresponds to the female sexual organ. The cross is the symbol of the masculine, thus the rose cross, the primary symbol of the Rosicrucian order, is a symbol of union, and of the sacred marriage. The rose cross also represents the union of the natural world (the rose), and the world constructed by man (the cross).

The rose of the rose cross has five petals, and is therefore a pentagram. The petals represent the five senses, among other meanings. The pentagram, the symbol of witchcraft, has been called the Witches' Rose, because of the fivefold nature of both the pentagram and the rose. It's difficult to observe with modern hybrid roses, but if you look at the older varieties, you will find the petals usually number in multiples of five—that is, five, ten, or fifteen petals.

Lakshmi, the Hindu goddess of love, the most beautiful goddess in the Hindu pantheon, is said to have been born from a rose composed of 108 large and 1,008 small petals. She is always pictured either sitting on a rose, holding roses, or both.

A Christian legend says that the rose was thornless in the Garden of Eden. Once Adam and Eve were expelled, the rose grew thorns. Although the rose was associated with goddesses of love (including physical love) in ancient times, by the Middle Ages the rose was a symbol of the Virgin Mary and so came to symbolize purity and innocence. Rosary beads were originally made from rose petals. The word "rosary" comes from the Latin, *rosarium,* a rose garden. The first rosaries were Buddhist and had 99 or 108 beads. Catholic rosaries have 165 beads and are sacred to Mary.

The fairy tale *Beauty and the Beast* starts with a rose. While Beauty's sisters ask for rich clothing and jewels, she asks her father only to bring her back a rose from his voyage. During his travels, while looking for the elusive rose, he is caught in bad weather and has to spend the night in the Beast's castle. He goes into the Beast's garden and finds a perfect rose and picks it for his daughter. The Beast catches him taking it, and demands Beauty come to him in exchange for the rose. The rose and Beauty are, in effect, interchangeable.

Here are some final beliefs about roses. The Romans believed that rose petals floated in wine would protect against drunkenness. In medieval Europe, roses were worn as protection against the evil eye. An old German love charm says:

Take three roses and wear them over your heart
for three days. Then steep them in wine for three days.
Strain the wine and give it to the one you desire.

Perfumes and oils derived from roses may be one of the oldest scents used by humans. Rose petals are used in cooking, and yield rose petal jam and candied rose petals. Rosewater, made from rose petals, is also an ingredient in foods and magical spells. The fruit of the rose, or rose hip, is used in many ways—to flavor jellies, preserves, and syrups. Tea containing dried rose hips is rich in vitamin C.

In all, roses, originally a symbol of love and beauty, have come to be widely used for their medicinal properties. And even in these harried modern times, roses are still the most popular flower to give your sweetheart to express your love.

The Goddess in Brazil

by Mavesper Ceridwen

The country of Brazil is a very ancient civilization, with archeological remains that date back to more than fifty thousand years. The study of these ancient civilizations is still very recent and much remains to be found about how ancient Brazilians lived. Since there is little information regarding the ancestors, the best source of information on traditional Brazilian shamanism exists in historical registers.

Magical Brazil

Brazil is a huge and diverse country. There is a deep contrast in its natural beauty, which ranges from equatorial and tropical forest to flat wastelands and regions of stunted vegetation regions. These differences in natural forms corresponds to the diversity of the country's indigenous spirituality. That is, the native culture was transformed by its contact with Portuguese Christian groups 500 years ago and sent into hiding—thus obscuring Brazilian indigenous mythology.

The Jesuits of the day had many mistaken ideas regarding the legends and beliefs of native Brazilians, and for many years the ideas of these people were lost under this blanket of confusion and misrepresentation. It is only in recent times that anthropologists and ethnologists have begun studying the remaining indigenous cultures, discovering quite interesting data. For example, among the Yanomamis, a tribe from Alto Xingu, there is a sacred language spoken only by women, and kept unknown from men. Why this is so is not exactly clear, except it likely indicates the presence of a not-too-distant goddess-centered religious system. On the whole, more study needs to be done to clarify the old systems of belief. Therefore, it is the duty of the Pagans of Brazil, and of all people who value Earth's spirituality, to foster such studies and so fully understand our roots.

As a Brazilian Pagan, I have been collecting Brazilian indigenous legends and myths, selecting texts from many peoples and trying to identify in those texts the different faces of the Goddess. Although it is correct to state that Brazilian Indians did not know gods in the religious sense of the word, instead personifying natural phenomena in the way of animist religious systems, there are similarities in the myths of Brazilian indigenous tribes and other Goddess-based religions. In comparing these myths, we see are able to observe in the indigenous tribes self-ritualistic work, based in ancestor customs, allied to the knowledge of magical use of herbs and other native materials from Brazil. Furthermore, there are strong similarities between their myths and those of other goddess traditions. Let us take a look, for example, at the legend of the Desanâ tribe about the foundation of the world.

The Foundation of the World Myth

At first, the world did not exist at all. Darkness ruled the Earth. In the midst of this nothingness, a woman was born from herself. She was made from six invisible things, and so was called the Non-Created. She appeared mysteriously, suspended over magical benches and wrapped in ornaments that would eventually transform into a dwelling of quartz. She was called Yabá Beló, the Grandmother of the Universe.

This woman thought about how the future of the world should be. While she was thinking, she chewed magical herbs and smoked tobacco. Her thoughts started to materialize in the shape of a sphere, which began to rise in the air. Eventually, her thoughts began to absorb the darkness, until all the darkness was held in the sphere. This was the universe, yet there was no light. The only place there was light was the quartz dwelling of Yabá Beló, and she called it her Womb.

Her house was large, and Yabá Beló wanted to people her house. She chewed more herbs, and without thinking took a wad from her mouth. She mixed the wad of herbs with her saliva, and created the men of the white stone and called them the Five Thunder Beings. She saluted the immortal beings she had created, saying, "Hello, brothers." And they answered, "Hello, Grandmother of the Universe and of all that exists." They inhabited rooms in her big house and were guarded by a huge-winged bat. Yebá Beló told the Thunder Beings to create other mortal beings. However, the Thunder Beings, in their laziness, did not obey. Then, smoking more tobacco, she created a smoke being, which she turned into flesh. It was her grandson Yebá Ngoamãn, who saluted her, "Hail, O Grandmother!" And she gave him a crane with feathers, and male and female seeds. The crane, which later on changed into the Sun, looked like a human face. Yebá Beló released the Sun to light the world. After that, all creatures were created. The first women had a wonderful scent of pineapple.

The Universality of the Brazilian Goddess

The above legend is proof that the myths of the Great Goddess have a certain universality, and we must pursue further study of these obscure myths. One of the few things that tie together all the Brazilian Indians beliefs is the common idea that all things, all beings, have a mother. This mother, in most indigenous languages of Brazil, is designated Cy. This figure represents the Great Mother, the Mother of all, the one who personifies neverending maternity. Cy is the *terra brasilis,* the incarnation of the Earth that is copied in the pregnant wombs of all that exist. Cy is the lunar goddess, mother of everybody, the one who speaks from the Earth, from the ground we stand on, and from the womb we all came.

Another goddess mentioned in many Brazilian mythologies is the Big Snake. Also called Lady of the Elements, she possesses the powers of cosmogony. She is the generator of life and controller of the creation. Amazon legends say that her body is the river itself, and her sixty-one stops on the way to the sea represents the sixty-one tribes of Brazil.

Another myth told in many tribes is the myth of Mani. The legends say that the daughter of a Brazilian tribal chief showed up pregnant yet still a virgin. Her father thought about punishing her, but then he dreamed of a spirit who told him that the child was magic and would bring good luck to everybody. A girl was born, named Mani, who was very different from other children. For instance, her skin was so white it glowed. She also was born already speaking, and she has walked on her second day of life. All were charmed by the wise words of Mani, but she died before she was one year old and was buried in her mother's hut, as was the custom among her people. Her mother watered her grave every day, as tradition commanded. After a while, an unknown tree grew on the girl's grave. The roots were very white underneath their peels; they had Mani's color. They were called *manioc,* an important food plant for Brazilian Indians. In ritual, Mani, the Mother of the Corn, is torn into pieces so that it can give origin to the tree that sustains life.

Another important myth speaks of Uiara, or Iara, the Lady of the Water. Uiara is the mermaid of the rivers, and is the most celebrated Amazon goddess. In some places, people call her the female porpoise. Uiara is a gorgeous tanned woman, with black hair and hazel eyes. She possesses a unique beauty, and those who see her bathing naked in the rivers cannot control their instincts and throw themselves into the water. Not always do they manage to come back to the world of the living. Those who manage to return are forever haunted. It takes prayers and sorcery, and a shaman of great power, to take them out of a state of torpor. Some describe her as having a sparkling star on her forehead, which works as bait for the easily influenced.

At the margins of Jamundá river in Amazon at Serra de Itacamiabá, near a lake called Jaci-Uará, or the Mirror of the Moon, lived the Lawless women, or Iacamiabas. Icamiaba means originally "The Nation of Tits," and was a people composed only by women. These women were fugitives from Serra de Tunaí, seeking to live free from cruel Jurapari, the Son of the Sun. Jurapari punished those that disobeyed him with death. This legend is assumed to be about the dreams of women who wish to escape from a patriarchal society.

The women of Icamiaba wore braided hair. They worshipped Muiraquitã's mother, and her magical green stones, which were shaped as frogs, fish, or turtles and possessed magical properties of protection from the danger that surrounded the margins of the lake. When Jacy, the Moon, reached her throne in the sky, there would be a great celebration and the women would receive the stones by diving in the lake. Frogs are symbol of fertility, the creative power of the lunar goddess. Muiraquitã's mother gave the stones to the men who visited the Icamiabas and worshipped her once a year. These stones today are considered love charms, because they represent this rare moment of meeting for pleasure, the forever young love among the Icamiabas.

Overall, we can identify many countless faces of the Goddess in the indigenous traditions of Brazil. To comprehend that the Goddess is not only Ceridwen, Isis, Yemanjá, Freya, Zoe, and Ixel, but also that she is Cy, Mani, Yebá Beló, the Big Snake, and Iara, is to grow our knowledge of her. May the goddess from Brazil, and the Goddess under any of her ten thousand names, bless the Earth with peace.

Rhymes of Good Fortune

by Laurel Nightspring Reufner

Find a penny, pick it up.
The rest of the day you'll have good luck.

What is our obsession with the finding of lucky objects? We did it as kids—and gleefully. My daughters are currently taken with pine cones, which are excitedly gathered and handed over to Mommy, sap and all. And perhaps the only thing that keeps us from obsession as adults is that we probably feel a little silly about it.

Lucky Stone Folklore

Perhaps this desire for lucky objects is genetic. Consider that it is only the rare small child who doesn't go through the rock collection phase. It doesn't matter what kind of

stone or rock it is—driveway slag, river rocks, pea gravel: They all delight. Fortunately, as they get older children become more discerning, and only certain kinds of stones will do for good luck. Eventually they have to be holey, white, round, or otherwise extraordinary.

Truth be told, my husband still scours the school playground gravel for small stones with holes in them, although I seriously doubt he'd admit to gathering them for good luck. Most people keep their holey stones, but in some areas they are only lucky if you get rid of them. First you pick the stone up, then spit on it, and then throw it behind you while saying the following:

> *Lucky stone! Lucky stone! Go over my head,*
> *And bring me some good luck before I go to bed.*

Here is some more folklore about stones: If you see a piece of coal lying on the road, you'd better not pass it by or you'll have bad luck. In fact, coal is treated much like holey stones when it comes to luck and wishes; you should pick it up, spit on it, and then pitch it over your left shoulder while making a wish. If you are the first one to find the coal, then you wish will come true. If you want your new find to bring you luck instead of wishes, then tuck it in a pocket and carry it with you, as per the saying:

> *If you see a piece of coal, pick it up,*
> *All the day you'll have good luck.*

Straight Pin Folklore

Finding a straight pin nowadays isn't all that big of a deal, unless it is stuck in the carpet where you were about to put your foot. But in fact, such pins were once prized treasures. They were difficult and expensive to make and buy, and so a woman's "pin money" was important. Therefore, finding a pin would indeed have been good luck. To leave one lying on the ground would be akin to walking past money. Consider also the solemn oath sworn on pain of sticking a "needle in your eye." Here are two rhymes about straight pins.

See a pin and pick it up
All the day you'll have good luck.
See a pin and let it lay
Bad luck you'll have all that day.
Pin, pin, bring me luck,

Because I stop to pick you up.
Find a pin and let it lie,
You shall want before you die.
See a pin and let it lie,
Before the night you will cry.

If you find a pin, you are supposed to put it in your collar or lapel and wear it as long as you can. Alternatively, you can perform some pin-wishing magic. Making sure the pin is pointing towards you, pick it up with your right hand and stick it into the left shoulder of your clothing while making your wish. After you've worn the pin awhile, give it away to someone or else the wish won't come true. And be forewarned, some people believe that a pin should never be approached or picked up by its point, but only by the head.

Other Lucky Things

Find a feather, stick it up,
All the day you'll have good luck.

Buttons, coins, and four-leaved clovers are all also considered lucky to find. So are feathers considered lucky, especially the ones, as the above rhyme states, found stuck upright in the ground. Eagle feathers are especially lucky—but be sure to leave them were you find them, unless you have a permit to possess them.

And since they aren't all that prevalent today, finding a horseshoe is probably luckier now than it used to be. Some sources claim that you have to pitch the horseshoe over your head and make a wish, although I only see that leading to bad luck depending on where the horseshoe lands. And most of us probably already know that if you want to put a horseshoe up for good luck somewhere on your property, you need to nail it down with the points up so the luck doesn't run out.

Some lucky things, such as the first star in the night sky, cannot be picked up. Remember searching for it as a child and getting so excited when you beat your friends to it? Children today, as well as the young at heart everywhere, still enjoy this particular search.

Star light, star bright,
First star I see tonight,
Wish I may, wish I might,
Get this wish I wish tonight.

As many of us know, it is out intent that makes something lucky or unlucky. Children seem to have an uncanny knack for this, finding something during the course of the day that is unusual and makes them feel special. To find an unusual thing gives an extra little boost of confidence that today will be a good day. This is, of course, some of the greatest magic of all, for when we feel more confident our luck does seem better.

What about the penny that we started with? I still pick them up, most of the time. But only if they're lying faceup.

The Magic of Dandelions

by Nuala Drago

There is much lore about the modest dandelion; even its very name has a rich history. Ancient apothecaries called them *dens leonis,* meaning "tooth of the lion," which the plant's serrated leaves are said to resemble. In French, dens leonis translates to *dent de lion,* from which the name "dandelion" was derived. But the French also have a less polite nickname for the plant, *pis en lis,* which means "pee in the bed." This is from the plant's age-old reputation as an effective diuretic. In fact, in many parts of England dandelions are called *pissibed* for the same reason.

Fortunately, dandelions are identified by more pleasing names as well—including wild endive, fairy herb, bitter herb, buttercup, and fairy clocks. The scientific name is *Taraxacum officinale,* but no matter what you choose to call this vibrant yellow harbinger of spring, it is one of nature's most versatile, intriguing, and valuable plants.

Dandelion Legends and Facts

According to an ancient Celtic legend, dandelions are the children of the Sky God and the Earth Mother. They awaken each dawn to unfurl their blossoms in the morning Sun and to bask in the warmth of their father's life-giving rays. Their faces turn to follow him from east to west in his journey across the sky until he leaves them at day's end, when they close their petals tightly—as though donning a nightdress—and bow their heads to sleep, secure in the bosom of their mother.

Because of their illustrious ancestry, dandelions are endowed with a powerful connection to the supernatural realm. The bond is further enhanced by the fact that dandelions sink their roots deeply into the earth, visiting the underworld, the realm of the gods and goddesses who have the power to cull the old and the sick from among the living. Their yellow flower heads, too, are associated with solar deities such as Belenos, Lugh, and Ogmios. On the whole, it is thought, the dandelion draws nourishment from Sun and soil, and shares the secrets of life, death, and rebirth with the wild spirits who inhabit the region in between. It is said these secrets are passed to any creature that ingests the dandelion, resulting in increased extrasensory abilities of the mind; intuition and telepathy.

While this legend may seem a colorful blend of myth and fable, there is still much wisdom to be extracted from it. In fact, in Celtic countries, where the fairy faith is alive and well, many believe in the healing forces and supernatural powers of dandelions, particularly their ability to cure diseases inflicted by fairies and malevolent spirits. It is also believed that ingesting dandelions in one form or another on a regular basis may even impart the ability to communicate with the dead.

Such beliefs are shared in many lands and cultures. This is not surprising, since the dandelion has been a recognized and reliable source of food and medicine for man and beast for more than six hundred years. It was a staple in the pharmacopoeias of many Eastern countries by the tenth century; as early as the 1500s, European apothecaries were prescribing dandelions as a cure for maladies such as skin blemishes and liver ailments.

In ages past, when people had to forage or grow their own food, they worked hard. Harsh living conditions depleted their bodies. Winter stores of fresh foodstuffs were placed in grain pits or root cellars to be carefully rationed; if fruit and vegetable supplies ran out before spring, the result was often scurvy, a painfully debilitating disease caused by vitamin deficiencies with nasty symptoms such as bleeding gums, tooth loss, anemia, malaise, nosebleeds, muscle cramps, joint pains, and bruising.

How fortunate for the afflicted that long before summer berries could be gathered or new crops of fruits and vegetables could be planted and ready to harvest, dandelions provided them with a welcome release from the physical weakness, pain, and pallor of their illness. Only a couple of generations ago, it was commonplace in many households to drink a spring tonic prepared from dandelions. This concoction was an all-purpose elixir used to combat illnesses such as respiratory infections and to lift the spirits of those who suffered from depression and fatigue, especially after the long winter indoors. Families also made dandelion beer or wine as a delicious, restorative apéritif.

Nutritionists today can tell you that dandelions are brimming with such nutrients as bioflavinoids, calcium, potassium, iron, niacin, choline, folic acid, magnesium, sulfur, and zinc, to name just a few. They also contain an entire alphabet of vitamins, all at higher levels than many other commonly cultivated greens, including spinach and chard. Health experts will also tell you that dandelions may even help to reduce serum cholesterol and promote good health by cleansing and rejuvenating the body.

Dandelions are good for animals and the environment too. Although dandelions are said to produce bitter honey, they are an important source of food for bees in the early spring because they bloom long before most other flowering plants. Many animals such as deer, rabbits, and bears seek out the green leaves and flowers, while the airy seed tufts they generate at the end of their growing cycle are a valuable food source for songbirds.

So, if the magic of dandelions appeals to you, it's easy to take part in it. But take care; be certain that any fresh dandelions you use are free of pesticides or herbicides. Consider buying them from a reliable source such as a restaurant supplier, or, better yet, growing your own organically. As with any fresh produce, be sure to wash dandelions thoroughly if you are going to eat them. Gloves may be helpful when you handle them because the milky sap of the stem and root may stain or irritate your skin. And, if you are adding dandelions to your diet for the first time, go slowly until you know how your body will react, because dandelions can have a diuretic or laxative effect.

At first, you may simply wish to add a few dandelion leaves or blossoms to your tossed salads. The leaves also make an excellent substitute for watercress in tea sandwiches and may be substituted for part or all of the spinach in many recipes. You may also try adding the tops and greens to soups, breads, and casseroles. Your personal tastes and intentions should guide you, and experience will soon teach you valuable lessons—such as the right time to harvest dandelions for the best flavor and texture. In general, spring dandelions are preferred because as the season progresses they tend to become bitter.

If you enjoy hot beverages, dandelion root may be used as a substitute for coffee and tea. Scrub several roots well, blot them dry, and dice them into tiny pieces. Spread them on a baking sheet and roast in a 350°F oven until they are very dark brown and crisp enough to be crushed to resemble instant coffee. Use a teaspoon of crushed root per cup of hot water, adding milk and sweetener to taste. If you don't have the time or inclination to harvest and prepare your own dandelion roots, dandelion tea is available through health-food stores and catalogs. The powdered root is also available in capsule form.

For the truly ambitious, however, dandelion wine is a most rewarding project. A good recipe produces a pale-yellow, clear wine with the aroma and flavor of a fine liqueur. This can be enjoyed for its own merit or as the perfect compliment to many celebrations and rituals.

On the whole, dandelions are particularly appropriate as food, beverage, and decoration in spring festivals such as Beltane, which celebrate the return of the Sun. They are also appropriate at Samhain because of their association with the underworld. Because they are prolific and persistent, they are ideal for fertility rituals as well as spells for strength, perseverance, or wealth.

Unfortunately, there are those who will always consider the dandelion to be nothing more than a noxious weed. For those who follow the traditions of natural magic, however, the dandelion is a beautiful source of natural energy, a vibrant entity representative of natural cycles and universal forces, and a reminder that all living things are connected.

For Further Study

Asala, Joanne. *Celtic Folklore Cooking.* Llewellyn Publications, 1998.

Cunningham, Scott. *Magical Herbalism.* Llewellyn Publications, 1991.

The Magical Allure
of New Orleans

by Cerridwen Iris Shea

A friend of mine says she can't spend more than three days in New Orleans, because the city makes her want to take off all her clothes and dance through the streets, singing. I don't have quite that reaction—though I do want to rearrange my life so that I can spend a part of every winter in New Orleans—but I understand what she means. There is something lively, lusty, and slightly nefarious about the place. It has inspired books, movies, music—and rituals. It is a city with many cemeteries, all above ground—true "cities of the dead." And yet, it is one of the liveliest cities on earth.

The wide mix of cultures is one reason New Orleans is so special. The city has been both French and Spanish, and the African slave population brought their culture into the mix as well. German, Irish, Scottish, and Italian also have all contributed to the flavor of the city. With such mixture, the city became a collection of individualists. This is the city of Pere Antoine, Marie Laveau, Jean Lafitte, Louis Armstrong, Jelly Roll Morton, Dorothy Dix, Lillian Hellman, Huey Long, and Harry Connick, Jr. This is a city of the senses, where all the six senses are assaulted and seduced constantly and simultaneously.

Because, of course, a great deal of the life force of the city comes from the dead. In a city of over forty cemeteries, caring for the dead is a full-time job. There has long been a "keeping up with the Joneses" mentality as far as the care of the family tombs. Because of the water table and the heat, many graves must be above ground. When someone dies, he or she is put into the family tomb and sealed in for a year and a day. If another family member dies within that year, the tomb cannot be opened. A vault in the wall of the cemetary is rented. After the year and the day, the family vault is opened. The heat has created somewhat of a crematorium effect within the tomb, and the body is mostly ash. The ashes are swept down into the bottom of the tomb with a tool called a shaft—which is where the expression "given the shaft" originates—then the relative who was put in the rental unit can be moved into the family tomb and sealed in for another year and a day.

Some of the tombs in New Orleans are not built above ground, but are below ground with heavy stone lids. When the water table rises, the coffins also rise and bump the stone tablets, which makes a knocking sound that often spooks the unaware.

Another story one of my cemetery guides told me is that what we think of as patio furniture originated in New Orleans cemeteries. Because tending graves was such an enormous part of family and social life, especially on All Saints' Day, there tended to be large gravesite gatherings. These often included elderly relatives and pregnant women. Furniture was brought out to the cemetery so that they could sit and rest while they caught up with the relatives. Instead of dragging the house furniture back and forth, special furniture was created only for outdoor use. This furniture was later adopted for patio furniture. While I've found printed confirmation of many of the stories I was told in my New Orleans sojourn, I haven't been able to confirm this one—but I enjoy it anyway.

Marie Laveau, of course, is still a potent influence in the city. New Orleans Voodoo (or Voudoun, depending upon to whom you speak) has grown up quite separately and differently than

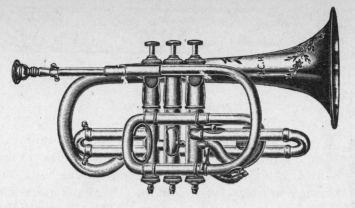

Haitian Voodoo. Marie, born in 1794, and her daughter, also named Marie, became powerful women in the city. Their strong beliefs and their ability to make others believe in them have allowed them to exert a considerable influence. Marie the elder must have been quite a strong woman and a strong healer; she gave birth to fifteen children and lived to the age of eighty-seven at a time when dying in childbirth was common. Marie was also a great friend of Pere Antoine's and attended Mass every day. A magical person traveling to New Orleans should always stop at Marie's tomb in St. Louis Cemetery #1 to pay respects. You will feel her influence instantly. (Make sure that you visit as part of a tour group—it's still unsafe to visit the cemeteries alone.)

The allure of New Orleans is a celebration of the individual, both living and dead, coexisting peacefully. The veil between the worlds is thin here, all the time. The ancestors are always talking, and they do demand that you listen. For a magical person, time in New Orleans is a necessity. It's more than a desire of the senses, it's a desire of the soul.

For Further Study

Florence, Robert. *City of the Dead: A Journey Through St. Louis Cemetery #1*. The Center for Louisiana Studies, 1996.

Garvey, Joan B., and Mary Lou Widmer. *Beautiful Crescent: A History of New Orleans*. Garner Press, 1998.

Gehman, Mary, and Nancy Ries. *Women and New Orleans*. Margaret Media, Inc., 2000.

Independence Day Ritual

by Jenna Tigerheart

July is full of opportunities to celebrate our independence. July 4, of course, is Independence Day in the United States, and an excellent time to celebrate our personal freedom. July 14, on the other hand, is Bastille Day, which is celebrated in France. This day marks the beginning of the French Revolution, in which the French people put an end to the rule of the monarchy. This month is a good time to celebrate our freedom in ritual and practice.

The following ritual is meant to be a vibrant and energetic ritual for a group. It includes a time of reflection and sharing. However, if you are working alone on this ritual, you can write down reflections and burn them during the energy raising to share your energy with the universe.

The Ritual

Start this ritual by gathering the following items on and around your altar. You can replace any of these items with one that is more personal if necessary.

Sandalwood Incense

An eagle symbol (a picture, a feather, and so on; in a pinch I have used a U.S. quarter showing the "tails" side up).

A red spirit candle

A chalice that holds water from a sacred place

Oak leaves

Color-coordinated candles for each of the four elements

Centering & Cleansing

Set up your altar with the eagle in the east, the candle in the south, the chalice in the west, and the oak leaves in the north. Place your elemental candles in their directions (white air is east, yellow fire is south, blue water is west, and brown earth is north). Light the incense and use it to cleanse the sacred space. Once the space is cleansed, use the incense to cleanse the participants as they enter the circle. Concentrate on the cleansing, leaving all concerns regarding the mundane world outside.

Once everyone is inside the space, cast the circle, saying:

> Power of east, breath of air, winds of change, eagle fair,
> Bring your vision and be here now. (Light white candle)
> Blessed be!
> Power of south, flames of fire, warmth of love, freedom's desire,
> Bring your healing and be here now. (Light yellow candle)
> Blessed be!
> Power of west, blessed water, cup of dreams for each son and daughter,
> Bring your dreams and be here now. (Light blue candle)
> Blessed be!
> Power of north, body of earth, tree of life, time of rebirth,
> Bring your grounding; be here now. (Light brown candle)
> Blessed be!

Then, light your spirit candle, and say:

> We light this spirit candle for the spirit of freedom—a spirit we must pursue and cultivate. We can only be free if

we wish to be free and we try to be free. Spirit of freedom, come and be here now. Blessed be!

Now get comfortable, and share with one another your personal freedoms, whether small or large. This is a time to share with everyone and celebrate what you have.

Once everyone has shared, it is time to raise some energy for freedom. Freedom is not easy to attain and requires much energy. Transformation can be very difficult in a society that is set in its ways. So pull out drums, guitars, voices, and any other musical instruments, and use them. The following chant can be used as part of that energy raising.

Eagle's gifted eyes, see where freedom lies,
Flames of sacred fire, bring us our desire,
Cup of sacred dreams, lead us to life's streams,
Body of our birth, show us our true worth.

Once the energy has been raised, direct it outward all over the country to help our society gain freedom. Speak the following "Declaration of Freedom":

Freedom is precious and rare in our society. So many work so hard to put themselves or others into prisons from which they cannot escape. Only those who wish to escape can escape and gain their freedom. Only through freedom can we truly be all we can be. Prisons take many forms: isolation, discrimination, and lack of confidence. Let us work toward freedom from these prisons. No more discrimination. Racism, ageism, sexism, be gone! We are tearing down the prisons and we will be free!

Finally, open the circle by saying:

Hail east! The winds of change are upon us.
Let freedom be ours. Hail and farewell!
Blessed be!
Hail south! Through the fires of love we will be free!
Hail and farewell!
Blessed be!
Hail west, the cup of transformation is ours.
Let us seek freedom! Hail and farewell!
Blessed be!
Hail north, the cycle of life is never-ending.
So may our freedom be never-ending. Hail and farewell!
Blessed be!

May our circle remain unbroken even as we leave this
place. May the spirit of freedom go ever in our hearts.
May we merry meet, and merry part, and merry meet
again! Blessed be!

Lammas

by Anna Franklin

The feast of Lammas, celebrated on August 1, originates in the ancient Celtic festival of Lughnasa, a word which translates as "the games (or assembly) of Lugh." Lugh was a popular god associated with the harvest and the Sun. The Celts held tribal gatherings at this time of year, which included competitions and games, contracts and legal rulings, and even trial marriages.

The cult of Lugh rose to prominence in Ireland from the middle of the Iron Age onward, brought by Britons fleeing from the Roman invaders. He was known as Lud in England, Llew or Lleu in Wales, Lugus in Gaul, and Lugh or Lugaidh in Ireland. Many places were named after him. Lyons in France was called Lugdunum, and London was named from Lud, while other examples include Leiden, Laon, Loudon, and Liegnitz.

It is possible that this festival was dedicated originally to mother goddesses that represent the land and earth itself—Talitiu, Carman, Macha, and Rhiannon. Their festivals also occurred on August 1.

The Anglo-Saxons invaders of Britain adopted Lughnasa, and called it Lammas, a word derived from the Anglo-Saxon *hlaef-mass,* meaning "loaf-mass." This festival marks the first harvest, when the first of the grain is gathered in, ground in a mill, and baked into a loaf. It was a popular ceremony during the Middle Ages, but died out after the Reformation.

Whether you call the festival Lammas or Lughnasa, it marks the end of the summer season of growth when the heat of the dog days ripens and dries the grain in the fields. Though the weather is hot and sultry, the Irish reckon it the start of autumn, as growth is ended and the harvest begins. In fact, it was considered unlucky to pick any fruit, reap any grain, or dig up any vegetables before Lughnasa. In parts of Ireland, the nearest Sunday to Lughnasa was known as Cally Sunday; it was traditional to lift the first new potatoes on this day. The favored dish at this time was one known variously as ceallaigh, cally, or colcannon. This consists of boiled potatoes mashed, mixed with butter or milk, and seasoned with onion, garlic, or cabbage. It was believed that if you ate a good meal on Cally Sunday you would not go hungry for the next twelve months.

It is possible that the original Lughnasa assemblies and fairs were wakes, mourning for the death of summer, or the death of the Corn God. The seasonal Lammas fairs in England were called wakes, and the tradition of games at a funeral is very ancient. (The original Olympic Games were funeral games held every fourth year at Olympia.) Traditional Witches celebrate Lughnasa with various games and competitions in honor of the death of the corn god. The winner becomes the champion of the Goddess and swears to sacrifice a loaf of bread at the end of the harvest.

Modern Pagans today celebrate Lammas as the first harvest, giving thanks for Earth's bounty. A loaf of bread is baked in the traditional plait or sheaf shape. It is blessed, divided up, and the first portion is laid on the altar or on the ground, as an offering to the gods.

In an age when crops can be imported all year round, we tend to forget just how important this time was to our ancestors— the failure of the harvest meant starvation and death. As we thank the gods for the beneficence of the harvest at Lammas, we should offer up a prayer of thankfulness them. If you can afford it, make a charitable donation at this time to benefit those who are less fortunate than you.

Magical Seashells

by deTraci Regula

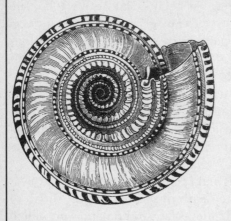

Unicorn horns and sunken ships, cups and saucers for fairy tea-parties—the seashore tosses up magic with every rippling wave. Seashells are beautiful flowers of the sea, and are used as magical adornments all over the world. Perhaps because of their organic nature, shells are always associated with deity. The following list details some of the uses and lore concerning seashells around the world. Whatever your magical or decorative need, there is a seashell ready to fulfill it.

Abalone shells have been used as ornament in many cultures. The reflective quality of the inside of the shell wards off the evil eye. Baby abalone shells are used whole in necklaces and other adornments. Paua shell, a blue abalone, is called the "sea opal" because of its beauty and resemblance to blue or black opals. Native American Pueblo Indians use the abalone to offer water to the Corn Maidens, and the California Pomo Indians believe the shining iridescence of the abalone represents lightning. Their god of lightning, Thunder Man, is said to have eyes of abalone shell. Thunder comes when he shakes his jacket, which is covered with shell beads.

Clam shells of all kinds symbolize Aphrodite. The giant clam was often used for disk beads.

Cowry shells are like miniature sculptures depicting the sacred gateway of life, the female genitalia. The obvious symbolic value of this shell has escaped few cultures, and cowries are found in burials from the beginning of human culture. The cowrie is associated with many divinities, both male and female, but usually it is employed as a supreme symbol of women and goddesses. The cowrie is sacred to Eshu, god of divination, and Olokun and Yemaja, sea goddesses, all of the Yoruba. In Greece, it was called the *concha venerea,* or "shell of Venus." Worn to prevent sterility and assure an easy birth, the cowry has been revered worldwide, and it has been a valuable item of trade. They are used widely as money as well as decoration, especially in Africa and Polynesia. Natu-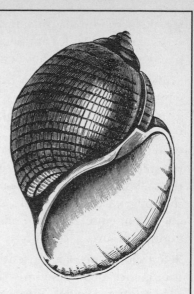ral golden cowries are found as votive objects in burials in Egypt and many other places. In the South Pacific, golden cowries were especially valued, and in some areas were only worn by men of high rank. For these ceremonial necklaces, the golden cowrie would be polished, but otherwise left unadorned.

Dentalium is a tubular, tooth-like shell popular as an adornment around the world. Alaskan Inuits traditionally wear long ear pendants composed of strands of dangling dentalium shells, tied off at the waist with an abalone shell.

Nautilus shells have many chambers, which allows this shell to be fashioned into beautiful ornaments. The inner "pearl" of the shell, a silver arched oval, is particularly popular in jewelry. Nautilus pearls were worn as headbands in the South Pacific and were said to increase the wearer's understanding. Modern mystics believe that these shells stimulate the third eye and enhance visions. An especially lovely adornment for moonlit rites, they can also be gently rubbed over the body to remove fevers and improve the skin.

River snail shells were sometimes worn as amulets by boaters on the Yangtze River and represented Nu Kua, the primal female force who may manifest as a giant snail. Snail shells also serve as containers for amulets which, when filled with magical herbs and stones, are then sealed and worn or carried.

Scallop shells, when worn on a string or thong, are an old symbol of St. James the Apostle, patron saint of Christian pilgrims. The presence of a scallop necklace offered some protection to travelers traversing brigand-haunted roads, because even those cutthroats thought twice before slaying someone in the midst of so sacred an activity as a pilgrimage. In general, the scallop shell inspired hospitality on the road. Who knew if that pilgrim were really just a pilgrim, or perhaps a saint or angel in disguise? Scallop shells also have symbolized Aphrodite, goddess of love.

Sea urchine spines are used in necklaces. Large ones, up to four inches long, sometimes show an attractive white and purple banding. Smaller ones are used as tube beads, and some species retain a purple color. All of the species of sea urchine spine represent protection.

Spondylus, or spiny oyster, shells are used to make beads in South America. Elaborate beadwork designs similar to later glass beadwork were created using these burnt-peach colored beads. The desirability of these beads made spondylus shells an object of trade and import between Ecuador, where it was commonly found, and the Incas in Peru. Spondylus shells also were used in Polynesia and New Guinea, where strings of them joined with a pendant formed a necklace called *soulava*. These were ritually traded in a ceremonial exchange called *kula* for another adornment, the Conus shell armband known as the *mwali*, which itself might also be adorned with spondylus beads. A variety of spondylus was also used to make the wampum beads of the Iroquois. These beads were woven into elaborate bands which contained the history of the tribe. These bands were "read" at ceremonies by the Keeper of the Wampum. Other bands were used as currency.

The Egyptian Trinity: Isis, Osiris, and Horus

by Denise Dumars

Trinities occur in many belief systems; in fact, the number 3 is considered magical in numerous contexts and cultures. For instance, ancient Egyptians worshipped a trinity that represents what we might call the "nuclear family" of the gods.

Horus, the hawk-headed Egyptian god, is the son of Isis and Osiris. The three of them together make up what is usually referred to as the "Egyptian Trinity." Mother, father, child . . . what could be simpler? But the mythology of this trinity is much more complex than one might think.

The legend goes like this. Ra, the Egyptian supreme being, is portrayed as a curmudgeon who withdraws after creating the universe. Two of his children, Nut, the sky goddess, and Geb, the earth god, wish to marry and have children. But Ra does not want any more beings to be created, and he says no. The couple appeals to their uncle, Thoth, the Moon god, who is also the god of writing, gambling, and academic subjects. He forms a plan in order to help them.

He asks Ra to gamble with him. Thoth requests that, if he should win, he would like as his reward permission for Nut and Geb to marry and procreate. Ra takes his challenge—and loses. And so the Egyptian pantheon is propagated when Nut gives birth to Osiris, Isis, Nephthys, Set, and Horus the Elder.

The Egyptian "Adam and Eve" therefore are Isis and Osiris. According to legend, humanity descends from the children of Horus, their son, and the goddess Hathor, a goddess of love, beauty, and joy. In fact, the representation of Isis nursing became the model that artists would use centuries later to depict the Madonna and Child. In general, Egyptians looked at their gods as a very closely interbred family. Isis is queen of both heaven and Earth. Osiris is the king of the new race of men, and of the afterlife. The myth states that Isis and Osiris were brother and sister. They were supposed to have fallen in love in the womb, and were considered husband and wife after they were born. Set was their brother, and Nephthys, Isis's twin sister, became his bride. But all was not well within the royal family. Set was jealous of his brother's kingship and schemed to take his place in the world. Nephthys pined for Osiris while her warlike husband schemed and plotted Osiris'demise.

Before his death, Nephthys, disguised as Isis, succeeded in seducing Osiris. She bore Osiris' child, Anubis, the jackal-headed god who became the god of embalming. Set and his henchmen assassinated and dismembered Osiris, scattering the pieces of his body where they believed they would never be found. Horus, therefore, was both born and conceived after his father's death. In time, Isis searched far and wide for pieces of Osiris's body and re-membered him (both literally and figuratively), but the one part of his body that she never found was his phallus for, according to legend, it had been eaten by a fish. But Isis is the goddess of magic; she was able to fashion an artificial phallus for her husband's body and thereby become impregnated by him. So, as in many myth systems, Osiris represents the sacrificed god who must die for his people. In this respect, Osiris is also a vegetation god, a god of sowing and reaping, and he is sometimes depicted with green skin as a symbol of this attribute.

When Horus grew to manhood he vowed to avenge his father's death and protect his mother from Set's wrath. He overcame Set in battle and delivered him as a prisoner to his mother. He asked her to execute Set for his crimes, but she declined, stating that to do so would make her as bad as he. And so the actions of Isis become an early example of "turning the other cheek."

It is very interesting to note that Isis, therefore, gives birth to a child by an absent god, which is relevant in its implications for another religion which was yet to come at the time of the ancient Egyptians. Plutarch gave us the version of the story of Isis and Osiris that we know today. Egyptian texts vary as to the details, so most modern books on Egyptian religion will cite or quote from his account. We do know that the afterlife was very important to these desert people. Perhaps because they lived in such a harsh environment, the idea of a meaningful afterlife was very attractive. They spent a lot of time preparing for it. Also, the fact that Osiris rises from the dead is reminiscent of later Christian beliefs. As Normandi Ellis says of Osiris: "His death and rebirth illuminated the path from darkness to light, from unconsciousness to enlightenment."

This left Isis as the major goddess of Egypt, and her worship spread quickly to many other lands. Horus and his wife Hathor populated the world. Statuary and paintings often depict Isis and the adult Horus caring for Osiris in the afterlife. But the major depictions of this trinity are often missing a figure: Osiris himself. It is the symbol of Isis with her child Horus that we remember, and which has followed us through the centuries as a powerful symbol of mother and child, and of life everlasting.

For Further Study

Budge, E. A. Wallis. (translation). *The Egyptian Book of the Dead*. Dover, 1967.

Ellis, Normandi. *Awakening Osiris*. Phanes Press, 1988.

Regula, deTraci. *The Mysteries of Isis*. Llewellyn, 1995.

Buffy, Summer Goddess of the Gym

by Barbara Ardinger

Although Witches are thought to be "large women in colorful clothing," the Inner Witch is really a buffed-up woman of mighty power who can step and stretch and pump and jiggle with the best of them.

All honor, then, to Buffy, girl of the golden gym, vigorous goddess of toned muscles and firm body. Buffy revs up our cardiovascular system and assures that the makers of leotards and athletic shoes will ever have customers. Younger sister to Nike, the Goddess of Victory over flab and fat, Buffy enthusiastically exhorts us to "just do it." Buffy is known to go the head of the workout room, and cry like a banshee: "Go for the burn," and "No pain, no gain." She bolsters us as we stare into the mirror and wonder who in the world that flushed and trembling woman can possibly be.

All honor and glory to Buffy, whose highest priestess is Jane and whose highest priest is Richard. Chant with her: "Step, kick, bend. Stretch, stretch, stretch. Tuck your tummy, squeeze your buttocks. Reach, reach, reach for the stars. Step, step, step!"

For pure vibrant energy and wondrous luxury, Buffy's Golden Gym rivals the healing temples of old. Let us follow our personal coach, and Buffy acolyte, lovely Sadistica, as she gives us a mini-tour.

"You start here," Sadistica tells us as she leads us into the locker room. "Just go ahead and put your clothes in this locker." She pretends not to notice that our leotard is a bit shabby. "The showers are over there. Now walk this way."

She leads us into a silent room filled with elaborate and devious machines of torture. "This is the weight room," she continues. "This is the place where the bodybuilders hang. Let me introduce you to our two personal coaches, Testostero and Pheroman. These guys will pump you up."

Shuddering at the thought, we move on. "Here's the aerobics room!" Sadistica says, shouting over the roar of disco music. "Classes every hour on the hour! Stair training! Kickboxing! Spinning! Discipline!"

Just as we're about to succumb to complete and utter deafness, she leads us into the sauna, where we see beautiful people sweating, then into the massage room, where we see another beautiful person being rubbed down. "That's Chirapsia," our guide whispers. "She knows how to locate every nerve in your body."

The beautiful person on the table groans. Sadistica smiles. "You won't believe how you feel after she's done working on you."

Sadistica leads us to the lounge-snackshop-gift-shop. "I just love it here," she confesses. "I love the smoothies and shakes and granola. But mostly I love the, you know, people you can meet here. They're all so fit and gorgeous."

Yes, indeed, it's time to shape up. It's time to meet new people. All honor and all that jazz to Buffy, goddess of the golden gym, goddess of the buffed-up body, goddess of glorious good health.

Buffy rules!

Goddess Magic

by Abby Willowroot

Magic, real magic, is all around us. We are so busy that we often don't even notice it. But the simple secret to noticing and tapping into magic is easy to learn.

Celebrating the Goddess is a wonderful way to begin seeing and exploring everyday magic. Goddess magic can also bring powerful visions and insights as it transforms your life. The essence of Goddess magic is learning to remember what your ancient ancestors knew—that is, to reclaim your birthright of wisdom and sacred connections to the power of the Great Goddess.

The ancient rituals and celebrations of the goddesses often involved oracles, seers, and others with psychic gifts. These specially gifted women acted as guides and heralds of the magic that was occurring. Their task was to make the community ready for the magical experiences they would share. Today we sometimes rely on professional psychics to help us see the magical situations in our own lives. However it is sought, vision and insight awaits you.

Your Own Rituals

Insight and openness are the keys to Goddess magic. Working with your own tarot cards, Goddess energy rituals can help you to be your own oracle. There are many good tarot decks that are filled with energy of the Goddess. Selecting one of these and using it daily will enhance your mystical abilities. The cards help you to look beyond the obvious and see more deeply into a situation. The more you practice with the cards, the clearer and surer your vision will become. The cards also help you to see that all things are more complex than they first appear to be. Understanding this complexity will help you to create powerful Goddess rituals and spells.

One very positive benefit of practicing Goddess magic is the deep sense of confidence it gives you. It is the confidence of knowing you are an essential part of the sacred cycles of life, that you are needed. You will experience the confidence of learning to trust your own inner voice. Your sacred place in the universe will become abundantly clear as you work with this powerful magic.

Triple Goddess Magic

There are many different types of Goddess magic. There is the initiating, dynamic magic of the maiden; the abundant protective magic of the mother, and the wise magic of the crone. Each one of these types of Goddess magic can be used by all ages. When you use this magic, you are calling upon the forces and wisdom of the sacred aspects of the Triple Goddess.

For powerful workings, it is often good to balance energies by invoking the Triple Goddess in all her stages. This ensures that your working will be blessed with clarity of vision and perspective. Generally, the powers and visions we possess are colored by where we are in the goddess cycle. If your age places you in the maiden stage of the cycle, you will bring different perceptions to a ritual than if you were in the mother or crone stage, and so on. No matter which cycle you are in, it is important to work to balance the energy so that the Goddess energy you invoke represents the clear wisdom and power of all three of her aspects.

Spells that call upon the Goddess in this balanced way temper action with wisdom, courage with compassion, and enthusiasm with insight. This is the path to the craft of the wise. It provides good groundwork for any ritual. Once it is done, you can call upon any specific goddess you wish.

The Goddess in Various Guises

The great goddess Isis is a powerful goddess to call upon for rituals of transformation and change. Calling on Isis for her special magic must be done with great reverence and an open heart. You can also call on Isis in matters of the heart and love. When calling on her it is good to use dark-blue and orange candles, though white candles are appropriate as well. In an Isis ritual, use an incense with a heavy, earthy scent like musk.

Hygeia is an ancient goddess of healing. Her special magic is associated with healing, cleansing, childbirth, and renewal. Hygeia is also a goddess who can be called upon for increased abundance and prosperity. When calling on Hygeia it is good to use white, green, or red candles. Your incense should have a light, clean scent—like pine, sandalwood, or similar.

Hecate is the ancient one of death and rebirth. Her special magic is associated with profound transformations. Calling on Hecate is done only rarely, but when she is invoked, special care must be taken to bless all and never hold negative thoughts. Hecate presides over the mysteries of all life. The candles you use should be green, black, or white. Your incense should be subtle and not too sweet-smelling.

Gaia is the Earth and protectress of all life. Her special magic is related to cycles, seasons, plants, and healing. Gaia may also be called on for new life rituals, and to understand the ways of nature and her creatures. Call on Gaia for rituals to heal the environment. And when calling on Gaia, it is best to do it outdoors, sitting on the ground. The candles used when invoking Gaia should be blue, green, or brown. White candles may also be used. Let the air be the incense of Gaia.

Luna and Selene are Moon goddesses, bringers of psychic vision. Their special magic is the gift of seeing beyond space and time. Call on them to connect with the ancients, expand psychic skills, and access the sacred flow. You can also call on the Moon goddesses for rituals to heal the oceans and waters of the Earth. When calling on the Moon goddesses use white or purple candles. The incense may be fruity or floral, but should have a light scent.

Kuan Yin is a goddess of mercy, protection, and compassion. Her special magic is healing and understanding through compassion. Her special gifts expand the heart and bring insight through all the senses. The candles used when invoking Kuan Yin are white, light blue, or bright yellow. The incense associated with Kuan Yin is light—such as rose, lilac or sandalwood.

These are just a few goddesses; there are many others you may choose to call upon. Whichever goddess you work with, it is important to begin with balance and prepare yourself for working with the powerful energies of Goddess magic.

Before beginning any magical working, it is important to take time to prepare your body and spirit. Simple preparations include a warm bath or shower, a short meditation asking that your intent be pure, a glass of water to enhance your psychic abilities (drinking water enhances psychic vibrations and receptivity), and a cleaning and blessing of the space where you will be doing your magic.

Goddess magic is available to you at any time. The blessings of the Goddess flow freely once you are in sync with her ways. Everyday, you have many opportunities to be in harmony with the Goddess, in how you treat yourself and others, and in the ways you speak and act. The more you live life in ways that match your ideals, the closer you are to accessing true Goddess magic all the time. This magic becomes a part of who you are, and you become aware of the world as a changing place, your positive energy and healing visions make it a better place. You have the power, if you want it, to become walking, breathing, living Goddess magic!

Myth of Cailleach

by Kristin Madden

Place names from Scotland to Wales, Ireland, and the Isle of Man recall the pre-Celtic goddess, Cailleach, whose name means "veiled one." Neither invasions to these lands by other cultures nor conversion to Christianity of people can erase our awareness of her presence here. After all, it was she that dropped huge boulders from her apron as she passed through the countryside, so forming the local cairns and mountains.

Cailleach has been known as the Old Woman, Daughter of the Moon, Daughter of the Winter Sun, the Hag of Beare, and even the Queen of the Faeries in Limerick. There is a story that she may have originally been a Spanish princess named Beara. Cailleach was a goddess of weather and winter. She raised and calmed the winds. In many tales, it was she that threw the thunderbolts. Her magic branch, also seen as a wand, staff, or hammer, brought snow and frost whenever it touched the land. This wand was so powerful that countless humans attempted to gain it through trickery or steal it outright. None were successful. Normally described as a crone, or hag goddess, Cailleach is often pictured as a fearsome old woman with blue or blue-black skin, one

eye, and sometimes red fangs. In Scotland, she was seen as a hag with bear's teeth and boar's tusks. Always dressed in gray, she was known to wear a plaid shawl over her matted hair. However, in time she has come to embody the Celtic triple goddess in stories that tell of her transformation into the bride at Imbolc.

Scottish folklore tells us that she hid her staff under a holly tree each Beltane and turned into a gray stone. It is said that if Imbolc is fair, she emerges to gather sticks for the fire that will warm her through a cold winter. If it is cold and wet, she stays in until Samhain and allows the summer to be warm. Some legends hold that instead of turning into a stone, she becomes a beautiful maid at winter's end.

Cailleach was the original spirit of Samhain. As an immortal being, she renewed her youth each Samhain. When all has been harvested, the remainder of the fields belongs to Cailleach. The last sheaf of harvested corn is crafted into a dolly, called the *cailleach*. This doll was shown publicly in some areas. In others, it was placed in an honored spot in a farmer's home for the protection of the community and ensure a fruitful harvest in the year to come. Alternate traditions fill the apron of the cailleach with bread, cheese, and a sickle, or feed her to livestock.

In Irish folklore, there were three great ages: that of the yew, of the eagle, and of the Hag of Beare. She was older than the oldest of animals, and she loved countless human men who would die of old age even as she became revitalized in an endless cycle, like Earth itself.

It is interesting to note that this ugly hag goddess is strongly associated with sexuality. In one story, she arrives at a home, begging to warm herself before the fire and is refused. A man named Diarmid took up her cause and convinced them to allow her in. Later, she climbed into his bed, and he allowed her to do so merely folding the blanket between their bodies. To his shock, she transformed into the most beautiful woman he had ever seen.

The hag is known to hold, and grant, power of rulership as well. In the story of the nine hostages, Fergus kisses the hag and is rewarded with sovereignty over Ireland just before she again turns into a beautiful young woman. In a story of the sons of Eochaid Mugmedn, five brothers set out on a manhood quest. They get lost and one is sent to find drinking water. What he finds is a frightening black hag guarding a well. She promises to give him water if he will kiss her. He refuses, as do all his brothers except Niall. Niall gives her a big hug and kiss. When he looks again, she has turned into an astoundingly beautiful woman that calls him King of Tara and vows that his descendants will rule after him.

As Mother of All, Cailleach was guardian to a host of wild creatures, including wolves, pigs, goats, wild cattle, snakes, and birds of prey. She tended her special flock of deer along the rough and rocky coasts. With this herd, she showed great tenderness and nurturing, bringing them fish and seaweed with her own hands when food was scarce. She guarded them against predators, both animal and human. In turn, they provided milk for her.

As the Mistress of the Wild Beasts, she is a shape-shifting goddess. In Scotland, she manifested as a crane carrying sticks in its mouth to forecast storms. She is commonly known to take the shape of an eagle, a cormorant, a gray mare, and a great gray stone. She is so deeply associated with the Earth that she may inhabit any boulder or mountain. She is similarly associated with water and wells. In a story from Argyll, she watched over a well at the summit of Ben Cruachan. Each night, she staunched its flow and prevented it from overflowing by placing a boulder over it. One night, she fell asleep and neglected to place the boulder. The well overflowed, flooding the valley, and killing everyone and everything in its path. The valley became Loch Awe and Cailleach felt her guilt so strongly that she turned into a stone.

Cailleach may be seen as the *bean nighe,* the fairy woman that is the washer at the ford, though this image is also connected with Morrigan. Cailleach was reputed to wash her cloak in a whirlpool at the end of summer. In this aspect, she is associated with the cycles of death, rebirth, and transformation as she washes the clothes of one that is about to die. One of her Gaelic names is the *cailleach-oidhche,* meaning "crone of the night."

Whatever the legends of Cailleach may have been based on, it is clear that her power and memory are as immortal as she is reputed to be. The land holds her name and spirit for us, just as the inevitable cycles of life do. Through her, we can come to terms with death and rebirth, remembering that we do not end with the death of this body. She reminds us that we each hold strength and magic, no matter our age. She is a key to the beauty and power of elderhood, something that has been largely lost to us in modern society.

Navel-Ring Charging Spell

by Ed Fitch

Although this ritual is intended for the navel-rings that are popular nowadays, it can be adapted for other pierced parts of the body.

On the night of the Full Moon, set your rite in a quiet and solitary place. Place an image of the Goddess in the ritual area, with a candle set before her, and a goblet or cup of your own favorite wine. You may add flowers and other offerings as you feel are appropriate. Place one candle each at the north, east, south, and west corners of the ritual area. Next to the northern candle place the card of the tarot Queen or Page (depending on your preference) of Pentacles. Next to the eastern candle place the card of the Queen or Page of Swords. Next to the southern candle place the card of the Queen or Page of Wands. Next to the western candle place the card of the Queen or Page of Cups.

Place your athame before the image of the Goddess and a small vial of olive oil. Also next to the image place folded a polishing cloth. Have music appropriate to your goals ready to play. Polish your fingernails and toenails in your personal power color. When all is quiet prior to your rite, bathe in a candlelit place, bearing strongly in mind that the water is cleansing body, soul, and spirit. Look frequently at your navel-ring as you bathe, and watch the glint of the candlelight on it.

Now, dress in raiment and jewelry that are magical to you, but which leaves your navel-ring open to the view of the gods. (Or wear nothing but your jewelry, if it pleases you and feels magical.) Start the music and begin the ritual.

Go to the north. Light the candle and strike a dramatic and magical pose to best display your navel-ring before the elemental powers, saying:

Powers of the earth, be with me on this night,
And give me your magic and power.

Go then to the east. Light the candle and strike a dramatic and magical pose to best display your navel-ring before the elemental powers, saying:

Powers of the air, be with me on this night,
And give me your magic and power.

Repeat with the south candle, substituting "fire" for "air." Repeat with the west candle, substituting "water." Then step before your image of the Goddess, and light the candle before her. Strike a dramatic and magical pose before the image, and say:

My lady, my sister, creatrix of all magic,
Be with me as I cast this spell of power and of strength.
And through this talisman of power that I wear,
Grant me the power that I draw from thee!

With the cloth, buff your silver ring, saying:
O patroness of beauty, fascination, and charm,
Imbue strength, power, magic, and wonder
Into this ring of power. Draw through it thy power,
That I may journey far and with your protection
in magic, in beauty, and in wonder.

The repeat thirteen times as you polish the ring:

Power of my lady, power be with me!

Anoint your ring with the oil, saying:

So mote it be!

Sacred Sites of North America

by Elizabeth Barrette

Shelves upon shelves of books extol the virtues of all the temples, shrines, fissures, mazes, holy mountains, and other such sacred sites that can be found in the far corners of the world. You could fill an entire library with tomes about Egypt, Greece, or Great Britain, yet the numerous sacred sites of North America remain largely uncelebrated. Well, I've been all over the western two-thirds of the United States, with a few excursions to Canada and Mexico besides, and I can tell you there's no shortage of magical and spiritual places to visit here.

Native American legend refers to this continent as "Turtle Island," my favorite name for it. Tribal cultures once populated virtually the entire span of the region, from Alaska to what we now call Meso-America. They left behind hundreds of constructs such as earthen mounds, and they created numerous myths about the sites. The European cultures that followed these Native ones have added to the structures and lore. There's quite a range of sacredness underfoot if you know how to look for it.

The Far North

Alaska holds the Denali wilderness, crowned by the majestic Mount McKinley. The highest peak in North America and the second highest on Earth, it measures 20,320 feet at the summit. Page Bryant, in her book *Terravision,* lists this place as an electrical vortex and sacred site. Denali has a powerful and fragile beauty. Northern ecosystems are very delicate, for life must struggle against the challenges of the climate and does not recover well from additional stress. Yet life persists here, even in the face of freezing temperatures and desert-level precipitation. It makes this an ideal pilgrimage if you need to meditate on surviving adversity, particularly the amorphous environmental kind, and appreciating small blessings amidst hardship.

Western United States

At Grace Cathedral in San Francisco one can find one of the most elaborate labyrinths in North America. A labyrinth is a single winding path, not a branching path like a maze. Although the cathedral itself is Episcopalian Christian, labyrinths are considered sacred in many religions. This one is open to the public. The church also carries out a fair amount of interfaith work, making it a comfortable place to visit for people of any tradition. Consider walking a labyrinth when you feel confused and need to find your way through the choices you face.

The Grand Canyon in Arizona is not only a national landmark, it is also a sacred site for indigenous cultures such as the Navajo, Hopi, and Havasupai. One of the more accessible sites, it offers everything from camping to mule trains and rafting trips. It also is home to Sipapu, the place of emergence mentioned in Hopi mythology; this site lies at the convergence of the Colorado and Little Colorado Rivers. *Terravision* lists the Grand Canyon as an electrical vortex, and Sipapu as a magnetic vortex; in other words, this place is a balance of masculine and feminine energies. The whole region

has a patient, timeless feel. Go here if you're tired of modern life's hectic pace.

The Black Hills, or Paha Sapa in local native dialect, in South Dakota mark one of the most sacred areas for the Dakota nations. *Terravision* cites it as an electrical grid. Within this region stands Harney Peak, historically a favored location for a vision quest. Today you can hike up a nicely maintained trail to the old fire-watch tower on the peak, and there are little niche caves up in the rocks too. You can make it up and down again in one day, or camp on top; I've done both. The forest is mostly Black Hills spruce, with a scattering of other evergreens and deciduous trees, draped with soft gray-green moss. The tall trunks feel like the pillars of a cathedral, and human sounds don't carry very far in the hush. It makes you want to whisper as you move through the trees. If you seek guidance through dreams, or a place to feel humbled by the presence of nature, go here.

Central United States

Among constructed sites, my favorite is the Baha'i House of Worship in Wilmette, Illinois. Surrounded by lush gardens and sparkling fountains, this nine-sided building evokes a deep and abiding peace. The white concrete of its walls is shaped into exquisite patterns, from abstract lacework to symbols from many different religions. The sign out front says "All Are Welcome," and yes, they mean that. The Baha'i faith is a true world religion that works and plays well with others, based on the idea that humanity is one. This is a wonderful destination for those of you who enjoy studying different religions. It's also the place to go if you ever need a direct line to the Creator, however you conceive Him/Her/It/Them. Sit in the seat directly under the center of the ceiling, and you'll be in the center of the most impressive energy vortex I've ever found inside four walls.

Mammoth Cave National Park in Kentucky holds the largest known system of subterranean tunnels and chambers in the world. The earliest exploration dates back about 4,000 years, and we still don't know the full extent of the system; the mapped portion alone stretches more than 350 miles. The park service offers a diversity of tours. Caves are sacred to many earth-based religions. Spelunking is a sacred experience like no other, from the breathy echoes to the enveloping darkness. If you seek the womb of the Great Earth Mother, you'll find it here.

Cherokee myths describe a wide variety of natural and constructed locations with spiritual significance. *Gahuhdi*, or "The Finishing Place," lies within the Cohutta Mountains of Georgia. Here, a serpentine rock wall winds along the southern side of the mountain. Two associated legends name this as the place where Groundhogs' Mother killed the Uktena monster and also where a hunter killed the Ustuhtli monster, both described as snakelike creatures. Consider this as a destination if you face a single, powerful opponent and want to cultivate your "dragonslayer" spirit.

Eastern United States

Carmel, New York, also known as Indian Rock or Turtle Rock, is an ancient ceremonial site. The main stone stands about thirty feet high, decorated with pictures of a sun wheel, an arrow, a bird, and a turtle. A large flat altar stone rests nearby. Like so many sites, its origin remains something of a mystery. We can infer some of the beliefs and practices of the people who once worshipped here, but not the details. Still, this site stands out as an important piece of history, yielding some of the more picturesque examples of Native American spirituality. It's a good place to go if you feel cast adrift and need to reconnect to who you are and where you come from.

Mexico

The southern region of our continent holds a scattering of ancient and interesting sites. One that I've seen in person is majestic Teotihuacan, at which are found a pair of blocky pyramids known as the Temple of the Sun and the Temple of the Moon. It's quite a hike if you want to climb to the top of either of these structures, but well worth the effort; the view is incredible. While the indigenous religions of this region were pretty bloodthirsty, they're also among the most colorful on the planet. At this site you can still see a lot of the splendid carvings and paintings that people made in the name of their relgions. The entire complex is vast, with various other structures and broad avenues you can walk along. This site has special appeal for people of Mexican heritage, but the solar and lunar energies are strong enough here that it is worth it to go just for these.

For Further Study

The Baha'i House of Worship offers a website with information about the faith and its sacred sites:
http://www.us.bahai.org/how/

Bryant, Page. *Terravision: A Traveler's Guide to the Living Planet Earth*. Ballantine, 1991.
Lists numerous sacred sites around the world, sorted regionally.

Cousineau, Phil. *The Art of Pilgrimage: The Seeker's Guide to Making Travel Sacred*. Conari Press, 1998.
This book explores the subjective experience of the spiritual journey.

Grace Cathedral has a website with a search function to help you find a labyrinth near you:
http://www.gracecathedral.org/labyrinth/index.shtml

Magical places of Mexico come to life on this website:
http://www.earthwisdom.com/mexico.html

The National Park Service maintains this page for Mammoth Cave:
http://www.nps.gov/maca/home.htm

Rossman, Douglass A. *Where Legends Live: A Pictorial Guide to Cherokee Mythic Places*. Cherokee Publications, 1988.
Details places sacred to the Cherokee people in Tennessee, North Carolina, South Carolina, and Georgia.

Belly Dancing, the Rite that Honors the Goddess

by Emely Flak

O n a warm, sultry evening somewhere in a busy metropolitan hub, someone plays some music with a Middle Eastern beat. Women dance to the music to celebrate their collective femininity and individual shape. Bare bellies shimmy, bare feet rustle across the polished wooden floor; the women take pride in their varied appearance. All of them are beautiful and resplendent in a rainbow of floating chiffon interspersed with noisy gold and silver accessories.

Such is a belly dancing class in an Australian adult learning center, the latest craze across many industrialized Western countries. In such classes, women of all sorts gather to dance and so rejoice together and reconnect to ancient goddess energies.

History of Belly Dancing

Although difficult to pinpoint its beginnings, belly dancing evolved from ancient spiritual movements that honored fertility. As the survival of our species relied on our success in reproducing, our ancestors devised rituals such as the belly dance to gain favors from the fertility goddess. The earthy, sensual movements are said to unite the body with the spirit of the Earth. This dance evolved into what the French named *danse du ventre*, or "dance of the belly," which was first demonstrated in the United States at the Chicago World Fair in 1896 by dancer identified only as Little Egypt. The Americans translated its French name into "belly dancing." We now associate the belly dance with Middle Eastern tradition.

This dance form has been labelled as obscene and primitive due its subtle and not so subtle sexual overtones. Despite efforts over the ages to eradicate this body-centered, exotic dance form, the belly dance has survived to enjoy a revival with many contemporary Western women.

So what is it about the dance that has attracted a high level of interest? Multicultural influences in Western society have enabled us to experience a diversity of food, languages, and customs. In turn, this has made us more culturally sensitive and less judgmental. It is quite common for diners to be entertained by a belly dancer on a busy night in most Middle Eastern restaurants. Meanwhile, growing interest in the dance has also been linked to the increased independence of women. Belly dancing can be seen as an empowering activity for women.

Details of Belly Dancing

Belly dancing is designed specificaly for the shape of the female body. The hips undulate in isolation from the rest of the body in a circular motion. The circle, a symbol of protection, represents the Great Mother Goddess in a tribal context. The hips move in the shape of the figure eight, making the movements hypnotic. Kinesiologists have recognised that figure-eight body movements that cross the center line of the body activate neurons connecting the left and right brain hemispheres. The dancer also isolates upper body movements, alternating with vibrating shimmy movements. Combined with the fluid actions carried out by the arms, belly dancing engages all parts of the body, including an internal massage of the reproductive and digestive organs. Belly dancing involves low-impact exercise, and it strengthens back muscles. Belly dancing is a healthy physical workout that suits women at all stages of their life. Furthermore, by dancing barefoot, the belly dancer connects with the Great Mother Goddess, with the Earth, and with nature.

This dance form has evolved over thousands of years and varies a great deal in the use of accessories. The props used, like swords, veils, candles, and even snakes, have magical and primitive roots. Some dancers use finger zills adding interest, color, and sound to the performance. Dancers apply their individuality and freedom of expression through their choice of accessories and their costume.

Even today, some traditions continue to recognize the fertility element of this dance. At an Egyptian wedding, the bride and groom often engage the services of a belly dancer. The couple place their hands on the dancers stomach to ensure their own bounty. Interestingly, the fertility aspect of belly dancing has also emerged as a useful exercise for childbirth. Fernad Lamaze, in his childbirth classes, recommended pelvic rocking movements, similar to those in belly dancing, to shorten the duration of labor and to ease the pain of giving birth.

In a culture where slim, emaciated bodies are promoted as the paragon of feminine beauty, belly dancing is an art form that reveres the curvy female contour. Abundance in flesh is considered a bonus and belly dancers of all sizes and ages discover and enjoy confidence in displaying their shape. Women dancing together create an atmosphere of empowerment and trust. Now studied and practiced as an art form, many belly dancers in Middle Eastern restaurants, cabarets, and functions are women who have discovered a passion in keeping this ancient dance ritual alive.

Lunar Ritual

by Jonathan Keyes

Way back in the last Ice Age, long before modern civilizations flourished, prehistoric man carved notches on the bones of reindeer and the tusks of mammoths to represent the phases of the Moon. It is hard to imagine the awe and reverence these early people likely had for the heavens and its cycles. Shamanic rites and rituals were performed in concordance with the movements of the stars, and although we know little of these early ceremonies we know they formed the basis of religious philosophies in subsequent centuries.

As civilizations grew, ancient cultures in Babylon, Egypt, and Greece studied the stars and observed correlations between the movements in the skies and the patterns of human behavior. The planets became associated with gods and goddesses, and elaborate rituals and ceremonies were held according to astrologically judicious times to honor these deities and seek good favor. Alongside these ceremonies, the folk practice of honoring the solar and lunar holy days developed as well. Solar rituals, known as sabbats, take place on the equinoxes, the solstices, and the midpoint days between them. Many of the sabbats are most well-known to us today in their Christian form—Easter has replaced old Spring Equinox celebrations, and Christmas has replaced the Winter Solstice, or Yule. Often sabbats are times when the greater community gathers together to celebrate, give thanks, and ask for blessings.

Lunar rituals also have a long history and an ancient association with magic, witchcraft, and spellwork.

Rituals with the Moon are deep and intimate. They are often done privately or with a small group of close friends such as a coven. Rituals according to the Moon are known as esbats. New Moons are associated with times of death and renewal. Waxing Moons are associated with strengthening, nourishing, and building energy. This would be a wonderful time to help someone who is frail or weak build and gain health. Full Moons are times of fruition and great planetary energy. This makes them a perfect occasion to conduct many rituals, cast spells, empower tools, and make magic. Waning Moons are a good time to let go, lose weight, kick a bad habit, and banish negative energy.

Along with knowing the phase of the Moon, it can be very helpful to know what sign and element the Moon is in at any given time. Each sign and element is correlated with particular themes. By knowing these themes, we can augment our magical work by performing a ritual according to astrology. For this article I will focus specifically on the New and Full Moon times for lunar ritual. The New and Full Moons are like the sunrise and sunset of the month. They represent times when powerful transformation can happen. The New Moon is the seed point of the month, when we can set intentions and pray for our plans to take root. The Full Moon is a time of abundant power and energy that we can work with to transform our lives. Here is a brief list each New and Full Moon, and their element and sign at the exact moment of the change in phase, for the current year (based on the Eastern Time Zone). A complete run down of Moon phase and sign can be found in any good astrological publication, such as Llewellyn's *Daily Planetary Guide*.

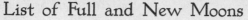

List of Full and New Moons

New Moon	January 2	Capricorn/Earth
Full Moon	January 18	Cancer/Water
New Moon	February 1	Aquarius/Air
Full Moon	February 16	Leo/Fire
New Moon	March 2	Pisces/Water
Full Moon	March 18	Virgo/Earth
New Moon	April 1	Aries/Fire
Full Moon	April 16	Libra/Air
New Moon	May 1	Taurus/Earth
Full Moon	May 15	Scorpio/Water
New Moon	May 30	Gemini/Air
Full Moon	June 14	Sagittarius/Fire
New Moon	June 29	Cancer/Water
Full Moon	July 13	Capricorn/Earth
New Moon	July 29	Leo/Fire
Full Moon	August 11	Aquarius/Air
New Moon	August 27	Virgo/Earth
Full Moon	September 10	Pisces/Water
New Moon	September 25	Libra/Air
Full Moon	October 10	Aries/Fire
New Moon	October 25	Scorpio/Water
Full Moon	November 8	Taurus/Earth
New Moon	November 23	Sagittarius/Fire
Full Moon	December 8	Gemini/Air
New Moon	December 23	Capricorn/Earth

Each time we honor the New and the Full Moon, we develop a relationship to the natural rhythm of our environment. Like the tides that roll in and out according to the Moon's pull, we have times of increased power and times when we feel less whole. Women have a more keen sense of this as their menstrual cycles and hormonal levels mimic the ebb and flow of the Moon.

Once we know what Moon times are associated with certain signs and elements, we can then formulate rituals that incorporate astrological factors. In this article, I will focus on the elements and their correspondences. When we conduct a ritual, we may have certain things we are working on such as finding a job (earth), looking for love (fire/water), increasing our creativity (fire), or assisting our health (all elements depending on the part of the body). In the table below, I list a number of correspondences between the elements and daily life.

Elemental Correspondences
Earth

Season: Winter

Time of day: Midnight

Holidays: Yule (Winter Solstice), Imbolc

Direction: North

Signs: Taurus, Virgo, Capricorn

Planets: Venus, Saturn

Colors: Brown, green

Physical correspondences: Stomach, spleen, bones, intestines, teeth, skin

Ritual objects: Stones, salt, drums, animal fur and figurines, plants

Associations: Work, nourishment, grounding, center, money, gardens and crops, stability

Air

Season: Spring

Time of day: Dawn

Holidays: Ostara (Spring Equinox), Beltane

Direction: East

Signs: Gemini, Libra, Aquarius

Planets: Mercury, Uranus

Colors: Yellow, sky blue, white

Physical correspondences: Nervous system, lungs

Ritual Objects: Feathers, knives, athame, bells, wind instruments (flutes)

Associations: Vision, sight, communication, language, thought, breath

Fire

Season: Summer

Time of day: Noon

Holidays: Midsummer (Summer Solstice), Lammas

Direction: South

Signs: Aries, Leo, Sagittarius

Planets: Sun, Mars, Jupiter

Colors: Red, bright yellow, gold

Physical Correspondences: Heart, blood, liver, circulation

Ritual Objects: Wand, candles, pipes, incense

Associations: Playfulness, passion, sex, self-expression, creativity, dance, joy, laughter

Water

Season: Fall

Time of Day: Dusk

Holidays: Mabon (Fall Equinox), Samhain

Direction: West

Signs: Cancer, Scorpio, Pisces

Planets: Moon, Neptune, Pluto

Colors: Blue, blue-green, silver

Physical correspondences: Lymph glands, fluids in the body besides blood, immune system, reproductive system, urinary system

Ritual Objects: Bowls, water, cups, cauldrons, shells, silver, bodies of water, sea creatures

Associations: Dreams, intuition, imagination, psychic work, trance, death, love, emotions, intensity, transformation

Setting up a Ritual According to Astrology

Setting up a ritual according to astrological conditions can be fairly easy. One way to do this is to honor current element associated with the Moon by putting out associated objects. If the Moon is in Cancer, a water sign, then use sacred objects associated with water on your altar or in your ritual space. It is helpful if these objects are personally meaningful; for instance, a picture of a nearby waterfall mixed with small sea creature figurines and a bowl of water can set the mood for a water ritual. Light a few blue or sea-green candles to encourage a peaceful atmosphere. Work on emotional issues, boundary problems, or immunological disorders.

The ritual space that you set up should be meditative and encourage transformation in the appropriate areas of your life. A ritual when the Moon is in a fire sign can add a needed burst of vitality, confidence, and energy. A ritual when the Moon is in an earth sign is grounding and assists in practical matters. A ritual when the Moon is in an air sign can help us connect to the community and speak from our hearts more clearly. Each Moon time is an opportunity for transforming our lives and strengthening our body, mind, and soul in a variety of ways.

To prepare for the ritual, take some time to clean the space you will be working in. This means literally sweeping the floors (if the ritual is done inside), taking out the trash, and arranging the furniture. Cleaning helps prepare a space for new energy and vitality to come in. Next, take a shower and put on fresh clean clothes as a way of honoring this special time. It can then be helpful to smudge or light incense in the space as a way of clearing the energy and preparing it for magical work. During the ritual, it can be helpful to honor the element that you are working by incorporating prayers to the element.

By incorporating astrology into lunar ritual, we add an additional tool that can be helpful for augmenting and transforming our lives. We connect to a tradition that is ancient and we integrate ourselves with the movement of the Moon through the zodiac that surrounds us. In the end, working with astrology and the cycles of the Moon will broaden and strengthen our magical practice.

The Monkey Man of India

by Sheri Richerson

According to probes by forensic experts and psychiatrists, the monkey man of India, which gained so much notoriety a few years ago, is nothing more than a "mere figment of the imagination of emotionally weak people" *(Times of India)*. But could this monkey-like creature with metallic claws be real and living still? After all, why would a substantial reward for his capture be offered if he weren't real?

The Story

In the first years of the millenium, there were 350 reports from the people of India who saw a strange, monkey-like creature. According to most accounts, this creature attacked and scratched many people. Evidence was presented of various wounds, and the nation began to wonder what sort of creature they had on their proverbial hands.

Today, we live in a world dominated by mass media that can travel instantaneously to all corners. Whether or not a story is true, a kind of mass hysteria can be created by an unsettling urban legend that is passed on via the Internet.

Prior to now, ideas and fears took some amount of time to sink into public consciousness. In practice, a story had to be repeated over and over again to sink in. Of course, with each story's retelling, each teller added his or her own thoughts to the original story. In a country overcrowded with wild monkeys, and a mass consciousness much more aware than before of threats to humanity, it could easily be that stories get blown out of proportion before we have a chance to check up on them.

These thoughts all come from rational thinking. Yes, I believe that a story, true or not, can put fear into people. We know that when facing something unknown, humans often exhibit a natural fear. An idea can be planted into someone's mind often enough that they begin to believe it is real. I don't know if this is the case here, or if the monkey man is an actual creature, but let's explore the facts. Let's take a look at the legend behind the famous monkey man, and you can decide for yourself if he's real or just a figment of an overactive imagination widely circulated over electronic media.

The Legend

As we begin this current tale of the monkey man of India, you must first realize that his story pops up every couple years. This in itself could be cause for much debate or even alarm—just what is it that makes him suddenly appear? How do the people distinguish the monkey man from the hundreds of other monkeys on the streets?

According to one source, "I first heard about the monkey man as a young child. We hurried to the local village where he was reported to be. When we got there, we saw that the monkey man was no more than a mere primate with rabies. He would go into a village and begin to attack anyone he could find."

Another local resident had this to say. "We were taking an evening walk when we walked into this huge man-monkey," he said. "The monster sprang up twenty feet from a crouching position and grabbed the branches of a tree and vanished before me and my children could even scream."

These accounts would explain certain common aspects of the tales. Rabies, of course, would easily explain all the bites and scratches. His superbeing abilities to leap and escape may explain why he can't be captured. Why then do so many confuse such a creature with a mystical half-human hybrid? Why don't the authorities do more to capture him? Or is it possible the authorities know more about this creature than they are letting on to a terrified public?

According to legend, two well-known monkey-man deterrents are light and water. These are the very commodities that the poor New Delhi suburbs can't get on a regular basis—due to shortages in plumbing and electricity—which allows for further speculation. Could the monkey man be a creature of political invention? Could this creature be a sublimated wish desire?

We may never know the complete truth behind this creature, as with Loch Ness and Bigfoot. Like these more famous creatures, the monkey man has been variously described as a kind of giant chipmunk, as a monkey creature, as a gruesome man, and as something approximating a bear. The only explanation for the various descriptions that I have is either we have a monster or an alien on the loose capable of changing shapes, or else the people who see him are so hysterical that they cannot properly give a description. The only thing that seems consistent in the description is that everyone questioned seems to agree the monkey man wears a helmet.

Many local people compare the monkey man to our Frankenstein, a hideous monster that was created by a mad scientist. Once the monster came to life he killed the man. The monkey man has run rampant ever since his first appearance, having free reign in the city wherever he appears. This can be traced back to the ancient monkey god, Hanuman, who was quite a mischief maker. Maybe the monkey man is the reincarnation of the ancient monkey god who is returning from the great unknown to take care of unfinished business.

Of course, there is also the Wildlife Protection Act of 1972 which allows the monkeys to have free rein with impunity from hunters or poachers. And in a country where Hindu ascetics put on tails and pretend to be monkeys, how likely is the real monkey man ever to be found?

Until the mystery is solved, the now all too familiar cry of "the monkey man is here" will ring out over rooftops at night. The headlines of the world newspapers and websites will continue to help keep this legend alive in the minds of people all over the world.

Butter Lamps: The Safe Alternative for Your Altar

by Dr. Jonn Mumford

A recently released MSNBC story on candles, details the environmental and personal pollution provided by some brands sold to the consumer. As the following excerpt, by Francesca Lyman, from January, 2001, details:

> No one ever mentioned the controversies over burning candles that have flickered in the news throughout the last year: That candles with lead wicks can give off toxic emissions. One study, by researchers at the University of Michigan, found that such candles give off emissions that exceed Environmental Protection Agency-standards for outdoor air. . . Don't burn candles with a shiny metal core in the wick unless you know it's lead-free.

Given the custom of using candles both for ritual and for ambience, I would like to introduce you to the use of magical ghee, or clarified butter, in lamps as an alternate source of light for your altar and other magical purposes.

Indian ghee lamps, often popularly called "butter lamps," provide a very pure, very nontoxic flame that make splendid focal points in magical ritual. Ghee lamps are perfect for use as altar lamps and are wonderful for romantic interludes as well. The flame is nontoxic and pure, and gives no smoke when properly adjusted. It also is part of an ancient magical tradition.

Ghee, or clarified butter, is a delicious, if choles-terol-laden, substance preferred for Indian cooking. Ghee is a semiliquid form of butter from which the water and milk solids have been removed by heating and straining. Indians refer to it as "liquid gold," and it can be bought at any Indian market in larger cities. (The recipe for turning unsalted butter into ghee also appears at the end of this article.)

The Lamp

Providing you live in a city with an Indian ethnic com-munity, it would be simplest for you to go to an Indian shop to purchase your ghee lamp, and the cotton wicks appropriate for the size and type of the lamp. There are two types of ghee lamps; one variety is a shallow *yoni dish,* in which ghee and a special cotton wick is placed and lit. These lamps may be made of brass or clay. The other type of lamp has a special wick holder in the center so that the straight cotton wick points upright, rather like a candle. In this type of lamp you can also burn grape seed or sunflower oils, both of which are, in homeopathic magic, sacred to Surya or the Sun. Think of sun-ripened grapes and sunflowers to see the reasoning.

Homemade Wicks and Butter Lamps

Since you may not always be able to find a ready-made ghee lamp, you may have to master the fine art of mak-ing a cotton ball wick on your own. Here are the accoutrements necessary for a homemade ghee lamp: a supply of ghee, a shallow metal dish (half an inch maximum depth, no more), pure cotton balls.

Note: I rushed out today just in case I was so out of touch with the real world that real cotton balls no longer existed. I had visions of finding only synthetic, teased plastic balls rather like cotton candy, but I discovered you can still buy real cotton balls these days. Just make sure the package says they are pure, 100-hundred percent cotton and nothing else.

Procedure

Melt a little ghee gently in a saucepan. Remove it from the heat and drop in a few cotton balls so that they become thoroughly saturated. Remove the cotton balls and gently squeeze the excess ghee out of them. Take care not to distort their round shape, then twist the top-third of the cotton ball into a point, leaving the other two-thirds as a ball-shape. The point, which will be your wick, should be no more than an inch in length.

Now, pour the remaining melted ghee into the metal container, and place the ball flush up against an edge with the wick extending horizontally over the side or lip. Brass ashtrays are ideal since they have ready-made lips to hold cigarettes. Otherwise, with pliers you can make a lip in your small metal container. Remember the dish must not be more than half or three quarters of an inch deep or the cotton ball may drown in the ghee.

Light the point, or wick, of your cotton ball, and a lovely flame will appear. When you get the knack of this, the lamp will burn on the altar for an hour or more—depending on how much capacity your container has to hold ghee.

Making Your Own Ghee

1   pound unsalted butter

Break the butter into smaller pieces and melt it over medium heat in a stainless-steel or glass saucepan. Stir to encourage slow and even melting of the butter without risk of burning. While stirring, turn the heat up and allow the melted butter to reach a gentle boil. Once it is boiling, turn the heat to low and simmer. Bubbles will rise to the surface of the butter, and a foam will gather as a crust on the top. You may skim this off, or leave it alone; these are milk solids which will eventually settle to the bottom.

Allow the butter to simmer until all the bubbles stop rising (which indicates the water has been boiled off), and you are left with milk solids on the bottom and hot, clear golden oil on top. Turn off the heat source and remove the ghee with a soup scoop or ladle, being careful not to disturb the milk-sediment on the bottom. Golden ghee is the pure oil fat left over after the water has been boiled out of the butter and the milk solids have been decanted.

Assuming you have a steady hand and the pan has a handle, you may gently pour the clear ghee directly into a heatproof glass or steel container with a lid for future use. Allow to cool before sealing.

Ghee is remarkable in that it does not become rancid and indeed will keep months unrefrigerated. Kept in the fridge, you can be sure it will last six months or longer. One very famous cook recommends freezing ghee to prolongs its life to a year or more. Ghee is highly valued in ayurvedic medicine as a restorative and a vehicle for carrying medications.

Ghee takes temperatures of up to 375°F before burning, and when used for frying it gives a rich flavor. Ghee is particularly good for cooking spices, as it encourages the release of the medicinal and culinary components of them.

The Japanese Festival of Tanabata

by Lynne Sturtevant

Tanabata, in Japan, is a time to focus on improving your skills and to ask for success in business and love. The holiday, also known as the Star Festival, celebrates an ancient legend known as "The Romance of the River of Heaven." The story is rooted in the belief that each star is an immortal being with the power to influence events on Earth.

In the story, Shokujo, the star Vega, was the daughter of the Celestial Emperor. She lived on the eastern bank of the River of Heaven, which we call the Milky Way, and she wore a silver gown embroidered with stars. She spent each day at her loom weaving fine silk kimonos for the many gods who lived in her father's palace. Shokujo was so devoted to her task that many knew her only as the Weaver Princess.

One day, the emperor told Shokujo it was time for her to marry. He introduced her to Kengyu, the star Altair, a handsome young cowherd. Shokujo and Kengyu fell in love so fully that they ignored their responsibilities. The cattle grew thin, and the gods face a lack of new clothing. The emperor demanded that Shokujo and Kengyu return to their duties, but they did not obey. They could not bear to be apart for even an hour.

Their disobedience enraged the Celestial Emperor. He summoned the lovers to his magnificent throne room and ordered them to live on opposite banks of the river. Shokujo and Kengyu could not hide their sadness. The emperor was moved by their tears and the depth of their love. He decreed once each year they could spend one night together. Shokujo and Kengyu thanked the Celestial Emperor, but they had little hope for the future. The days and months passed. The two lovers always thought of each other. On the seventh day of the seventh lunar month, a flock of magpies landed on the eastern bank of the glittering river. They hopped up to Shokujo as she worked at her loom. "We have come to help you," they said. The birds stretched their wings until they formed a bridge to the western bank. Shokujo ran across the backs and wings of the magpies to Kengyu who stood waiting on the other side.

The next morning, Shokujo crossed the magpie bridge again and returned to her weaving. Before the birds departed, they said, "We will try to help you next year, but we cannot fly through a storm. If it rains on the seventh day of the seventh moon, we will not come." As the magpies flew away, Shokujo began to cry. Her tears fell to earth as the heavy rains of summer.

This story has passed through hundreds of generations. Tanabata, the festival that celebrates the legend, today is a family holiday especially loved by children. In the past, on the night before Tanabata, children were given India ink, brushes, and strips of brightly colored paper known as *goshiki no kami*, or the "papers of the five colors." Each color represented one of the five elements: blue for wood, yellow for earth, red for fire, white for metal, and black for water. The children composed poems in honor of Shokujo, the Weaver Princess, then copied them onto the paper strips. They also wrote notes to Shokujo and asked her to help them improve their handwriting. The children also made paper dolls called *teruteru bozu*, or "make-it-shine boys," which they hung near a door or window before they went to bed.

On Tanabata morning, the children rose early to check the weather. If the "make-it-shine boys" had done their jobs, the weather was clear. If the dolls had failed and it is stormy, the magpies will not fly to heaven. Shokujo and Kengyu will not meet.

At sunset on Tanabata, the family moved outdoors. The elders lit paper lanterns and everyone gathered around a low, lacquered stand that held rice wine, pickles, cold noodles, and other lucky foods. A ceremonial tray known as a *sambo* was filled with

fresh flowers and burning incense to honor deceased ancestors. A spool of colored thread was always laid next to the sambo. Bowls of water were placed on the stand. When the sky was completely dark, girls dippped mulberry leaves into the bowls and gazed at the reflection of the stars on the surface. The manner in which the leaves curled predicted how soon they would marry.

Unlike many ancient festivals that disappeared as the centuries passed, Tanabata evolved. When the Japanese abandoned the lunar calendar, the holiday's date was permanently set on July 7. Children and adults still tie strips of paper to bamboo branches and set them outside. But not many people ask the Weaver Princess to help them improve their handwriting or sewing. One category of wishes hasn't changed, however. The Weaver Princess still receives requests for luck in love.

To make Tanabata strips, you need construction paper in the five colors (blue, yellow, red, white, and black); thread, ribbon, or yarn in the same five colors; scissors, glue, or tape, and a pen. Simply cut strips of construction paper, write your wishes on the strips, then tape or glue thread, ribbon, or yarn to the strips. Tie the strips to a branch or large stick, or attach them to trees or bushes outside your home. If that's not practical, tie the strips to a coat hanger and place it where the strips will catch the breeze.

To create the "make-it-shine boys," you need paper of any color; scissors, tape, or glue; and thread, ribbon, or yarn. Decide how large you want the paper dolls to be, then cut strips of paper twice that length. In other words, if you want the finished dolls to be four inches tall, cut strips eight inches long. Fold the strips in half and cut them as shown. Cut through both thicknesses of paper to create the sleeves of the doll's kimono. Cut through only one thickness of paper to make the doll's head. Fold the head up and attach a thread, ribbon, or piece of yarn as a hanger. Hang the "make-it-shine boys" with the Tanabata strips or display them separately in front of an open window.

Articles for Fall

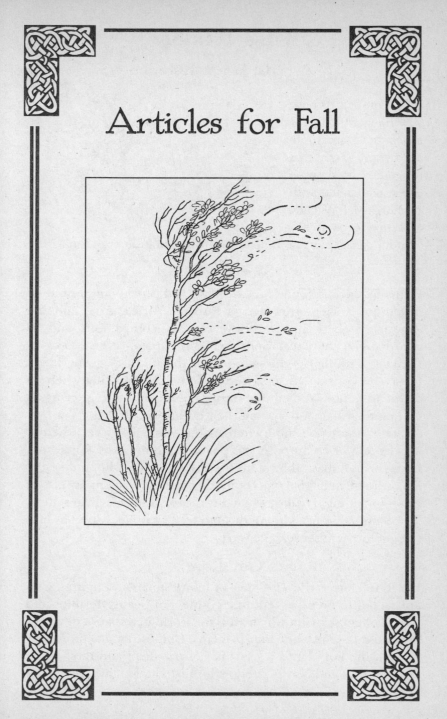

Feline Folklore

by Marguerite Elsbeth

Domestic cats have been with us for more than six thousand years, and in that time they have come to be associated with certain deities, Witches, and magic. Is it any wonder cats capture so much of our imagination even today?

Sacred Cats

Feline images are found on cave walls and carved out of stone in numerous ancient sites across Europe, Africa, Asia, and the Americas. These images show cats as companions and as guardians to the Great Goddess. Some images even show cats flanking a mother goddess figure in the midst of giving birth. Cats were considered so sacred to some cultures that when an Egyptian house cat died, the entire family went into grieving by cutting their hair and shaving their eyebrows.

Once there was a time when anyone who killed a cat, whether accidentally or on purpose, was put to death in Egypt, Rome, and Great Britain. Bast, the cat-mother, is a goddess who, unlike the fierce lion-headed Sekmet, embodies the benevolent aspects of cats—including fertility, sexuality, love, and life-giving heat. Twice-annual festivals are dedicated to Bast in her aspect as mistress of love and sensual pleasure.

Cat Lore

World folklore is rife with tales of feline spirits and figures. Cats are sacred to Freya, a Teutonic goddess of beauty, fertility, and independent sexuality who travels the world in a chariot drawn by magical cats. One of the four principal Chinese animal protectors is Shih, the lion. He is a guardian of the dead and their living descendants, and is associated with rain. The Mochica people of

Peru revere a feline who appears as a wrinkled old man with long fangs and cat whiskers. The medieval idea that the cat has nine lives, or that Witches may turn into cats nine times, may come from the ninefold goddess, an element of Egyptian myth.

The belief that cats can see ghosts, spirits, or fairies is found all over the world, and can be traced back to the Egyptians, who believe cats store sunlight in their eyes, and use it to see at night. Fears developed about cats in the Middle Ages because they were sacred animals to Pagan peoples. Cats—along with bats, owls, and toads—were thought to be Witches' companions who carried wicked messages and aided with spell casting.

Numerous legends tell of human beings who transform into the shape of a cat. Male wizards, magicians, and shamans may be gifted with this power, but usually the shape-shifter is a woman, and a Witch. In fact, Witches are said to shape-shift into cat form whenever the Moon is full, and good men were once advised to lay consecrated salt on their doorstep at this time, lest Witches compel them out into the night to join in their revels. Many tales also tell of men who shot a black cat in the paw, only to find the local Witch with a bandage on her hand the next morning. During the widespread Witch trials of Europe in the sixteenth and seventeenth centuries, cats were burned, hung by the neck, or drowned alongside their mistresses, for the above reasons.

The people of the British Isles believe cats are fairies in disguise, or at least are in league with the fairies. It is also said that fairies and ghosts can see through the eyes of cats, or that to look deeply into the eyes of a cat is to see fairyland. Cats alternate with the hare in legend as the underworld's messenger, and are sacred to the Celtic goddesses of the moon in the British Isles.

In certain areas of Europe and America, black cats are considered unlucky, while in other areas black cats bring luck, and white cats are feared. In Britain, tortoiseshell cats bring their owners luck, and in Russia blue cats bring luck. If a black cat crosses your path, greet the animal politely, and stroke it three times. Then leave the cat and go on your way. If you abuse, insult, or ignore the cat, no good luck will follow. An old saying about black cats is: "Whenever the cat of the house is black, the lasses of lovers shall have no lack." It was said that if the household cat sneezed

near a bride on her wedding day, she would have a happy married life. In eastern Europe a cat in the cradle foretells a safe birth, but a cat jumping over a coffin creates vampires. Also, while some people believe sleeping with a cat brings good luck and the Great Mother's protection, others believe that cats suck the breath of the sleeper, causing illness or death.

Cat Weather

Welsh sailors believe that a ship-cat's cry portends stormy weather; other sailors believe having a cat on board, or even mentioning the name of a cat, stirs up the wrath of the sea. In Indonesia, bathing a cat is one method of bringing on a rainstorm; in the American South, kicking a cat brings rain, or rheumatism. A sneezing cat means rain is on the way, and three sneezes in a row portends a cold for the cat's owner.

Meanwhile, a cat running wildly about means wind or a storm on the way; when the cat quiets down, the storm will soon blow over. A cat washing its ears foretells rain. When a cat is restless, and moves from place to place without settling, it may become windy. A cat sitting with its back to the fire portends frost. When a cat spends the night outdoors and cries loudly, bad weather's on the way.

Cat Dreams

While some believe real black cats are unlucky, black cats in dreams are lucky. Tortoiseshell cats in dreams mean luck in love. Ginger cats indicate luck in money and business. White cats bring

310

luck in creativity, spiritual matters, and divination. Cats with black and white markings indicate luck with children, or the birth of a child. Tabby cats mean luck for the home, and all who live there. Gray cats tell you to listen to your dreams. Calico or multi-colored cats bring luck with new and old friends. And two cats fighting in a dream indicate a looming illness or quarrel.

Bird Magic

by Jonathan Keyes

When we observe birds in the natural world, we immediately recognize their connection to the wind currents and the air. They swoop, dive, and hover in the skies and show us the power of their sight, their sharp instincts and multi-faceted talents in hunting, guarding, communicating, and nurturing.

Birds come in all shapes and sizes, with different characteristics individual to each one. A cardinal's beautiful red coloring reminds us of the creative and dynamic principles in nature and give us a glimpse at our own expressive and fiery qualities. A sweet yellow meadowlark sings its beautiful song and reminds us of gentle and cheerful energy.

Birds can be categorized according to their coloring, their size, their expressive abilities, and inherent nature. When we work with bird medicine, we work with a symbolic force, and we work with a transformational energy made manifest in the physical plane. As potent symbolic animal forms, birds can help us nourish our own internal strengths, and can lead us to a balancing of the parts of our nature that are lacking or weak. As a bodybuilder lifts weights, we can work with the wisdom and power of bird medicine to lift up our souls and strengthen our sense of clarity and balance.

Some Bird Ritual Ideas

Birds have the ability to shape and guide its feathers for maximum efficiency and allow the strength of its wings to carry it off the ground. When we feel weighed down and tied up in the confusions of everyday life, we can look to birds for the inspiration to lift ourselves up and to leave the mundane world behind through potent magical ritual. Birds give us a sense of transcendence and magic, because they can navigate the airy plane.

Since ancient times, birds have been revered and associated with deities. One primary myth is that of the phoenix. In Greek mythology, the phoenix was a powerful bird that rose from its own ashes after being burnt in sacrifice. This bird gives us a sense of the power to overcome obstacles. Furthermore, in Western religious lore, angels are seen as having wings. There is an ancient connection between the sky realm and heaven. Angels are heavenly messengers sent from above. There is often an association of the heavens and harp-playing angels up in the clouds. These connections give us a sense that the sky world is sacred and more pure and holy than the mundane earthly realm. Birds are our link to this heavenly world because they can soar to the heavens.

The air realm is connected to breath and oxygen. Breath is vital to our health. When we take the time to slowly breathe and draw in chi to all parts of our being, we are enlivened and relaxed. Birds can help remind us to slow down to truly draw in the air element. They help remind us that deep, slow breathing adds immense enjoyment and peace of mind.

Bird Medicine

There are a number of other ways to connect with bird medicine. Here are a few.

Observation: One way to connect with birds is to spend time observing their habits by bird watching. Birds have very particular habits and routines, and examining them can be marvelously entertaining. Even with binoculars, you need a keen sense of sight to see all the colorings and markings in birds. Overall, this practice augments our skills of patience, observation, and brings delight at the wonders of the universe.

Studying and Drawing: Once you have watched them in the wild, you can get to know these creatures more by studying in natural history books and by drawing them in a special notebook. This will enhance your ability to understand their powers and characteristics and how to incorporate these characteristics into your own life.

Feather Medicine: If you can, gather a feather from the bird you are attracted to. This will help solidify your connection to that particular bird. Make sure you find the feather or are given it. Some feathers, like those of the eagle, are actually illegal to own, so take care. Feathers carry the energetic properties of the bird. When you place the feather on an altar or a sacred place, it will remind you of the bird's medicine. Use the feather in rituals, and when you make prayers, honor the energy of the bird. Speak aloud its attributes and strengths. Make offerings to the spirit of this creature whenever you can. Offering tobacco, hair, or special herbs to the spirit of the bird; this is a way to give something back for the teachings and lessons you are receiving.

Birds and Their Healing Properties

Here is a brief introduction to a number of common birds.

Crow

Description: This highly intelligent bird is found all over the world. They are observant creatures that will work together in groups to scavenge food and ward off predators. They have an intricate communication system and domesticated birds have learned to count.

Properties: The crow is associated with magic and can be a powerful totem for exploring deeper mysteries. Its black color signifies the wisdom of the night and the Moon. Crows are also associated with death and transformation, and can teach us observation skills. Crow is also a protective totem for banishing negative energy.

Eagle

Description: This magnificent creature is one of the largest of the birds. As a bird of prey, it takes aim and swoops down on carrion, waterfowl, or fish for its meal. Eagles hunt with precision and spend hours soaring high up in the air or perched in tall crags and trees.

Properties: The eagle is a powerful totem for those needing vision, insight, and the ability to make quick decisions. Eagles encourage us to aim for our goals and achieve them. As large creatures, they help us develop confidence and help bring out the warrior in all of us.

Great Blue Heron

Description: These long-legged and long-necked water birds fly with grace and majesty. You can often find these creatures wading in water or sitting perched by a river bank or lake, searching for fish to prey on. Their sharp beaks enable them to spear fish easily.

Properties: Great blue herons are important totems for those needing more grace, beauty, and poise in their lives. They symbolize the dichotomous between delicacy and power, and they strengthen our innate wisdom.

Hummingbird

Description: This delicate and intensely swift bird likes to feed on the nectar of flowers and can be seen zipping madly from one to another. Its wing speed is unbelievably quick, and we marvel at the bird's ability to hover in midair above a bush.

Properties: This little bird is capable of finding the sweet nectar in life. If you are lacking in cheer and playfulness, the hummingbird can help you. It is also helpful for working with flower medicine and for increasing your vibratory level. If you are feeling dull and lethargic, hummingbird medicine will energize and vitalize you.

Owl

Description: There are many different kinds of owls, but all share the same nocturnal habits, the same deep-set eyes, and ability to swivel the head almost completely around. With their incredible sense of sight and hearing, they make great hunters, swooping and gliding down silently so as to surprise their prey.

Properties: Owls have long been associated with the Moon and the dark mysteries. When we want to explore the deeper realms of our unconscious, or study arcane lore such as tarot, astrology, or the Qabala, owl can be a wonderful guide. Owl can be an ally for doing rituals under the light of the Moon and is also associated with death and transformation. This bird is also a powerful totem for healers and shamans. Owl will help you be silent, watchful, invisible, precise, wise, and powerful.

Enjoy Bird Magic

The magic of birds can be powerfully transformational and healing. Through studying the traits of birds, we can incorporate their positive attributes into our lives. By honoring the tremendous power of bird medicine, we can be more in harmony with the natural world, and we can be inspired be these creatures of the sky realm.

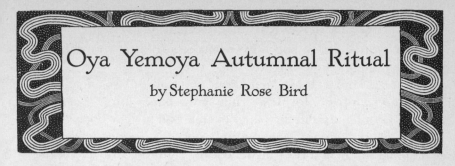

Oya Yemoya Autumnal Ritual
by Stephanie Rose Bird

Devout practitioners of Ife, a spiritual practice which began in Yoruba land in Africa and migrated to the Americas with slaves and immigrants, know Oya is not to be taken lightly.

As the orisha, or goddess, of weather and change, Oya is fierce and can bring unanticipated upheavals. Oya is patron of feminine leadership and strength. As an orisha of the air, she is capable of clearing spaces of murky thoughts and bad intentions. Since Oya is embodied by weather and edges, she represents the energetic forces required to transform from one state of being to another. She may be just the orisha to invoke as you shape-shift (mentally or physically) while giving up bad habits or during weight-loss programs.

To invoke Oya, build an altar. Start on a Wednesday during the ninth month or the ninth day of the month. Collect about one-quart rainwater from a storm, and find a tree branch that has been struck by lightning or was brought down during a storm. Clear a space in your office, studio, workout room, study, or library, and hang the tree branch by a purple ribbon over the space where your altar will be. Wash two plums, one smooth ripe eggplant, and a small cluster of grapes in the rain water. Place them in a copper or burnt-orange-colored bowl of ceramic or glass; place the bowl on top of a red satin or silk cloth. Set a glass of red wine on top of the cloth near the bowl. Put some of the rain water in a small black bowl on top of the cloth. Arrange all nine elements of the altar pleasingly. Come to the altar when you wish to invoke the orisha Oya. Greet her by saying:

Kabiesi! Greetings to her majesty!

Ask questions for the guidance or strength you need in your life. But be prepared, because you never know how Oya will answer.

The Bonfire and Elemental Cleansing

For this ritual, list the negative habits or attributes you which to purge using the following wording: "I am _____" (for example, "I am jealous," "I am lazy," and so on). Use a lead pencil on brown paper for this. Crumble the paper into a loose ball using both hands. Put the paper trouble ball in your pocket.

Next, build a fire using natural wood in a hooded grill or on natural sand near a river or the ocean. Light the fire, and recite as you walk in a circle counter clockwise:

As leaves depart all manner of tree
Autumn is time to purge what's lurking in me.
Oya, great orisha of swift change and weather
Help loosen the binding thoughts which are my tether.
Flickering leaves, migrating birds, and fire of orange gold
Lift from my spirits the ills that I hold.

Throw the paper trouble ball into fire with your dominant hand, saying:

Yemoya, Ologun, sweet Mother of Earth
Let your sweet waters speed my cleansing and rebirth.

Throw a bucket of saltwater onto the flame to extinguish it.

Oya's Whispering Winds Rinse

Oya represents the most dramatic forces of nature. The swirling of her skirts have been known to create tumultuous winds, fierce thunderstorms, and even tornados. Oya is also the orisha aligned with capriciousness, breeziness, and the powerful Amazon women of myth. Her bright spirit is most evident during the winds of autumn. At this time, you should enjoy the potent blend of flowers, herbs, fruits, seaweed, and ferns which encapsulate the magic of the harvest season; and the following hair rinse recipe will help you do so. Since Oya is the Nigerian orisha of weather, give the rinse a proper kick by using filtered rain-storm water. Pay homage to Oya as you set your tresses free.

1½ cups mountain spring or rain water (filtered)

2   tblsps dried maidenhair fern (optional)

2   tblsps dried slippery elm bark

½ tsp dried horsetail (shave grass) herb

1 tblsp calendula flower petals

2 tsps dried coltsfoot herb

¼ cup dried Irish moss (whole pieces)

2 tblsps grapefruit seed extract

1 tsp flaxseed, evening primrose, hemp, or safflower oil

½ tsp grapefruit essential oil

¼ tsp neroli essential oil

8 drops patchouli essential oil

¼ cup red grape juice or burgundy wine

Bring water to a boil. Add maidenhair fern, slippery elm bark, and horsetail. Cover; reduce heat to medium. Decoct for 40 minutes. Pour hot decoction over calendula, coltsfoot, and Irish moss. Infuse 30 minutes. Meanwhile, in a small bowl blend grapefruit seed extract, the oil of your choice, and the essential oils. Strain the herbal infusion over a bowl using a thin woven sieve. Add the grape juice or wine to the infusion, followed by the oil blend. Mix and shake well before using. This can be sprayed on as a leave-in treatment or used as a final conditioning rinse. This recipe makes approximately eight ounces of rinse; its shelf life is 30 days if refrigerated.

Golden Apple Goddesses

by Diana Rajchel

The goddess Eris threw a great curve ball with her golden apple. She chucked the fruit into a wedding she wasn't invited to, and so began a squabble between Aphrodite, Hera, and Athena that was the spark that set off the Trojan War. The apple, which had been marked "for the fairest," was awarded to Aphrodite, who had offered the best bribe to the judge, Paris. Paris, a shepherd, was given the hand of Helen of Troy by Aphrodite. As Helen was already married, this little incident started a war that eventually got Paris killed.

What about the Apple?

Mythologists such as Thomas Bulfinch have focused on the end result of the decision about that apple, philosophizing on what the Greeks felt men would do for love. But why, exactly, was Aphrodite the fitting recipient for the apple? In other tales, Aphrodite used golden apples to bribe a priestess she wished to swipe from Artemis, goddess of the hunt. Aphrodite reputedly hated to see beautiful women waste themselves in celibacy, and hated even more to see her powers dishonored. She often worked mischief on even the greatest of gods, either by herself or with the help of her son, Eros.

In another story, a young man fancied a dedicant of Artemis for his wife, but she was not a willing party to the attentions of any man. This young woman's father was a king. While he wished to indulge his daughter's desire to remain independent from men, he also needed an the alliances her marriage might bring. So, as a compromise with his daughter, the king said that she could run a race with her suitors; if she lost she must marry the winner. The daughter ran many races and left her potential mates lagging in their pursuit. The young man who set his sights on the king's daughter appealed to Aphrodite, and the goddess was more than happy to provide the man with help. She gifted him with one of her golden apples. During the race, when he pulled apace with his beloved, he tossed a golden apple behind him. The young woman stopped to pick it up, and he won the race and her hand. Aphrodite had disrupted this woman's life by planting a golden apple in her path, much as Eris disrupted the wedding party.

With a little imagination, we could picture Eris and Aphrodite asseparate aspects of the same goddess, much in the same way that Artemis, Selene, and Hecate were triple aspects of the Moon. Eris and Aphrodite both caused disruptive events; both provoked unexpected emotions and created unexpected events that transformed the lives of humans. Both had a certain puckish personality, and both seemed able to overrule the will of the most powerful of gods. Tellingly, both could claim golden apples as a symbol.

In some traditions of shamanism, in some forms of Wicca, and in Jungian psychology, Aphrodite and Eris would represent one aspect of the shadow self. Aphrodite absorbed the socially

acceptable attributes of the personal; she was beautiful, a mother and sometimes a wife, and she focused on pleasure and indulgence. Eris was the opposite. There are no extant accounts that tell of her appearance, but it is known that she lived to alter the best-laid plans, and that she is the source of vibrations that keep humor in the world.

A companion to the theory of the shadow self is the theory of the anima/ animus. Anima/animus is the concept that all individuals harbor some aspect of the opposite sex within their personalities. In Celtic and Wiccan-inspired myth interpretations, the apple represents the divine feminine, while the gold color of the apple would normally correspond with the Sun and the male aspect of divinity. When these elements are brought together, it could suggest a symbol of the male and female divinely combined, even within a Hellenic cultural perspective. The gold was a color associated with Apollo and the male gods, and the apple itself was a symbol of the feminine, the potential that leads to birth. In the *Principia Discordia*, the apple is a five-principled symbol called the Sacred Chao. It is considered a little bomb of the bizarre and sometimes serendipitous that lands upon a person, and, perhaps with the five points on the sliced apple's core in mind, the *Principia* claims that the elements of chaos occur in five steps.

The commonalties of both Eris and Aphrodite suggest the unified personality of the empowered sexual woman—particularly in regards to the shadow self in union with the social self. On the dark side, such a woman plays sometimes nasty jokes on rivals and enemies; on the brighter side, she is an unexpected delight that brings erotic fulfillment. She is the element of the unexpected, the love that happens while someone is making other plans. Both the Eris aspect and the Aphrodite aspect of the Goddess have positive and negative qualities, and each has qualities that would be assumed to be negative that can, in the right situation, turn out to be positive.

The multiplicity of personality aspects among the goddesses is the principle behind the worship of dark goddesses. Each person has within him or herself an aspect not typically considered socially acceptable. For instance, a person with Aphrodite/Eris traits might have a propensity for brutal honesty, a willingness to make a scene, or a tendency to tease and disorganize in the manner of either goddess.

Someone developing spiritually learns to embrace those "negative" aspects and apply them in normal life in a positive way. For example, a person who might have been intimidated by love partners in the past can tap into their Eris self, and start an argument in a restaurant, much to the surprise of the partner. While this behavior might appear on the surface negative, particularly in the chaos that might ensue, it changes the balance of the relationship by making clear to the abusive partner that there is a dangerous side to your spirit.

A person who wishes to explore these aspects of the social and shadow self could follow this simple ritual. Take an apple, some toothpicks, and a black and gold candle. Light the black and white candle, saying:

Light and dark are part of the same.

Take a moment to meditate on the apple. Hold it between the candle flames, and notice the parts you see, and consider the parts you can't see as you rotate that apple so that part is always cast in shadow. Say:

I turn my face and show the world
Another side of myself;
Aphrodite the golden girl
or Eris the wicked elf.

Take a knife, and split the apple in half. Pull out each seed, and consume the apple. Chew slowly, and savor the fruit. Meditate on the way you sometimes show the world one portion of your personality, and at other times display a different aspect of yourself. Save the seeds and put them in a muslin bag. Carry these as a charm when you need to draw on differing aspects of your personality in situations you find challenging.

When listening to stories of Aphrodite or Eris, remember that even love can bring chaos, and chaos, sometimes, love.

The First Kantele

by Therese Francis

The Finnish lays, or *kantele,* are sung poems that can each last for hours. The following is a prose version of the making of the first kantele. It does not do justice to the original poetry, though the charm for safe passage through the rapids gives a small taste of the poetry's style. Unlike English poetry, Finnish poems are structured and repetitious, and do not rhyme; all action is in present tense.

The Kantele

Old Väinämöinen finally finds the seven charms for his new boat—the charms for protection, speed, weatherproofing, and more. And on that day, old Väinämöinen sets out in his new boat, along with his friends of the Kaleva District, to North Farm. There they intend to demand a portion of the treasures from the magical *sampo.* He easily steers the charmed boat through the water, with the music of the sea in his ears.

The first day he steers through the inland waters, the next day he steers through the fen, and then on the third day he finds the rapids. He moves into the rapids, where the boat is caught up in the whirlpool. Fortunately, Lemminkäinen remembers the charm for safe passage through the white waters. He moves to the front of the boat to sing:

> *Stop, rapid, foaming,*
> *Stop, mighty water, surging,*
> *Maid of the rapids, girl of the foam,*
> *Sit down on a rock in the seething water*
> *With your embrace calm the waves*
> *Wrap the eddies in your hands*
> *Quiet the foam with your grasp*

So that it will not splatter on our chests
Nor splash on our heads.

He sings a sweet love song to the maiden of the rapids, enticing her to calm the waters for their passage. He entreats her to turn the rocks to moss, that the boat may pass over any danger unharmed. And as she is charmed, she does so. She calms the waters so that old Väinämöinen easily steers the boat through the water's course. He steers between the boulders and over the swells. He steers to the broad waters, never losing speed or getting stuck.

But just as Väinämöinen steers the wooden vessel out of the rapids into the broad waters, it grounds on something. The boat is stuck there in the water, even though it should be in open sea. Something solid holds the boat, refusing to release it.

Craftsman Ilmarinen and reckless Lemminkäinen stick oars into the sea. They are unable to move the boat. They try to pry the boat loose from whatever it is stuck on, but are unsuccessful.

Old Väinämöinen scolds them, saying: "You reckless sons of Lempi! Bend over and see what the vessel is stuck on. Is it a rock or a rotten tree trunk or some other obstacle? When we know that, then we will know what to do."

So Lemminkäinen looks under the boat. He says: "The boat is not on a rock nor on a rotten tree trunk. The boat is on a pike's shoulders, on the shoulders of the dog of the water."

"Well," responds wise Väinämöinen, "rocks and rotten tree trunks and pikes are all of the waters. Take a sword and cut us off."

And with that, reckless Lemminkäinen swings his mighty sword over the edge of the boat, down into the water. And promptly falls in.

Craftsman Ilmarinen reaches into the waves and pulls Lemminkäinen out by his hair. "Everyone is created to be a man, to wear a beard," he scold the younger man. The craftsman draws his blade from its sheath and, holding to the edge of the boat, swings the sword into the water at the pike.

The blade breaks into bits. The pike doesn't even notice. Steadfast old Väinämöinen speaks up. "There are not the markings of half a man on you. Whenever the need arises, whenever a man's spirit is called for, then your spirit is just so-so, your whole activity diverted elsewhere."

He draws his sword and swings it into the water at the pike's head. His sword gets caught on the pike's gills. He pulls with all his strength. The sword cuts the pike in half. The bottom portion falls to the ocean floor but the ribs stick to his sword. He swings his sword, with the pike ribs attached, into the vessel.

With the pike gone, the boats starts to move again. Old Väinämöinen steers it to an island. He throws the pike onto the land and asks who is to have the honors of cutting up the meat. Everyone on the ship says that Väinämöinen caught it, therefore the honor is his. So he does. Ten of the women from the ship have a cooking contest; the pike is so large they each have plenty for their dishes. Everyone eats heartily.

When the cooking and eating is done, Väinämöinen says: "This pike bone would make an excellent fishbone harp. Who here has the skills to make a fishbone harp?" But none on board have such skills. So old Väinämöinen takes on the task himself. He uses the pike's jawbone for the harp's frame, and the pike's teeth for pegs. He turns hair from a demon's gelding into strings. Now the fishbone harp is ready.

Many come to hear the new instrument—young boys, married men, little girls, and aged women. But each person that attempts to play it only gets squawks and sputters. None of the assembled can get a harmonious sound from the harp.

Finally, an old man asks the harp: "Why do you make this racket? Will the Finnish lays never again be sung beautifully?"

And the fishbone harp replies, "I will only play for the

one that made me. No other may hear my luscious sounds under his fingers."

Tthe assembled call to Väinämöinen to take up the harp he has made, to entice music from its strings. So he takes up the kantele and runs his fingers across the strings. A beautiful melody fills the air. Joyous noise surrounds the area. The animals and fish and birds assemble to hear the wondrous song. Väinämöinen sings, and every thing is enchanted.

So pure is the tone of the fishbone harp that tears stream from all the eyes of the listeners, and even the singer himself. Large drops build up on his face, then fall to the ground and roll to the sea. They fall through the clear waters into the black ooze. At last, old Väinämöinen speaks: "Can any of the assembled young men, the handsome youths, gather up my tears from under the clear waters? I will give a birdskin-lined fur coat to any that can gather my tears back to me."

But none of the assembled men can gather the tears from the blue, clear waters.

A raven comes forward. Väinämöinen says: "I will give you a birdskin-lined fur coat if you can gather my tears from the clear waters and return them to me."

The raven dives into the water, but cannot gather the tears. A blue goldeneye swims up the Väinämöinen. Again the old man says: "I will give you a birdskin-lined fur coat if you can gather my tears from the clear waters and return them to me."

The goldeneye dives deep under the clear waters and into the black ooze. He gathers the tears. He brings them to Väinämöinen's hand. They have already changed to other things. They have grown into beautiful things, swelled up as pearls the color of bluish fresh-water. They are now blue pearls to honor any king, to be an everlasting joy for rulers.

Steadfast Väinämöinen returns to the vessel, the well-charmed skiff. Old Väinämöinen continues his journey to North Farm.

And that is another song to be sung another day.

Magical Ways to Chop Firewood

by Roslyn Reid

There's an old saying in the back country that wood warms you twice—once when you burn it, and before that once when you chop it.

Long ago in a land called New Jersey, I was one of many apartment-dwelling Pagans who celebrated the fire festivals with candles. Then I moved to a house with a real fireplace. Great, I thought, now we can do Yule and Beltane properly, sitting on the floor and toasting the Goddess next to a cozy, roaring wood fire... Any of you Pagans who already have a fireplace know I had a lot to learn.

Unless your first fireplace is gas or electric, there is much to know. First and foremost, you will discover that firewood

does not come cheap. Presplit firewood, which burns well, is in high demand, and therefore costs dearly. And contrary to what you might think, you can't save money by buying firewood out of season—it's no cheaper in the summer than in the winter. This is because wood needs to season, or age, for around a year before it is considered optimal heating fuel. Consumers have to pay for the cost of this time, or else who will?

The only real bargains to be found on firewood are unsplit wood, unwanted trees, and green wood, which is fresh and unseasoned. Green wood is cheap or free because it can contain as much as 65 percent moisture;

therefore it will actually need to consume heat to burn rather than producing heat of its own. Even cheap, green wood is a bad deal if you have nowhere to let it sit and age.

Although I recommend buying wood already split, unsplit firewood can be had at, pardon the expression, fire-sale prices, sometimes even free. At our house, it seemed like trees and parts of trees suitable for burning were falling down in the yard all the time, although most freshly fallen trees are green wood. Also, the parks in this area open up once a year for residents to take out downed trees or to cut down dead trees for firewood. The wood is free; but again, you must split it yourself.

If you decide to go the cheap route, first make sure you know what you're getting into—you will need to be in good shape to handle heavy pieces of wood. To give you a better idea of the intense physical labor involved, boxing champion George Foreman says that chopping and hauling firewood is his best workout. Acquiring a chainsaw may a good idea, though it is a very dangerous tool. In any case, you will still need an axe for splitting small logs, along with a maul, and possibly an adze. The maul is necessary for splitting larger chunks of wood into a usable size. The adze is used for splitting off thin kindling-sized pieces, which are needed to start a fire.

The high moisture content in green wood keeps it from falling apart easily, so it can be difficult to split. Although firewood ages faster when split, it's also easier to split when it's aged—so you can't win. Properly aged wood produces a ring when struck. A thud indicates the wood is not dry enough and needs more aging. Cultivate an ear for the right sound.

The lesson to be learned is that the Goddess is always ready to help you by letting nature take its course. Wood starts to split naturally when it dries, and you will observe fine cracks radiating from its center at that time. If you don't see them, put it back on the woodpile and wait a little longer—patience is a great virtue when it comes to dealing with wood. When the time is right, take your maul or wedge and look for a good strike spot on the wood. Start with the biggest crack—one good whack is usually all it takes.

And speaking of the Goddess, here is where the Pagan method of chopping wood comes in. What's different about it? Well, you will soon learn the truth of the old adage that nothing is as easy as it looks. The actual woodchopping process begins before you ever touch a piece of wood. First you must determine just who the head forest deity is in your area. Do a little ceremony of your choice near the woodpile some evening to meet up with the deity. In some areas it may be possible to discover the names of local deities, and even what they may have looked like, by doing historical research at the library.

Next comes the blessing of your tools. Take your axe, maul, and adze—and the chainsaw, for that matter—cast a circle, and place them inside. Consecrate them to the Lord or Lady of the Forest according to whatever procedure you currently use. One may even carve or write sacred text, such as runes, on their handles of the tools if so desired. On metal-handled tools, these can be scratched in with a pin.

You are ready to start splitting the wood, though you must perform an incantation to the forest deity every time you chop. In the old days, one customary practice was sacrificing a fowl to the fallen tree. These days, when most fowl comes from the supermarket, this would be meaningless. For modern Pagans, an incantation to the deity will suffice. I have never found it necessary to go as far as casting a circle and calling the deity inside; but if this works better for you, by all means do it.

If ever you forget your incantation, you will find yourself expending great effort for very little return. My favorite incantation for chopping wood is: "O Great Lord of the Forest, guide my arm!" You should notice the difference right away. In addition, be sure to ask for protection from the deity, though wearing safety gear, such as goggles, gloves, long pants, and sturdy boots can help. (Note: Do not wear safety gloves when using a chainsaw, as this is actually more dangerous than using your bare hands.)

Oh, and it would be a nice touch to offer something to the fire your deity helped create.

Durga's Story

by Natalie Harter

Once, many years ago, the world was frozen in crisis. Demons ran rampant, destroying everything in their path. The defeated gods took refuge in the Himalayas and waited for a miracle. But they knew a time had been foretold when demons would wreak havoc upon the world, and that only a woman could vanquish them. They cowered in hopelessness.

In time, the goddess Durga heard the troubled cries of the gods, and emerged in the midst of the battleground, riding atop a fierce lion, armed with weapons in each of her ten hands. She had come to fight the great demon Mahisasura and his legions. Her battle cry shook the earth, and she waged war against the demons for many days. With each sigh from the goddess, hundreds of female warriors rose to her aid. Finally Durga was triumphant, and Mahisasura seemed defeated.

But killing a being of such power is not easy, and Mahisasura assumed the form of a ferocious buffalo demon and returned to battle. Each time he was slain by the hand of the goddess, he reappeared in a form more terrible than the one before. And at last, Durga cut off his head. Assuming her victory, the gods gave their thanks, and she returned from whence she came.

Shumba, the lord of the demons, set off with his younger brother, Nishumba, fast in search of Durga, not intending to set to war with her, but rather to seduce her. Shumba asked that Durga be his bride, but she replied that she had taken a vow in her youth to only marry the one who could defeat her in battle. Enraged, Shumba and Nishumba waged yet another war against Durga, but as always, she was difficult to defeat. Upon hearing that Shumba asked some of his evil legions to drag her to him by the hair, Durga's face grew black as night, and the goddess Kali emerged from her forehead. Kali vanquished every demon in her sight, and met their appetite for destruction with her own. Defeat seemed at hand, but the demons had one last weapon to deploy.

The demon Raktabija was the last remaining, but he had a hideous advantage, for each time he shed a drop of blood, a thousand more demons stood ready for battle. Kali, in all her fierceness, licked up every last drop of Raktabija's blood until nothing remained. Eventually, Nishumba was killed and only Shumba was left. Still arrogant, Shumba challenged Durga to fight him alone, without her warriors at her side. At this challenge Durga rode out to Shumba astride her lion alone and engaged him in what was to be the final battle. Time stood still as Durga and Shumba fought, and while the battle was horrific, in the end, the goddess pierced the demon's heart with her dagger, and victory was finally hers. The prophecy was fulfilled, and the world returned to the joyous place it once had been.

Durga's Festival

The story above comes from the Devi-Mahatmya, a classical Sanskrit text comprised of seven hundred verses that tell of the greatness of the goddess. It is in honor of this story, and of Durga's triumph over the demons, that the people of Nepal celebrate their annual festival, Dasain, or Durga Puja. This ten-day festival of thanks to the goddess is marked by gifts, prayer, and theater. The color red pervades the holiday, visible in the tika powder used for blessing, the hibiscus flowers offered to the goddess, and the blood shed in her honor. Blood sacrifice is still common practice for many Hindu holidays, but nowhere is it more present than at Dasain. Beginning on the New Moon in October, and continuing for nine nights, Dasain's magnitude is comparable to Christmas in the West, though its sentiment is more similar to Thanksgiving. It is a harvest festival and a time of sacrifice to recharge the universe.

On each day of Dasain the temples are crowded at dawn and dusk, and in the evening masked dancers perform the story of Durga's victory in the three cities of Kathmandu, Patan, and Bhaktapur. On the first day of the festival, Ghatasthapana, which means "preparing the sacred jar," people construct altars to Durga and plant grain seeds in small containers. On the eighth evening, Kalratri, or "black night," the festival reaches a climactic point as the great blood sacrifices commence. Every family that is able sacrifices an animal to Durga, the most favorable sacrifice being a black male goat. Priests slaughter water buffalo in temples at night, and the sacrifices continue through the ninth day. Motorcycles, taxis, and even the noses of each of the planes in the Royal Nepal Airlines are sprinkled with sacrificial blood. On the tenth day, Vijaya Dasain, or the "day of victory," the household shrine constructed on the first day is opened and the sprouted grain is given as a symbol of abundance. Tika, a sticky substance made of dry rice, yogurt, and red powder is applied to the forehead in blessing. Families dress in new garments and visit relatives, and many line up at the palace to receive tika from the royal family.

Durga's Message

Like many Hindu gods and goddesses, Durga is contradictory. Her name, translated, means "one who is difficult to know." She is both divine mother and warrior queen. She is personifies wisdom, knowledge, and memory, and embodies the powers of the gods. She is one of the most revered aspects of shakti, the divine female energy.

Durga's story, over fifteen hundred years old, will be timely and relevant as long as hatred and selfishness run rampant in our world. Durga is able to finally defeat Shumba when she does two things: when she stands united, absorbing all her aspects back into herself, and when she pierces his heart. The path to victory is not a traditional one, as mere force will not suffice. It is only by opening the emotive center of the demon that she succeeds.

We can call upon Durga's energy, her shakti, when we need to rise above the demons in ourselves, and to withstand them in others. After her triumph, Durga vowed that if the world was ever again in danger of destruction she would return. When that day comes the people will surely shout "Jai ma," or "Victory to the mother," just as they do every night of Dasain.

Wicca in Brazil

by Mavesper Ceridwen

With the publication of the first translation of books on Wicca into Portuguese, the craft is growing noticably today in Brazil. There are thousands of Brazilians hungry for information, many of whom will adopt Paganism as their spiritual path.

The speed of the growth of Wicca in Brazil makes us ask: Why does this spiritual path, of European origins, with so many traditions developed by Americans, attract so many Brazilians?

This question is intriguing, especially considering that Brazil is known for several African-based religious traditions similar to many forms of Paganism. Nevertheless, the answer is not simple. In fact, Brazil is not a country of many living Pagan religions—Umbanda, though this is strongly influenced by Christianity; Candomblé, based on African traditions; and indigenous religious systems (as is more fully explained on page 242 in this edition of the *Magical Almanac).*

Wicca, however, with its tradition of living the sacred day by day, its eschewing of hierarchies, and integration with nature, is an attractive alternative to the dominant Catholicism of the counrty, even as it hearkens to the hidden spiritual traditions of the country. In Brazil, Wicca attracts people who have never been comfortable with patriarchal religions.

Furthermore, though Brazil is a diverse country and there are many races, in actuality it is rare to find a Brazilian who also does not have European roots. So it is not so odd to think that Brazilians may be attracted to a spiritual practice that calls on the traditions of witchcraft in Europe. Actually, in Brazil, just as the races have learned to coexist in relative peace, so do Brazilians easily adapt the gods and goddesses of other cultures to their own spiritual practice. For us, Brazilians, African gods are just as responsive and worthy of our worship as those of the Celtic, Egyptian, Indian, or Japanese.

I do not believe that practicing Wiccans in Brazil needs to question which pantheon to adopt. The pan-cultural posture is appropriate and seems natural to our cultural mores. Wicca is not a religion of North Americans or Europeans. Wicca is the religion of the whole Earth; the Goddess ignores the geographical and linguistic barriers. To practice Wicca in Brazil is the same as anywhere. Wicca is a universal religion.

Still, there are some barriers. Brazilian Wiccans need more information in order to know the foundations of Wicca enough so that we can find our special form of practicing it. We live now in a state of discovery, which require constant reflection. Our priority should be to recover the religiosity of our land, and adapt it to new spiritual practices. Many of us already study the goddesses and native Brazilian shamanism. These won't substitute an appreciation for Hecate, Brigit, or Yemanja in many hearts of Brazilian Witches, but will add to our understanding, and deepen our worship, of the various guises of the Goddess and her consort.

As well, we are also creating, through initiatives such as Abrawicca—the Brazilian Association of Wiccan Philosophy and Religion—an atmosphere of support to those interested in the Goddess's path. Already, hundreds of Wiccans have met at monthly public events, exchanging Pagan art, celebrating group rituals, sharing information in lectures and study groups, and generating circles and covens. From our participation in those activities, we are beginning to feel that we are part of a great world-wide Pagan community, increasing our conscience of what really means to belong to the Goddess's path.

To express how many of us feel about being Witches today in Brazil, I share with you the following blessing.

I Am Pagan in Brazil Today

I am Pagan in Brazil today and I live the Goddess's religion in love and honesty, walking and learning how to flow with the rhythms of nature. I try to live in beauty, so that beauty wraps me up. I know the Goddess and each day I understand her a little more, knowing this task fills my life with purpose and wealth. I meet the Goddess in each person's face who crosses my road, no matter who they are.

I am Pagan in Brazil today and my body hurts with every story of polluted water and forest, mistreated animals, and inhumane actions. I know the Moon in my own blood, even when the clouds hide it in the sky. I live the cycles of nature, and I celebrate the ancestral dates. I dance, I sing, and I commemorate the sabbats. I never stop smiling at each of the mysteries.

I am Pagan in Brazil and I use magic to improve my life and of others, learning from my mistakes and recognizing the universe as a miracle. I know the several worlds and learn the lesson of the cycles. I struggle to know myself, to welcome what I can integrate, to know the Dark Goddess in my life and learn to love her. As a Pagan, I also see the collective shadow of our nation. As a Pagan, I am nonconformist, universal, and a fierce defender of freedom. I am aware of the importance of defending the right of whomever thinks different from me.

I am a Pagan in Brazil and I watch uneasily as our religion becomes better known. I fight against ignorance, instructing all who are interested in Witchcraft about its truths. I hold that we are regular people, with regular lives, and are not mere diversion for spectators. I admire who stays faithful to the path even when facing difficulties.

I am an urban Witch who discovers nature in the most unusual places. I dance in parks. I look for the forest, the savannah, and the beach. I refuel my energy in the nature and I grant power to everything that surrounds me, making everything I do alive with my magic.

I am Pagan in Brazil, part of a growing movement of like-minded people who come to their practice in love and honor. I know the breathing of each living being of this planet, and the pulsation of each star beyond, beats in the rhythm of my heart, because I know that the Goddess is all life and every love, and I am hers and she is mine.

Making Your Own Magic Inks

by Laurel
Nightspring
Reufner

The use of ink dates back at least two thousand years, as traces of inks have been found among the ruins of ancient Chinese and Egyptian civilizations. Ink also has used in ancient magical ritual. In fact, most ancient magical treatises contained information relating to inks, their creation, and purification.

One early magical ink recipe used oak galls and iron (from iron nails.) Unfortunately, this is an acidic combination that will eat through paper over time.

There are different types of inks, but the following categories are entirely my own. Natural inks are the easiest to make, using mainly household ingredients. Pigments are composed of insoluble powders that are mixed with water or an oil to make a paint or ink. They are more labor intensive, but still use mainly natural ingredients. And finally, there are the commercial colored inks, usually made with dyes rather than pigments.

Natural inks are made from a variety of materials. You will have many ingredients on hand, and need to purchase only a few. Vinegar will help preserve your ink's color, but makes the ink slightly acidic. Salt helps preserve the mixture and adds a bit of magical protection. Gum arabic is a binding agent that will help thicken inks. Add it a little at a time. Use distilled or filtered water if at all possible.

Lampblack Ink

Lampblack

Water

Gum arabic

To make lampblack, you'll need a candle, a small container, a small card, and a spoon. The process will discolor the back of your spoon somewhat, so use one you don't mind ruining. Light the candle and hold the bottom of the spoon directly in the flame—after a few seconds you'll notice a black, sooty buildup. Using the card, scrape the soot off into the container and repeat the process. It takes some patience to get enough for a decent amount of ink. Once you're satisfied with the amount of lampblack you've collected, take a dropper and add hot water one drop at a time. Mix until the soot dissolves. Now add gum arabic a bit at a time until you reach an optimal consistency. Store in a small tightly closed bottle.

Walnut Shell Ink

12   walnut shells broken into very small pieces

1   cup water

1   tsp vinegar

Place the walnut shells and water in a ceramic or glass saucepan. Bring to a boil, then reduce heat, letting it simmer for about 30 minutes. Turn off heat and allow to sit overnight. Add vinegar. Store your ink in a small bottle in the fridge, shaking vigorously before each use. It will keep for several weeks before spoiling.

Berry Ink

½   cup berries

½   tsp vinegar

½   tsp salt

Mash berries through a strainer to juice them. Add the vinegar and salt. Some good berries to try include strawberries, blueberries, blackberries, elderberries, hollyhocks, and sloes. By experimenting with the type of berry used you can achieve a variety of colors. This ink does not last long, so you will need to make small batches. If you want to have berry inks through the year, try using your freezer to preserve the colors. Simply juice your desired colorant and freeze in ice cube trays. Once the cubes have set, simply pop them out into freezer bags and label with the contents and date. Later when you want a special summer ink, just thaw a couple of cubes, bring to room temperature, and add the rest of the ingredients.

Pigment Drawing Ink

Pigment inks are more complex and more expensive to make, but for a special spell, ritual, or writing, you can't beat them. Pigment powders are made up of special rare earths, clays, chemicals, or stones allowing you to incorporate stone and earth magic into your spells and rituals.

    ½ cup gum arabic

    1 cup water

    Powdered pigment

Mix the gum arabic with the water and allow to soak overnight. This will form the binder. Either use hot water initially or gently heat in a double boiler to allow the gum to more easily dissolve. When ready to make the ink, place the pigment in a glass bowl or nonporous surface, and add enough of the binder solution to the pigment to make a thick paste. Mix well. Put the paste into a small bottle. Note: Some of pigment powders can be hazardous to your health if inhaled, so use a face mask to keep you from breathing the powder. Most catalogs can give you more specifics for whichever pigment you purchase.

To write with your new inks, use either a small, fine-bristled brush or a pen. A good old-fashioned quill works fine, and a web search should turn up several sites with cutting instructions. You can also use pen nibs with quills. It takes a special metal collar that is slipped onto the end of the quill. You then simply slide the desired nib onto the collar. Or, use a fountain pen. There are two different types: one you dip, and one with a lever-filled reservoir. Quills and fountain pens come with a wide variety of nibs; learning to write with them adds a touch of elegance to your life

Whether bought from the store or made by hand, magical inks have many uses. If you're using colored inks, match the ink color to the intent of your working. Want to work with herbal energies? Make a decoction or infusion of the herb you want to work with and use it for the water in lampblack ink.

Hekt, The Frog-Headed Goddess of Rejuvenation

by Lily Gardner

Imagine what winter must have been like for prehistoric humans. In the north, light dwindled and the land froze. Plant life died and the animals grew scarce. Searching for water and food on the frozen landscape was fruitless. Imagine the joy and relief people felt when they witnessed the return of spring.

For ancient people, the frog came to symbolize spring. Like winter itself, frogs burrowed deep in the ground and appeared lifeless. And from the long winter frogs emerge renewed. In the lands to the south, frogs signaled the arrival of much needed rain. Prehistoric peoples used the symbol of the frog to express new life, fertility, regeneration, and the return of abundance.

The Mother Goddess was first represented as a frog figure in Paleolithic times. Engravings on bone of humans with frog limbs or frog heads date back as early as 7500 B.C. Later designs of the frog goddess showing vulvas or pubic triangles appeared in the Neolithic era. Concentric circles symbolizing regeneration were drawn on the bellies of these figures.

With the Egyptian civilization, the frog goddess acquired a name and a persona. Hekt was her name, and she was depicted as a woman with the head of a frog. Her traits closely resembled

what the ancients observed about frogs. Not only did the frog rise from the dead each spring, it metamorphosed from egg to tadpole to frog. Most astounding of all, if a frog's limb was severed, it would grow back. The Egyptians named Hekt "the Great Magician."

The frog signaled the beginning of the Egyptian agricultural year. Millions of frogs spawned after the annual flooding of the Nile transformed the arid countryside into fertile farmland. The cry of the frog was a joyous sound for the Egyptians.

Hekt represented the embryonic grain that died in the winter and was reborn the following spring. As wife of Khnum, who fashioned humankind on his potter's wheel, Hekt breathed life into the embryonic human and placed it in the woman's womb. There Hekt watched over the tiny baby as it formed through gestation and then was born. Women wore amulets carved in the likeness of Hekt as they went into labor. Hekt, in her role as heavenly midwife, was said to attend the birth of the Sun each morning.

As the grain died at harvest and its stalks withered back into the ground, so the frog went dormant at the end of the season. This part of the cycle was explored in the Osiris myth. Osiris, green god of vegetation, was killed and pieces of his body scattered through the land by his brother, Set. The goddess Isis searched the land and retrieved the pieces of Osiris. Paintings from this story of resurrection show Hekt assisting Isis. Hekt's powers of renewal and regeneration were needed to bring back the god of growing things.

Through the centuries, the frog goddess surfaced in other cultures. In the Celtic culture, the Sheila-na-gig figure was most likely an incarnation of the frog goddess. Sheila was a grotesque

crone figure with a frog face. Sheila is always depicted holding her vagina open with both hands. The Sheila-na-gig represented the life-death cycle in Ireland. By holding open her vagina, she symbolized the life-giver, but as the skeletal crone, she represented the death aspect of the Goddess. This duality was further symbolized by her frog face.

Frogs were sacred to Venus, Roman goddess of love and fertility. Her triple yoni symbol was often represented by three frogs, an apt symbol given the frog's fertilty and regenerative associations. As totem for Hecate, Venus's crone aspect, the frog represented the death and resurrection aspect of the Mother Goddess.

As Christianity gained power throughout Europe, death was no longer viewed as part of the natural cycle. Hecate, as the crone goddess, and her followers, the Witches, were demonized. As queen of the Witches, she struck terror in the hearts of people from the Middle Ages. Frogs were suspected of being part of the Witch's spellcraft, and as such they were feared and despised.

Another incarnation of the frog goddess was the Germanic goddess Holda. Her associations with Hekt seemed to focus on Hekt's role as midwife and protectress of young children. Some stories describe Holda as a beautiful white woman who rose from the fountain each day leading a train of crying babies. It was an old belief that croaking frogs were the souls of unborn children.

Holda also surfaced in stories of the Wild Hunt, an old belief that huntsmen, demons, and baying dogs rode the skies during winter storms. It was said by some that Holda led the Hunt, a train of unbaptised babies following her as she rode the skies.

The Grimm brothers recorded one tale of the frog goddess in their fairy story "Mother Holle." Holle lived in the bottom of a well, the common frog habitat in fairy tales. It is a story of transformation, a theme often associated with frogs.

Some form or another of the frog goddess was seen from Africa to Russia. Her prevalence bears testimony to how important she was in the human imagination. Even when the frog goddess was no longer worshipped, frogs were still considered powerful magic. The Japanese believe that frogs brought good luck. Shamans used frogs for weather divination. Pliny, the Roman philosopher, said that to wear a frog amulet gave one the power to attract friends and keep love. To meet a frog on the road is good luck for a gambler. It means that he will win money in his next game or contest. If you carve a frog on beryl, you'll make friends of former enemies.

Frog Goddess Ritual

Pray to Hekt in the spring. Ask for her protection if you are with child. Ask for her guidance if you are going through changes in your life or if you need a boost in your creativity. Hekt can empower your water spells. Honor her by placing frog images around your home or office. And when you make a wish on the first frog you see in the spring, if it's kept secret, it will come true.

For Further Study

Andrews, Ted. *Animal-Speak*. Llewellyn Publications, 1994.

Chevalier, Jean, and Alain Gheerbrant. *The Penguin Dictionary of Symbols*. Penguin Books Ltd, 1969.

de Lys, Claudia. *The Giant Book of Superstitions*. Citadel Press, 1979.

Gimbutas, Marija. *The Language of the Goddess*. Harper-Collins, 1989.

Monaghan, Patricia. *The New Book of Goddesses and Heroines*. Llewellyn Publications, 1991.

Walker, Barbara. *The Woman's Dictionary of Symbols and Sacred Objects*. HarperCollins, 1989.

The Iban of Sarawak

by S Y Zenith

A quick geography lesson about Sarawak: Tucked between the continents of Australia and mainland Asia is the world's third largest island, Borneo. The island is split between Malaysia, the oil-rich sultanate of Brunei, and the Indonesian province of Kaliman-tan. The Malaysia parts of Borneo, Sabah and Sarawak in the north, are separated by the South China Sea from mainland Malaysia.

The main cities of Sarawak have their share of modern high-rises and five-star hotels plugged into CNN. Yet Sarawak still echoes with headhunters, hornbills, wildlife, and pirates. Half an hour outside Kuching, the capital city, are distinctive regions of thatched-roofed hill villages, equatorial rainforests, rivers, jagged granite mountains, and deep caves. Mankind first inhabited the Niah Caves of Sarawak approximately 40,000 years ago; these people later built jungle shelters which evolved into the longhouses on stilts where several families live communally.

There are more than twenty-five ethnic communities in Sarawak today. The largest group is the Iban, which comprises around 30 percent. They were once notorious pirates and head-hunters but are mainly farmers today. The Iban are famous for their tattooes, textile-weaving, woodcarving, and intricate woven mats and baskets. Although a proportion of the Iban are Chris-

tian, they still maintain their original cultural identity, heritage and traditional beliefs, revering mythical and legendary heroes and deities. Two of their traditional practices include the deciphering of dreams and bird augury.

Well-known Iban festivals include the Gawai Kenyalang, a hornbill festival which commerates the bravery of warriors, Gawai Antu, a festival to appease the dead, and the big Gawai Dayak harvesting festival on June 1st. During these times, there is the customary observance of ritual, drinking of the local rice wine *tuak*, *ngajat* dancing, and displays of elaborate traditional costumes.

A respected Iban man is one who is eloquent in argument, courageous in hunting, and skillful in the use of the knife and the adze—a heavy chisel-like tool for dressing timber or shaping wooden items. A man skilled in handling these two implements is said to be able to mediate between the worlds of mortal man and spirits. By time a boy reaches adolescense, he typically carves his own toys and other objects. Decorative bamboo containers with stylized motifs of flora are permanent tokens indicative of a young male's affection for an unattached female. His etchings on these containers also signify personal accomplishment and refinement. To the Iban, the carving of a figure represents a connection with the spirit world. The person who carves it invokes and enters into a close relationship with a spirit. Only a man of experience and great powers is able to resist the presence of the spirit.

The skill most desired in the Iban woman is weaving. It is believed that designs are given to women by gods through dreams, hence they are objects of the heavens. When the Iban man is ready to retire to bed, he wraps himself in spiritual cloths known as *pua kumbu;* these assist his soul to travel to the heavens while his body sleeps so he may receive dreams that will help in daily undertakings. The two most important pieces of equipment to the weaver are the *belia* (beater) and the *jengkuan* (shuttle). Because weaving is of importance, it is guarded against michievious spirits. Men make equipment for weavers and inscribed them with protective figures. To be a master weaver, a woman has to learn the use of dyes, gain knowledge about designs and associated skills, then move through the ranks. As a mark of distinction, the master weaver wears a porcupine quill tied with red thread.

It is an ideal in Iban culture for a gifted carver to marry a talented weaver, because such matrimony is considered auspiciously blessed by the gods. Upon marriage, the groom may live with the bride's family or vice versa. After two years of marriage and if a child is born to the couple, they would move from the parental *bilik*, or a special apartment in a longhouse.

The man's role is to protect his family and fields from malevolent or predatory terrestrial and extraterrestrial entities. Usually prior to the time an Iban man is able to establish his own bilik, he would have embarked on a spiritual journey known as *berjalai*. A hundred or more years ago, such a journey would be a raiding party in search of human trophy heads and other bounty. In modern times, the man aims to earn a significant sum of money instead.

During the course of the journey, the man acquires a large number of amulets and talismans to protect from enemies, gain success in endeavours, guard against sickness, and so on. After returning from berjalai, a man is now able to carve figures of powerful spirits to be invoked when needed.

The crocodile and python are reptiles of immense power in Iban mythology and thus commonly carved on doors. These figures are believed to block entities of ill intent who would enter through the door. The iban also carve *agom* on their food storage bins for protection. Agom are small figures on pointed stakes that are inserted into the ground. These are also placed at the pathway to a rice field after planting. A ritual called the *permali umai* entails offerings to the gods and sacrificing a hen to purify the ground and all who participate. This ritual is conducted by an elder who calls on the gods for a bountiful harvest while cursing all evil spirits likely to interfere with the growing rice. The Iban god of fertility and of the earth is the Pulang Gana. This figure is carved in human form with teeth bared to frighten or consume malevolent spirits. Pulang Gana carvings on posts may be of either sex and have their organs positioned below their squatting body.

The riverine Iban are also skilled in the making of longboats reminiscent of their ancestors' tribal aggressions of days past. Iban ritual practices as a whole are interwoven with traditional beliefs, animism and shamanism, spirit worlds, taboos, and ancient customs passed down the generations.

Number 13 Lore

by Emely Flak

Someone tells you their address—1313 Elm Street. How do you react? Does this make you uncomfortable? If so, then you're not alone. Superstition about this number persists in Western society, despite the fact that there is no logic for fear of any particular number. Fear of this number has even earned its own name—triskaidekaphobia.

Many historians attribute the fear of this number to the fate of Jesus Christ who, surrounded by his twelve apostles, was the thirteenth guest at the Last Supper. However, pre-Christian Norse mythology also depicts unfortunate events following the arrival of the thirteenth dinner guest at Odin's banquet, which suggests triskaidekaphobia has deeper roots. According to legend, twelve gods feasted when the god Loki appeared and triggered an argument which resulted in the death of Baldur, the beloved god of light. In the end, these tales have led to current-day superstition that says if thirteen people dine at a table, one person will die within a year of the feast.

The fear of the number 13 has lasted through the centuries. The ancient Romans associated the number with destruction. Even children's fairy stories have been affected. Several versions of the story of Sleeping Beauty tell of the king who invited only twelve of the thirteen fairies to his table because he owned only twelve gold plates to set at the table. Each of the twelve fairies came and gave the king's daughter a magical gift, such as patience or beauty. The thirteenth fairy who was not invited, and who is often depicted as an ugly old hag, embarrassed the whole gathering by coming anyway. In retaliation for not being invited, instead of a gift, she brought a curse. On the princess's fifteenth birthday, Sleeping Beauty would die after pricking herself with a spindle. Even the twelfth good fairy, who was yet to bestow a gift to the king's daughter, was not able to undo this curse with her gift. She was, however, able to change the fate of death to a sleep of one hundred years.

Despite the fact that technology and scientific logic today dictate much of our understanding of the world, this simple superstition still pervades the Western world. Hotels and other multistory buildings in cities throughout many parts of the world even avoid having a "thirteenth floor." More recently, a fear of the number thirteen was fuelled by the ill-fated journey of the Apollo 13 space mission. On April 13, 1970, the oxygen tank on the spaceship exploded forcing an end to the mission, and the three astronauts nearly died. Many attributed this disaster to the prominent number 13 of the mission.

Additional superstition is aroused if the thirteenth day of the month falls on Friday. This has been attributed to Friday being the day on which Christ died on the cross. Put Friday and the number 13 together, and you have two bad omens. Interestingly, every calendar year will feature at least one Friday the thirteenth.

In the tarot deck, the thirteenth card symbolizes death. The first impression of the macabre skeleton on card number thirteen in the Major Arcana conjures up feelings of dread, no doubt fueled by the number of the card. Yet the death card remains a widely misunderstood part of the tarot deck. Those familiar with tarot interpretation understand that instead of representing a morbid physical death, the card often signifies transformation, the end of a cycle, and opportunity for rebirth, growth, and new beginnings.

Paradoxically, many people embrace the ill-luck of the number 13. Some dote on the number 13, and wear charms with the number inscribed on it. In the ancient religion of Mexico, the number was regarded as a lucky symbol of the Sun, and thought to represent omnipotent male energy. In the Qabala, the number 13 is also considered fortunate. Keen numerology students are aware that if you are born on the thirteenth day of any month, you are destined to be practical, alert, and intelligent with a high chance of success in scientific endeavors.

For Pagans and Wiccans, number 13 is regarded as significant and lucky. From a nature-centered spiritual perspective, the number represents the feminine essence and cycle, with thirteen lunar journeys, or full Moon cycles, occurring in each solar year. Many covens limit their group number to thirteen members.

Whatever your viewpoint on number 13, mixed reactions to this number over centuries have provoked varied emotions from trepidation to positive feelings. It's up to you to choose how you feel about this mysterious number.

Tending the Dead

by Cerridwen Iris Shea

Samhain is the time of year to honor one's dead ancestors and loved ones, set out meals, have a chat, and catch up on all the grave-tending one should have done during the year. It's a time to reconnect with those who have died, and to also deal with one's own mortality issues. Somehow, interacting with the dead makes one's own eventual demise somehow less intimidating.

Several years ago, I began performing a series of rituals around the time of Samhain that I call "Tending the Dead." It's grown so that a number of people across the world now work on it with me. Typically, those who are interested contact me a few weeks before Samhain, and we divide up a map of the world. Everyone is responsible for one specific area. I have basic ritual guidelines, but everyone who participates is responsible for crafting individual rituals to meet their needs and the needs of their specific area. In general, these rituals are inspired by the Mexican festivals for Los Dias de los Muertos, but they are not to be undertaken lightly. After all, these are underworld energies. To perform them, you need to have a strong sense of yourself as a magical person, combined with solid training

Samhain Practices and Rituals

I start preparing for Samhain early in October. I use a combination of Samhain, Halloween, Day of the Dead, and harvest items to decorate both at home and at work. At home, I set up a special altar for the dead, with photos and names of those who have died that I wish to remember. It also has candles flowers, usually marigolds, chrysanthemums, and white roses, and anything else I think might bring joy to the dead—such as food, water, chocolate, and so on. I also use black taper candles, which burn down during the course of each day and are replaced each morning. I usually start the rituals around 11:30 pm and finish by 1:00 am.

Rituals begin at midnight of October 31. The first night is reserved for children. I add candy and toys to the altar, and tailor the ritual toward children. I focus my energy on children who long for acceptance—I am a believer in nonconformity for children, and in treating them as unique and treasured individuals from an early age. The nights of November 2 is for adults, especially "unknown" ones who have no one to mourn for them. This includes plane-crash victims, homeless who may have died, runaways, victims of abuse, and the forgotten elderly. Instead of toys and candies, fruits, tobacco, cornmeal, and the like are placed on the altar. I also usually make a braided egg bread as an offering.

November 3 is for the animals. Dog and cat treats go on the altar, along with birdseed, toy mice, balls with bells in them, and so on. Because I am actively involved in horse racing, I also keep a list of horses who have broken down and died over the year, and I honor them at this time. I honor both the animals I know, and all the animals who are hunted without reverence, animals who are killed on the highways and roads, or just through sheer meanness or neglect. It is also important not to taint these rituals with anger, but to bless and honor the mistreated and downtrodden.

The final evening, on November 4, is to welcome the souls preparing to reincarnate. Milk and honey are put on the altar, white ribbons are tied around the black candles, and new baby decorations are interspersed with the skeletons and scythes.

In general, the structure of the rituals each night is similar. Set up the altar each night, and sweep the space with a besom. Light the altar and quarter candles; consecrate the elements and cast a circle by walking clockwise three times with a scythe. Construct a special circle casting call for this by saying: "The watchers of the directions are invited in to observe and protect."

I do a great deal of dragon work, so I also invite my dragons in at this point. Invite in the divine spirits of Cerridwen, Hecate, Anubis, Isis, and Ishtar. In general, the watchers and these divine ones are good to have around. Ask for their protection and assistance in your work, then state the purpose of that night's ritual. open the west gate, the gate of the dead, and invite in the souls you mean to honor that night.

Talk to them, but, most importantly, listen. Many will be confused. Some many not know that they are dead. One year, on October 30, a plane crashed in my area of the world, and I had 230 extra confused souls in my ritual a few days later. Make notes of what they ask you to do. Sometimes it might be to contact someone, sometimes it might be to actually carry out a task. Make no promises that night, but agree to think it over. Do not agree to do anything illegal or harmful to yourself or someone else. If the soul asks you to contact someone still living, try to find a gentle way to do so that will not be upsetting to the living person. Often, it is better to create an elemental (in a separate ritual) and send the elemental off with the message than to try to contact a stranger yourself. Do not be afraid. Remember that you have cast a circle where only good can enter.

Afterward, say farewell to the souls, and send them on their journey out of the circle, back through the west gate. I usually create a bridge of golden light out of the circle or a rainbow bridge to send them on their way. Now you must ground yourself; this is very important—or you will feel ill by the next morning. Take your time with this until you feel completely yourself again.

Bless the cakes and ale, and make your offerings to spirit. Thank Cerridwen, Hecate, Anubis, Isis, and Ishtar. Thank the watchers of the directions (and dragons, if you need to). Open the circle by walking it counterclockwise three times with the scythe. Extinguish the quarter candles, but let the altar candles burn all the way down (as long as they can do so safely). Put away the list of requests you may have accumulated. Eat something grounding. Make sure to take another shower before you go to sleep, or you may have trouble sleeping.

Eating is very important during all this. I usually have a good meal a couple of hours before the ritual and eat grounding food and protein right after it. Strength, stamina, and focus are keys to these days of rituals. If you fast, you won't be able to maintain the energy level required.

After the last day of these rituals, take down the Samhain decorations. You may choose to leave up, or add, any harvest decorations for Thanksgiving. This way, everything flows into each other, and there are fewer abrupt beginnings and endings.

Around the November 10, take out the various request lists and decide how to deal with them. Try to take care of everything before Thanksgiving.

Usually, there are very few requests. Use your common sense and discretion in deciding how to deal with them. If you have any questions, you can take them to Cerridwen, Hecate, Anubis, Isis, or Ishtar for advice.

These rituals sound like a lot of work, but they are actually quite a joy. I find that the dead appreciate any time and effort we make in their behalf, and they will reward your support and understanding throughout the year.

For Further Study

RavenWolf, Silver. *Halloween*. Llewellyn Worldwide. 1999.

RavenWolf, Silver. *To Light a Sacred Flame*. Llewellyn Worldwide, 1999.

How Music Came to the Earth

by Edain McCoy

Long, long ago, when the Earth was uninhabited by human life, the silent animals lived alone with the gods and goddesses of nature. It was a world of beauty, but also one of infinite silence. Only the rush and roar of Quetzalcoatl, the god of the wind gave sound to the Earth.

The deities found this lonely. There was no one to talk to but each other, and they didn't always get along. Even the animals of the earth could not communicate, neither with them nor with each other. It was frustrating and many of the deities began to sense that something was missing from their glorious creation.

One bright, cloudless day, the god of the sky, Tezcatlipoca, heard a beautiful sound coming from the palace of the sun god, Huitzilopochtli. He was so mesmerized by the sound and the many emotions it evoked in him that he sat outside the palace and listened for a long time. He found he wanted to stay all day, but he knew he had something important to do, and he knew he had to approach his nemesis Quetzalcoatl to get it done.

Quetzalcoatl was rumored to have breathed life into the animals of the Earth and was considered the most powerful of deities. Many disliked, even hated, Quetzalcoatl, but none denied his power.

Tezcatlipoca sought him out with some trepidation, but his mission was urgent he had to chance the wind god's displeasure.

"What do you want?" the wind god bellowed when he saw the intruder.

"I want sound."

"What are you talking about? Aren't the roar of my winds enough for you?"

"No. Nor are they enough for any of us. I want music."

"Music?" Quetzalcoatl's breath softened to a gale. "I've heard rumors of its existence, but I've never heard it before. How do we even know it's real?"

"It is."

"You seem very sure of yourself," Quetzalcoatl said.

"I know where the music is," Tezcatlipoca told him, "and I think you are the one who must go get it."

"Me?"

"Who else? You are the most powerful among us."

Tezcatlipoca could see his flattery was having an effect on the wind god as he thought over these words.

"Where is this place?" the wind god asked finally.

"Huitzilopochtli has it locked in his Sun palace, and I'm sure he thinks no one else knows."

"You heard this music?"

"It's beautiful. It can make you cry or laugh. It's just what our world needs."

"Then I'll go get it," roared the wind god. "But, Tezcatlipoca, how will I get there? The palace of the Sun is much higher than my winds can blow."

"And much higher than my sky too. Perhaps my brother Tlaloc, the rain god, can help us."

The two gods sought out Tlaloc, and found he tired of the only sounds he heard—his own waves slapping on the shoreline. He commanded the spirits and creatures of his seas to weave themselves together in a long rope that Quetzalcoatl could climb to reach the palace of the sun god.

When Quetzalcoatl arrived at the golden doors of the palace he heard the music Tezcatlipoca spoke of, and he was wholly enchanted. Summoning all his strength, he blew open the door of the palace and went inside.

Huitzilopochtli sat on his golden throne, drowsy from the spell of the music, when the wind god arrived. He sat up in fear and blazed forth a royal command that the music cease before Quetzalcoatl could hear it, but it was too late.

The wind god looked around at the diminutive flute players, singers, and drummers of the sun god.

"I've come to bring music to the Earth," Quetzalcoatl told the sun god. "All the deities agree that you must share it."

"Never," cried the sun god, "and you cannot make me."

Quetzalcoatl's anger swirled inside him like a hurricane. From his mouth came a cyclonic wind that engulfed the musicians and singers, drawing them into the wind god's arms. He kissed them all and hurried down the rope made from Tlaloc's creatures before Huitzilopochtli could recover and come after him with his blazing heat.

The singers and musicians looked about their beautiful new world and began to play and to sing.

The three gods who had envisioned this plot to bring music to the Earth held their collective breath and waited to see what would happen.

The sweet sounds of music flowed over creation and ignited it with the power of sound. The frogs began to croak, the birds began to chirp, wolves began to howl. In the oceans the whales began to sing. The Earth was full of the sounds of joy, sorrow, and beauty. The gods were pleased.

As the players and musicians mated, the Earth was soon populated with people to honor the gods. Even Huitzilopochtli was pleased with this turn of events. All the children of the Earth could now sing of their feelings to one another, and they could also use their music to honor the gods they loved.

And that, my friends, is how music came to the Earth.

Caloria, Fall Goddess of Potluck

by Barbara Ardinger

Potlucks are vitally important to Witches and other Pagans. Going to a ritual? Take something to eat afterward. Going to a drumming circle or a croning? The folks are sure to work up an appetite.

But the question is: What to take? How to accommodate vegetarians, carnivores, omnivores, and ecofeminists in this crazy modern world? Thanks to our found goddess manual (see page 95 of this edition), this gnawing problem is now solved.

True to goddess tradition, Caloria is a triple goddess. Low Caloria, who is dwarfish and simple, is our Virgin Vegetarian. Although her favorite dish is a casserole of brown rice, tofu, and lima beans, she has recently admitted that she is beginning to appreciate such gourmet fare as wild mushroom couscous and anything made with pasta, asparagus, or aubergine.

High Caloria, our Bountiful Mother, is luscious and delicious. Her greatest delight is to serve her children the yummy cheesecake baked by her high priestess, Sara Lee, or any savory dish whipped up by her high priestess, Julia Child. She also adds a tasty topping of pure love to any of the treats that arise from the ovens and barbecues of her many priests, who include Wolfgang Puck, Chef Boy-Ar-Dee, and all the good ol' boys on the cooking channel. High Caloria especially enjoys the glorious desserts created by Chocolata, one of the Found Goddesses of Ecstasy.

Eco-Caloria is she who inspires her grandchildren to eat off of china plates and drink out of glasses and china cups instead of using paper goods. Thus does she help us preserve the virgin forests and the Styrofoam mines.

When we know we're going to a potluck, therefore, always begin by invoking the goddess Caloria as follows:

> *Hail, Caloria, you who freeze and thaw and bake,*
> *Show me, please, the proper food to take.*

At the potluck, correct protocol is for every potential eater to carefully examine and comment on each offering. Then we join hands around the groaning table and give thanks to the goddess:

> *Hail Caloria, rich and wise—*
> *Feed my soul, but not my thighs.*

To learn what offering we may lay on the sacred potluck table, we next enter the goddess's sacred precinct and approach her sacred cave. As we open the door to the sacred cave and the inner light comes on, we take up our sacred plastic lidded bowl and look within for inspiration. It's easy to recognize when the goddess makes her will known, for then we feel the chill of her presence.

An alternative ritual honoring Caloria involves visiting her sacred marketplace and silently worshipping at the holy deli until one of the votaries of the goddess asks if he or she can help us. The votaries may, in fact, make suggestions. Proper protocol suggests the exchange of coins for culinary offerings prepared in situ.

Toe-Ring
Charging Spell

by Ed Fitch

On the night of the Full Moon, set your rite in a quiet and solitary place.

Place an image of the Goddess overlooking the ritual area, and place a candle before her. An image or symbol of the God should stand next to her.

You may add flowers and other offerings as you feel are appropriate. Place candles, ready to light, at the north, east, south, and west corners of the ritual area. At the center of the ritual locale place a flat foot-stone, and about it, touching the stone, place the cards of the tarot Queens or Pages (depending on your preference) with the Swords to east, Wands to South, Cups to West, and Pentacles to North.

Place a sword or dagger next to the stone and a small vial of olive oil or scented oil sacred to your patron goddess. Also a polishing cloth for the ring or anklet should be folded and placed neatly near the foot-stone. Have music appropriate to your goals, prepared and ready to play. Polish your fingernails and toenails in red, purple, black, or in your personal "power color." When all is quiet prior to your rite, bathe in a candlelit place, bearing strongly in mind that the water is cleansing your body, soul, and spirit. Wear the toe-ring or anklet. Look often at it as you bathe, and watch the glint of the candlelight or moonlight on it.

Dress in rainment and jewelry that are magical and "witchy" to you. (Or wear nothing but your jewelry, if it pleases you and feels magical.) Start the music and then dance into the ritual barefoot. Dance into the ritual area carrying a lit taper or fire-lighter. Dance about the foot-stone, then to the north. Light the candle and strike a dramatic pose, saying:

Powers of the earth,
Dance with me,
Give me your magic and power,
Here and beyond.

Dance back about the foot-stone, then to the east. Light the candle and strike a dramatic and magical pose, saying:

Powers of the air,
Dance with me,
And give me your magic and power,
Here and beyond.

Dance back about the foot-stone, then to the south. Light the candle and strike a dramatic and magical pose, saying:

Powers of fire,
Dance with me,
And give me your magic and power,
Here and beyond.

Dance back about the foot-stone, then to the west. Light the candle and strike a dramatic and magical pose, saying:

Powers of water,
Dance with me,
And give me your magic and power,
Here and beyond.

Then dance before your image of the Goddess, and light the candle before her. Strike a dramatic and magical pose before the image, and say:

My Lady, my sister,
Creatrix of all magic,
Be with me as I cast this spell
Of power and of strength.
Am I not beautiful?

Dance your way to the foot-stone, and dance around it sunwise (clockwise) thrice, ending before the foot-stone, facing the image of the Goddess. You may sit, if you desire, and remove your toe-ring or anklet. Polish it, saying:

O patroness of beauty, of fascination, of charm,
Imbue strength, power, magic, and wonder
Into this ring (or anklet) of power,
That I may journey far and with your protection
in magic, in beauty, and in wonder.
(Repeat the following thirteen times as you polish the metal.)
Power of my lady, power be with me!

Finally anoint your ring or anklet with the scented oil, saying:

So mote it be.

Now, dance with the polished toe-ring (or anklet) to the north quarter, rising on tiptoe to hold the ring up to catch the moonlight for the space of thirteen heartbeats, if possible. Repeat thus at east, south, and west. Go before the image of the Goddess, strike a dramatic and magical pose, and hold the ring or anklet up before her for the space of thirteen heartbeats, saying:

From you, O gracious one,
Do I draw protection, magic, and power.
May your strength
Ever flow through me.
So be it.

Then dance before the image of the God, and strike a silent pose before him. Dance back to the foot-stone, place your foot on it, and slide the ring onto your toe (or anklet onto your ankle), saying:

As I put on this ring (or anklet)
May I draw magic, beauty,
And wondrous power into myself
With every step that I take.

Take the sword or dagger and touch it (carefully) to your ring or anklet for the space of thirteen heartbeats. Then strike a dramatic and magical "power" pose, spreading your arms and calling in these or similar words:

Hear me, O great ones!
I have power,
Strength and beauty,

Which shall be with me
Wherever I go!
So be it!

Hold the "pose of power" for thirteen or more heartbeats, then dance to the candle at north, strike a dramatic and magical pose as you present your foot outward, tiptoe, saying:

Know of me—
I have power,
Beauty, and magic.

Dance then to the east, south, and west, repeating your magical presentation before each candle. Then dance to the image of the Goddess, strike your pose, and say:

I thank you, sister.
May your strength
Ever flow through me.
Thank you, Lady and Lord . . .
And blessed be.

If you feel it within you, a dance in the moonlight, in your own style, would be appropriate at this time. When you feel that the rite should end, put out the candles and depart.

It is proper to polish your toe-ring or anklet at each Full Moon, and to anoint it with oil.

This rite may be repeated each quarter of the year (Spring Equinox, Midsummer, Autumn Equinox, and Yule) or as desired.

The Elements of Spells
by Ember

When creating your own spells you are limited only by your imagination. The correspondences and styles for spellwork are many: Colors, elements, candles, stones, and herbs are just a few of the items you can use in spells.

Many people prefer simple spells such as candle magic, but blending this with other items can provide new and energized spells. This article concerns working with the four basic elements: earth, air, fire, and water. Combining them with your usual spell items allows for even more creative opportunities and will result in a more original and personal spell.

One method that works well is to create a spell jar, which expands on candle magic. To do this, partially fill a glass container with water and add stones or shells and sprinkle the appropriate herbs on the water. Dress a candle with oil that corresponds to your magical working and carve an appropriate symbol into it, then float it in the water. It goes without saying that these things are best done while visualizing your intent and within a magic circle. The spell jar provides an environment for combining all the elements: earth, air, fire, and water. When the candle has burned out, reuse its wax, keep the stones, and return the water and herbs to the Earth.

Of course, you may still tailor your spell around a specific element depending on the nature of your need. One method for earth-centered spells is to mix stones, herbs, and nuts with earth, and place a candle, or draw a rune, in a pile of this stuff while visualizing your intent. For a water-oriented spell, use sand and shells. When the spell is complete, simply return the items to the ground or sea. Save the candle wax if you can. This can be melted down and reused to make new candles.

Feathers are good to use in air spells. Place very small ones in sachets or pillows; mix with earth and sand mixtures; float on water; or anoint with a drop of oil and release in a strong wind. You may also create a bundle of feathers, herbs, and flowers then tie with a ribbon. The ribbon can be decorated with runes and oils and be of a corresponding color.

Depending on the other elements you would like to combine, float the bundle on water, bury in the ground, or burn it. Watch for natural items wherever you go. Look around for feathers, nuts, fallen leaves, rocks, shells, pinecones, sand, and water, especially in public areas such as beaches and parks; though always be sure you do not remove items from a protected area. Alternatively, you can buy some of these items in stores or order them via a mail-order source. But certainly it's more exciting and energizing if you can find them yourself in nature. Remember to take only what you will need for the moment and never dig up an entire plant.

However, harvesting a few seeds of the plant in the fall will allow you to grow it yourself. Collect just a jar of sand, small bottle of water, a couple of leaves, or rocks—and give thanks to the land as you do so. Grow your own herbs if you can, even the smallest patio or balcony can support a few containers of plants. These add to the power of the herbs in your spells and assure they are grown in conditions you can monitor and keep organic.

Be creative! If you pour your own candles, mix stones or shells in the wax. Being unique ensures variety and personal energy in all your spells. Happy spell-weaving!

Native American Magical Rituals

by Carly Wall

If you study native cultures, you will find that they all share the same spiritual beliefs based on nature. Intrinsic to their beliefs, they share a common acceptance of magic in their daily lives. Native Americans have followed these beliefs for well over 25,000 years.

For Native Americans, healing is an important aspect to spiritual practice. Native healing most certainly holds magical elements. First and foremost, the involvement of healing is given over to special men or women of the tribe who possess special powers—what we would term today psychic abilities or talents. They have been called "medicine men or women" and "shamans," and they employ symbolic rituals or ceremonies, and ritual purifications or purgings, as well as herbal remedies to heal.

Their belief system is such that they believed that in nature, all things are connected, and connected by spirit. Everything is alive, has spirit and awareness. Energy and matter is vibration and exists in an energy system of many levels, like a web. The universe of the shaman is divided into three parts: the upper, middle, and lower worlds. These classifications have nothing to do with the Western beliefs of heaven and hell. The levels are merely a part of the unseen world, and must be dealt with by experienced souls who ourney beyond them to what they deem paradise in order to obtain wisdom to use in the physical world.

The lower world, or underworld, is the first level encountered on the journey and where the power animals are found. You confront your dark side here; and the healing of emotions, memory, and the physical body all take place here. Each soul's journey is an individual experience. Access to the lower world consists of tunneling, burrowing, or the feeling of sinking.

The middle world, meanwhile, is the place of devas or nature spirits such as the fairy, the gnome, and such. Plant or rock spirits can be encountered here too. It is a thin veil that exists just outside the common world. This is the realm where magic can be worked; spells, curses, ghosts, and demons all exist just as we exist here.

The upper world is a place of wisdom, where one can encounter spiritual advisors or teachers, gods or goddesses. It is accessed when you need to find answers to questions. You can climb mountains, trees, or rocks to access this world, or feel that you are floating upward.

On the whole, the shaman's purpose is to create balance and harmony of the spirit for individuals in the tribe. They act as intermediaries between this world and the others for their fellow tribesmen and women. Sometimes, the shaman makes the journey into the other world to battle, work magic, and thus achieve balance in the universe, the goal of ultimate healing.

To do this, several Native cultures have used drugs to induce altered states, especially in conjunction with drumming or rattles. In olden times the drum was also called the "horse," because with the drum one could ride into the other worlds. The vibrations of these tools alter one's own vibrations and so lead one into a trance. This is a relaxed state of mind where one can enter light dream states. This technique is similar to other ecstasy states in which it becomes easier for the body and soul to separate and for the soul to travel into the other worlds to obtain knowledge, power, or healing. The shaman can also do this traveling for a person who is unable to do so him or herself. In this manner, the shaman allows his or her own soul to leave the body, and to discover knowledge or instruction that can then be used after the shaman returns.

Since life is energy and vibration, the loss of these forces leads to trauma and unbalancing. Illness can start this cycle, or a loss of contact with a power animal, or a foreign spirit taking up residence within the body. However it happens, this state of being can lead to bad luck, serious health threats, unhappiness, and death. To realign and balance, one must journey into the other world to discover the cause of this condition, and to gain the knowledge to put things right again. A power animal, or alterego of spiritual wisdom, is a helper in the other worlds. It is believed that everyone has a particular animal spirit connected with one's own energies. Discover this and you have an ally against the demons and dark spirits fighting to keep you out of balance and in the dark. If you have lost contact with your animal spirit, they say you are accident-prone, depressed, and listless. The shaman will ask the question, "What animal do you feel most drawn to, what animal do you dream of most often, appears to you in the physical world most often?" The answer gives insight into the power animal that resonates within you. Once you learn this, then your power animal and you can journey into the other reality to reconnect.

When unbalancing occurs, it is believed that part of the soul or life essence has been lost. It is then the job of the shaman or person to find this life essence and retrieve it. A welcoming ceremony is performed and the person must learn how to best work with this newly returned energy.

At other times, the cause of the problem can be an intrusive spirit or energy. If a person isn't vigilant, other energies can enter the body and take possession. An extraction is then called for. A shaman can journey or pass his or her hands over the body to detect the intruder, seeking hot or cold spots, or creatures or demons within the aura. With spirit helpers and power animals, the shaman can remove the energy, take it to a nearby body of water, and neutralize it. Using powerful psychic energies, he or she can then flood the person with cleansing energy, and so heal the individual.

There are other ways the shaman can work his or her magic. One way is through the use of plant magic or herbal healing. To do this, the shaman will take to the woods, find a plant that calls to him or her, sit and meditate by the plant to discover if this is the plant to be used. Herbs can be ingested, applied, or drunk in tea form. Certain herbs used in ceremony can be burned— sage, sweet grass, or cedar. Purification or purging is another form of healing ritual; it takes place inside a sweat lodge. Here, the healer and others come to pray, sing, and drum. During this time, water is ladled onto hot stones to produce steam in the belief that this will purge and cleanse the body of disease. Other symbolic healing ceremonies are also employed. They are different from tribe to tribe but most often employ the use of the medicine wheel, or a community singing that lasts from two to nine days and employs dancing, chanting, and drums and rattles.

These rituals ultimately are powerful. They employ the attention and concentration of human minds. Tools for helping focus this mind-power consist of various props, special clothing, music, and of course ritual itself. All of these help to bring all thoughts to one thought, thus focusing intention. An effective ritual must have a beginning and an end. It must also employ as many of the senses as one can, and the meaning of each step must be made known to all.

Of course, such ritual occurs in Native American culture through the use of stories. In them, special areas of power are laid out, the area is blessed. Special clothing, jewelry, food, and prayers or chants are used.

In the end, it is a recognition of nature and hidden worlds that leads Native American spiritualists to believe that there is always hope, a solution, a personal power that one can obtain if one is only willing to do the work, and to take the journey.

For Further Study

If you are interested in shamanism, you may want to read more in detail about it.

Andrews, Ted. *Animal-Speak*. Llewellyn Publications, 1994.

Meal Blessings

by Kristin Madden

Food! It nourishes us and comforts us. It is part of social ritual, and in some cultures the central focus of specific ceremonies celebrating the spirit and all manner of magical energies.

Most of us have a weakness for certain foods. The mere thought of gourmet treats can make some of us salivate; we feel better just by eating them. For example, chocolate often acts as rose quartz, making us feel soothed and loved. For some of us, good wine or coffee has this effect. For others, it is cake or lobster.

Many people today are very careful about the foods they eat. We may purchase organic vegetables or farm-raised fish. We might avoid the meat of animals that have received hormone injections or antibiotics. Those carnivores among us with an understanding of energy systems may take this a step further and only purchase meat from animals that were raised and killed in what they consider to be humane methods.

We all recognize the energy that we invest in our eating. After all, this is the reason that cake and ale are often shared at the end of Pagan rituals. However, we can carry the sacred meal over into our daily lives, and the preparation of food and drink can become a powerful time to work blessing magic.

Magic of Food

Food does much more than simply entertain our taste buds or comfort us when we are feeling down. Because we take in both the energy and physical matter of the food we consume, it can nourish us on many levels. Not only are we receiving the energy of the plant or animal matter that we ingest, we are also receiving energetic traces of those people that have handled this food.

Through preparing foods and drinks in a sacred manner, we invest them with beneficial energies that truly nurture the body and spirit. As "Kitchen Witches," we clear our personal energy of the tensions and worries of the day just as we would for any ritual. We bring our magical selves to the preparation of food and drink, charging our cooking or preparation utensils with blessings and beneficial energies.

As followers of earth-based religions, Pagans often develop a deep respect and gratitude for the blessings of Mother Earth and her children. While we understand that all species play a role in the food web of this planet, we also see the manifestation of spirit in the plants and animals we eat. Through the use of meal blessings, we honor their sacrifice and release any personal or unwanted energies before we begin our meals.

Keep this in mind when you come to your kitchen. Make every effort not to bring potentially harmful emotions to the preparation of food or drink. Begin by purifying yourself and your working area through the use of smudge, incense, or meditation. Count yourself down from ten to one or simply take a few deep breaths to center your energy.

Once your energy is clear, consciously direct blessings into the pots, utensils, and ingredients that go into your meal. Hold your hands out with palms open to these objects, take a deep breath, and visualize your love and prayers flowing hands into the food and drink. You may want to charge these items with specific prayers or simply send white light to your loved ones.

You may also want to direct a special mealtime prayer to the food and drink. The following prayer may be used in this way. It is a wonderful blessing for the whole family, bringing a sense of gratitude and honor to each meal.

Great Spirit,
We thank you for the gift of this food.
We send blessings of peace, love, and release to all whose bodies and
energies brought us this nourishment. We honor you in our enjoy-

ment and utilization of this meal.
May it bring us health and joy, reminding us of our interconnec-
tions with all that is.
As we receive, so do we give thanks for this gift.

With young children, it is best to keep prayers short, simple, and to the point as below.

Thank you, Great Spirit
Thank you, chicken and peas and milk (or other food items)
Thank you, Mother Earth
We love this food.

Unlike food that fills the stomach before it is digested, drink more instantly enter our systems. It is sometimes easier to feel and visualize a liquid filling our bodies and bringing blessings to every cell. Humans have been consecrating ritual liquids and charging them with blessings for millenia. We can use adopt the meal blessing above to carry forth a tradition of working magic through sacred drinks. You might also try this variation for more personal blessings.

Hold your cup in both hands and raise it to your third eye in the center of your forehead Allow the energies of Earth and sky to fill your being and pass through third eye into the cup. Offer this drink to the Great Spirit or God and Goddess. State that you honor them as you drink, and ask that they fill you with their blessings If you have specific prayers or energy you need, see it flow into the drink Ask that the liquid fill your being, permeating your cells and resonating with your energy field to help you manifest these blessings. With each sip, appreciate the consecrated liquid this drink has become. End by saying, "So mote it be."

For Further Study

Madden, Kristin. *Pagan Parenting.* Llewellyn Publications, 2000.

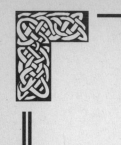

Products
and
Services

Celebrate Wiccan Days and Pagan Ways

Whether you're planning a ritual, Sabbat feast, or a birthday party, Llewellyn's *Witches' Calendar 2003* has all the information you need to make every day magical: Wiccan holidays; color correspondences; the best days to plant and harvest; the Moon's sign and phase; planetary motion, including retrogrades; and solar and lunar eclipses.

This year's calendar is packed with practical tips, folklore, herb lore, and art by Kathleen Edwards. Articles by popular Pagan authors include:

- **"Prophetic Dreaming" by Migene González-Wippler**
- **"Shamanism" by Richard Webster**
- **"Using Energy in Spell Casting" by Ann Moura**
- **"Pagans and Christians" by Gus diZerega**
- **"Creating a Hoodoo Garden" by Scott Appell**

LLEWELLYN'S *WITCHES' CALENDAR 2003*
36 pp. • 13" X 10"
ISBN 0-7387-0075-4/J072 • $12.95 U.S.
To order call 1-877-NEW-WRLD

A Planner for Young Witches On the Go

Stay on top of your school projects, social life, and work schedule, as well as sabbats, esbats, and coven meetings. Llewellyn's *Teen Witch Datebook 2003* is the first and only planner specifically designed for young Witches. Sixteen months long, this datebook features each week on a two-page spread; dozens of rituals and spells; Moon signs, phases, and times of change. Articles by well-known Pagan writers will inspire you:

- **"Out of the Closet" by Gwinevere Rain**
- **"My Life as a Witch" by Frankie Banfer**
- **"Joining the Dance" by Julianna Yau**
- **"The Art of Divination" by Yasmine Galenorn**

TEEN WITCH DATEBOOK 2003
168 pp. • 5 1/4" x 8" • spiral binding • 16 months
ISBN 0-7387-0198-X/J072 • $9.95 U.S.
To order call 1-877-NEW-WRLD

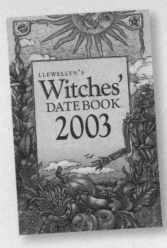

Celebrate the Seasons of the Witch

Make room for more magic in your life with Llewellyn's *Witches' Datebook*. Keep track of coven meetings, festivals, and your more mundane appointments. This enchanting datebook presents each week on a two-page spread. Comes complete with mini-calendars; a time zone map; holidays; historic dates; herb lore; Celtic moon rituals; best days to plant and harvest; and moon signs, phases, and times of change. Articles to enhance your practice include:

- **Sabbat rituals by Magenta Griffith**
- **Sabbat recipes by ShadowCat**
- **"Spellcrafting" by Yasmine Galenorn**
- **"Mabon" by James Kambos**
- **"Witchy Goddesses" by Patricia Monaghan**

LLEWELLYN'S *WITCHES' DATEBOOK 2003*
144 pp. • 5 1/4" x 8"
ISBN 0-7387-0076-2/J072 • $9.95 U.S.
To order call 1-877-NEW-WRLD